ARGONAUT LIBRARY
OF ANTIQUITIES

ANCIENT GREEK HOUSES

Remains of a nobleman's house recently excavated at Pella and partially restored. Early

ANCIENT GREEK HOUSES

*Their History and Development
from the Neolithic Period
to the Hellenistic Age*

by

Bertha Carr Rider
Classical Tripos, Cambridge, M. A., D. Lit., Lond.

ARGONAUT, INC., PUBLISHERS
CHICAGO   MCMLXIV

Library of Congress Catalog Card Number: *LC 64-23438*

12-14-67

EDITOR'S NOTE TO THE
FIRST AMERICAN EDITION

In the book world "Greek Architecture" and "Greek Temples" have long been the subjects of many books, from small pamphlets to the large photographic editions which grace so many American homes. But for all that has been published in this area the subject of the Greek house has remained almost untouched and is a virtually unknown field for layman and specialist alike.

The field of archaeological research on architecture, as can be seen in the select bibliography following, is lacking any work of reference quality on the specific subject of the Greek house. The numerous references to this book in later books and papers gives adequate testimony to its value and importance and makes it worthy of inclusion among the volumes of the Argonaut Library of Antiquities.

The original view of the author, *"that the history of the Greek house is continuous, and that similar types of houses prevail from the earliest period to the latest,"* is now a fact, the truth of which has been demonstrated by the finds of nearly every excavation in Greek lands. From Athens to Pella and from Olynthus to Dura Europos and Cyprus the archaeological search has revealed evidence of architectural continuity in every area where the Greeks once lived. Later writings on the subject of the Greek house (all based on Rider's work) are scattered through a host of archaeological periodicals, in many languages, but nowhere is there another book covering the subject so thoroughly.

The select bibliography will guide the student through this material for information and reference on the most recent discoveries, but as this work is also intended for the layman and the professional architect who may not wish to do such intensive research, the following paragraphs point out the most important references according to periods.

For classical Greek architecture in general the books by *W. B. Dinsmoor, A. W. Lawrence* and *D. S. Robertson* are basic references. But it must be remembered that the main concern of these authors was the monumental architecture rather than the domestic. The work of *J. W. Graham* is the most basic for prehistoric palaces, but here again little attention has been given to the houses of the average citizen while much is written on graves and royal dwellings.

For the Greek house of the fourth century B.C. as revealed by the excavations at Olynthus, see the writings of *D. M. Robinson* and G. *Mylonas*. The houses of the eight, sixth, fifth and fourth centuries B.C. found in the area of the later Agora in Athens are described by *D. Burr, J. Travlos, R. E. Wycherley* and *R. Young*. Travlos also gives details of most periods of Athenian houses as known from excavations. For the modern (popular) Greek house in connection with folklore see *G. Megas*.

The best available reference for the Hellenistic house in general is the book by *H. Fyfe*. Later discoveries can be studied in the works of *N. Moutsopoulos, P. Petsas* and *R. E. Wycherley*.

Again in *Travlos* and *Wycherley* as well as *R. Martin* the house as an element in poleodomy (city planning) may be studied. Finally, for a general recent view of the Greek house in all periods consult *L. Guerrini*. The other divisions of the lemma 'casa' in the encyclopaedia are also useful for a comparative study of the houses of other ancient peoples.

In order to preserve the value of this book as a reference, the pagination and figure numbers remain unchanged. It is hoped that this note and the bibliography will increase still further the usefulness of Rider's *Greek House: Its History and Development from the Neolithic Period to the Hellenistic Age*, now appearing in the Argonaut Library of Antiquities as *Ancient Greek Houses*.

The Editors

Chicago, Illinois
October 1964

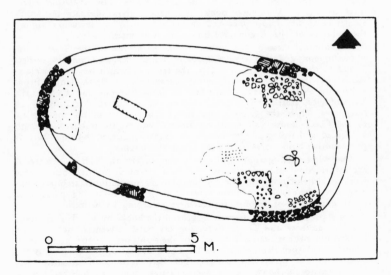

House, oval in shape, of the eighth century B.C.
Excavated to the north of Areopagus in Athens.

SELECT BIBLIOGRAPHY

American School of Classical Studies at Athens. *The Athenian Agora.* 2nd rev. ed. Athens 1962.

Blegen, C., *Prosymna: The Helladic Settlement Preceding the Argive Heraeum.* Cambridge, Mass. 1937.

———, "The Roof of the Mycenaean Megaron," in *Amer. Journ.* of *Archaeology* 49, 1945.

British Museum. *A Guide to the Exhibition Illustrating Greek and Roman Life.* 3rd ed. London 1929. (House and Furniture, pp. 103-116 and *passim*).

Burr, D.. "A Geometric House and a Proto-Attic Votive Deposit," in *Hesperia* 2, 1933, pp. 544-551.

Dinsmoor, W. B., *The Architecture of Ancient Greece.* 3rd ed. London 1950.

Fyfe. H., *Hellenistic Architecture,* London 1936.

Graham, J. W., *Palaces of Crete.* Princeton 1962.

———, "The Relation of the Minoan Palaces to the Near Eastern Palaces at the Second Millennium," in Bennett's *Mycenaean Studies,* Madison, Wisc. 1964.

Guerrini, L. "*Casa*: Grecia e Creta," in *Encicl. dell' Arte Antica* vol. II, pp. 378-392. 1959.

Hodge, H. T., *The Woodwork of Greek Roofs.* New York 1960.

Hutchinson, R. W., *Prehistoric Crete.* London 1962.

Lawrence, A. W., *Greek Architecture.* London 1957.

Levi, D., "Abitazioni preistoriche sulle pendice meridionali dell' Acropole," in *Annuario Sc. Arch. Ital. Atene* 13/14, 1930-31, pp. 411-498.

Lorimer, H. L., *Homer and the Monuments.* London 1950.

MacKendrick, P., *The Greek Stones Speak.* New York 1962.

Mackenzie, D., "Cretan Palaces," in *Annual of British School at Athens,* 1904-8.

Marinatos, S., *Crete and Mycenae.* London-New York 1960.

Martin, R., *L' urbanisme dans la Grece antique,* Paris 1954.

Megas, G., *The Greek House,* Athens 1949 (in Greek).

Moutsopoulos, N., "The Macedonian Palace of Vergina," in *Athene* (Chicago) 22, 1961, No. 1, pp. 33-38.

viii SELECT BIBLIOGRAPHY

Mylonas, G. E., *Ancient Mycenae*. Princeton 1957.

——, The Oecus Unit (*Excavations at Olynthos* vol. XII) 1946.

Orlandos, A., *The Building Materials of the Ancient Greeks* (in Greek) Athens, in progress.

Papagiannopoulos, Andrew, "Archaeologia kai Poleodomia ton Athenon," in *Technika Chronika*, 1959, pp. 3-8.

Petsas, Ph., "Pella. The Capital of the Macedonian Kings," in *Athene* (Chicago) 23, 1963, No. 3 & 4.

——, "Ten Years at Pella," in *Archaeology* 17, 1964, pp. 74-84.

Pfuhl, E., "Vorgriechische und griechische Haustypen," in *Festgabe H. Bluemner*, Zurich 1914.

Robertson, D. S., *Greek and Roman Architecture*. 2nd ed. New York 1945.

Robinson, D. M., "Praehistorische und griechische Haeuser," in Pauly-Wissowa-Kroll *Real Encyclopaedie* Suppl. VII (1939), cols. 223 ff.

——, The Hellenic House (*Excavations at Olynthus* vol. VIII'). 1938.

—— and others, *Excavations at Olynthus* (vols. VIII, X, XII). Baltimore 1929-1946.

Scranton, R., *Greek Architecture*. New York 1962.

——, "Greek Architectural Inscriptions as Documents," in *Harvard Library Bulletin* 14, No. 2, 1960, pp. 159-182.

Travlos, J., *Poleodomike Exelixis ton Athenon*. Athens 1960.

Wace, A. J. B., *Mycenae. An Archaeological History and Guide*. Princeton 1949. (Rp. 1963).

—— and Gardner, E. A., "House and Furniture," in Whibley's *Companion to Greek Studies*. 4th ed. Cambridge 1931.

Wycherley, R. E., *How the Greeks Built Cities*. 2nd ed. London 1962. (ch. VII).

Young, R., "An Industrial District of Ancient Athens," in *Hesperia* 20, 1951, pp. 187-253.

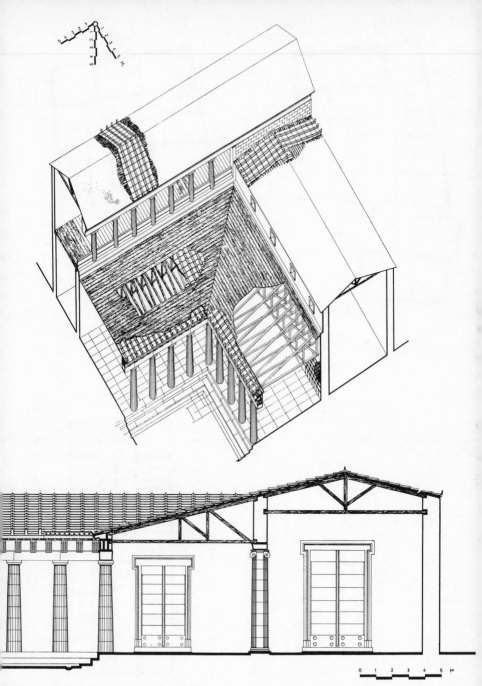

Bird's eye view and front view of the Macedonian palace
of Vergina. Early third century B.C. Restoration by Dr.
Nicholas Moutsopoulos, University of Thessalonike.

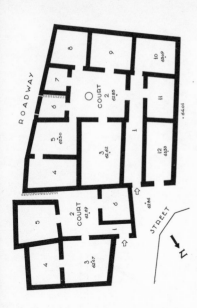

Two houses of the fifth century B.C. (D-C) to the west of Areopagus in Athens.

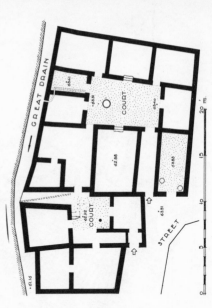

The two houses (D'-C') to the west of Areopagus in Athens after the mid-fourth century B.C.

Houses of the sixth century B.C. at the east foot of Agoraios Kolonos in Athens.

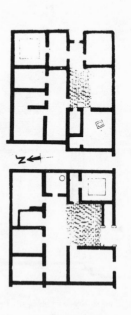

Two houses of Olynthus of the fourth century B.C.

PREFACE

THE rich nature of the recent evidence furnished by discoveries in Crete, Greece, and Asia Minor, on the subject of the Greek house of the earliest and latest periods, has given fresh impetus to the study, and many are the articles and tracts which have been written by English, German, French, and Italian scholars.

Among these the most important and penetrating are the writings of Professor Noack and Dr Mackenzie on the construction and plan of the Cretan palaces, and those of Professor Myres and Professor Gardner on the Homeric and classic house.

The articles on the subject are scattered throughout a host of archaeological periodicals in all languages, many of which are not even accessible to the student, and anything in the form of a continuous history or summary of the evidence and of the deductions drawn from it, does not exist in any tongue.

The aim of the following thesis has been to collect and present succinctly all the monumental evidence of importance from the Neolithic period onwards, as well as to give a summary of all the principal criticism to which it has been possible to obtain access, in order to enable the student of classic architecture to gain a general knowledge of the present state of the subject, within a reasonable compass.

Such a study is naturally, to a great extent, a work of compilation, and my object has been rather to order and review, than to suggest anything startlingly original in a field where so much is already but theory, and where the student is so apt to lose sight of the principal trail to devote himself to side issues.

At the same time my travels in Greece, Crete, the islands of the Aegean and Asia Minor, have enabled me to weigh all evidence carefully in the light of actual remains, and sometimes, where I dared, to criticise.

I have devoted my attention specially to the history from the prehistoric period to the fifth century, which interested me more particularly, and have only referred to the Hellenistic house to point out the certainty of its connection with the Mycenean, and to the Pompeian to show the last phase.

Much work is yet to be done in this branch, and we may hope for still more complete evidence from excavation, with regard to the later development of the Greek house.

It has become quite clear to me in the course of my research, that the history of the Greek house is continuous, and that similar types prevail from the earliest period to the latest. Such a view I may perhaps venture to present as original, for as far as I have been able to judge, it is nowhere assumed. The house of each successive period is rather described and discussed on its own merits than recognised as a link in a chain.

The complicated character of the race problems involved makes the whole discussion far from simple, but I think I have been able to show that the view I have put forward is not entirely *in nubibus*, but finds support and confirmation which can with difficulty be gainsaid.

Among the many works which I have consulted and to which reference is made in the following study, the most inspiring and suggestive have been those of the authorities already mentioned, to whom I here acknowledge my indebtedness throughout and tender my grateful thanks.

B. C. R.

LONDON,
1915.

CONTENTS

ILLUSTRATIONS

CORRIGENDA

P. 37, l. 13 and p. 38, l. 8. Read *en encorbellement*

CHAPTER I

INTRODUCTION

THE study of the Greek house, which but a decade
ago began with those shadowy indications of plan and
disposition found in the Homeric poems, has suddenly
been carried back into the darkness of untold centuries
by the amazing discoveries in Crete, and the consequent
revelation not only of an advanced pre-Hellenic civilisation
extending over thousands of years but of a complete
chain of evidence right back into the dark ages when
Europe first began to be inhabited by man.

This miraculous disclosure of a social era replete with
life and artistic interest, the very existence of which was
almost unsuspected before 1900, not only necessitates a
new survey of Greek development as a whole but leads
the question of the Hellenic house back into periods
where a comparison with the dwellings of widespread
and far roaming early tribes is essential, and even an
examination of the house in its most primitive form in
Europe.

It may be useful, then, at the outset to take a brief
review of the general conditions of those early ages in
Europe and the immediately connected area, North
Africa, once joined to it through Spain and Sicily, in
order to study the question of the probable origin of the
Greek house, its primitive form and its connection with
other synchronous buildings of a similar character.

R. G. H.   1

Though the presence of man in the Pliocene or last
division of the Tertiary period seems in the light of recent
discovery possible[1], yet no evidence from the nature of
the case can be forthcoming as to his dwelling; we can
only presuppose that it was natural and consisted of any
shelter which he found ready to hand and which offered
him a refuge from the danger of the moment[2].

With the Pleistocene or first division of the Quaternary
period the evidence is rich and full with regard to Palaeolithic man, who lived

ὥστε ἀήσυροι
μύρμηκες ἄντρων ἐν μυχοῖς ἀνηλίοις. (Aesch. *P.V.* 460.)

Like little ants in the sunless recesses of caves,

but had as yet no artificial shelter, and no graves or
burial customs which have left any trace. The wonderful
artistic activity of this stock is proved by such finds as
those from the cave of La Madeleine in Dordogne[3].

Our information concerning Palaeolithic man in the
East European area is gleaned for the most part from
North Africa, Asia Minor and Syria, for whether Crete
was in those remote ages the connecting link with the
African continent or not, it remains a fact that no vestiges
whatever of Palaeolithic man have been found in that
island[4], though the evidence is so singularly complete
from the succeeding period onwards.

The connection between Palaeolithic and Neolithic
man, though it seems natural to assume a continuous
evolution, has never been clearly proven[5], and must have
been interrupted by some sudden cataclysm, or perhaps
the last Glacial Age.

[1] Cf. Sergi's "Tertiary Hominidae"—*Europa*, p. 70 sqq.
[2] Meitzen, *Wanderungen*, III. p. 464.
[3] de Mortillet, *Le Préhistorique*, p. 411.
[4] *B.S.A.* VI. p. 25.   [5] Keane, *Ethnology*, p. 73.

However this may be, there is but little doubt that
Europe was repopulated after the last Ice Age by extensive
migratory movements from the South and South-East,
the seats of the earliest Neolithic culture[1], and that
streams of emigrants spread gradually across the Straits
of Gibraltar and up the Iberian peninsula to Gaul and
Britain, as well as up the Danube to Central and West
Europe. It need be a matter of no surprise, then, when
similar funeral monuments are found in countries so far
apart as Ireland and Greece, on the other hand it is quite
natural to look for analogies in structure where men of
the same common stock have been.

With the advent of the Neolithic culture, a much more
advanced state of civilisation is found[2], the troglodytic
stage is abandoned, monolithic and megalithic monuments
make their appearance over an extended area, human
dwellings of various kinds including lake dwellings are
constructed, barrows and sepulchral chambers are made,
and it is in this first period of extraordinary architectural
activity that our study of the house must really begin.

The constructive energy of these tireless builders in
stone is little short of miraculous, and many of their
monuments are still standing in their simple heavy
grandeur, to bear witness directly and completely with
regard to the manner and style of the early artificial
forms.

Before considering apart structures belonging to this
period built on Greek soil, it will be well to form an idea
of the parallel and often strikingly analogous arrangements
in other connected areas.

At the very outset arises the question of the true
relationship of the tomb and the house, and of the

---

[1] Ripley, *Races of Europe*, c. XVII. p. 463.
[2] Keane, *Ethnology*, c. VI.

deductions which may legitimately be drawn from the one with regard to the other.

The palaeolithic troglodytes of Belgium and France buried their dead in natural grottoes and caves like those in which they lived[1], so that at this epoch no distinction is to be made. For later periods it has generally been assumed that the tomb of any given age may be taken as evidence for the house of preceding ages[2], religious conservatism preserving for the sacred rite of burial the architectural forms of by-gone generations. The Esquimaux actually leave the dead in the house they occupied when alive[3]; most races, however, have found a resting place for them in the earth, either in some sort of depository or in a chamber imitative of the house of the living.

The further question arises as to which was ultimately the earlier form, the house or the tomb. Man in the early stages of his development is a superstitious being standing in awe and dread before his departed ancestors, so that even if the tomb, as seems quite possible, does not precede the house in historic development[4], it was yet so much more carefully and solidly built that it has come down to us intact through the ages, and provides us with some of the earliest architectural evidence we possess, where information regarding the actual house of the living is either inadequate or utterly lacking.

From the tomb, therefore, many of our deductions with respect to man's primitive artificial dwelling must necessarily be drawn. Its subterranean position is natural and fitting, so that an underground tomb built after a

[1] Lubbock, *Prehistoric Times*, p. 312.
[2] Cf. A. Buckland, *Journ. Anthrop. Inst.* IX. p. 152.
[3] Lubbock, *op. cit.* p. 128.
[4] Keane, *op. cit.* p. 126, note I.

house model does not perforce imply a previous underground dwelling, but is to be regarded simply as the
house of the living transferred to the silence and darkness
of the realms of the dead.

At the same time the view has been held (cf. Adler[1])
that such tombs have their origin in the hut dug out in
the hill-side, and point unmistakably to a stage when
the dwellings of the living were also subterranean.

Leaving aside the monolithic types of building such
as the menhirs, cycloliths, etc., which though eminently
characteristic of this age do not immediately concern
our subject, we will turn to the polylithic types built up
generally round a cell as embryo, in which the dead body
was laid.

In some cases the mortuary nature of the monument
can only be inferred, since it is often most difficult to
decide in the case of a Neolithic structure badly used by
the elements or by human hands, whether it was a house
for the living or a tomb, but in general the older types
would seem to be the dwellings of the dead. In any
case we need not insist on any distinction in the earliest
ages, for in some countries the evidence will be of one
nature, in others of the other, and both sepulchral and
domestic types are equally useful for the earliest styles of
building.

[1] Preface to Schliemann, *Tiryns*, p. xxix. Cf. "weems" of present
day in Scotland: Wilson, *Prehistoric Annals of Scotland*, I. pp. 107–8.

CHAPTER II

NEOLITHIC PERIOD IN NORTH AFRICA AND
WEST MEDITERRANEAN BASIN

LET us then take a rapid glance at the earliest constructions in *North Africa and the Mediterranean basin*, in order to form an idea of the prevailing types in the regions surrounding Greece through which she might be influenced in her primitive development.

In North Africa the simplest forms of the polylithic or cell type, viz. the cromlechs or dolmens, are found scattered all over the surface of the land along a coast line 1500 miles in length[1], from Tangiers and Lebdou to Tunis and Tripoli, and in view of the excavated finds no doubt remains that they were sepulchral chambers[2].

For example, on the plain of Gorra alone there are from two to three hundred burials[3], showing all the various primitive types. The very simplest form consists of a table or large slab without supports, and we may perhaps assume that the corpse was buried in a hole in the rock beneath[4]. In the next stage the rock tomb is closed in front by a slab, in some three artificial walls

---

[1] Rhind, *Archaeologia*, xxxviii. "On vestiges of ortholithic remains in N. Africa," p. 260.

[2] *ibid.* p. 254: pottery and bones were found in the cromlechs of Bainum.

[3] Carton, *Découvertes épigraphiques et archéologiques faites en Tunisie*, p. 328.

[4] *op. cit.* p. 331.

occur, and finally we reach the real artificial cell composed
of four sides on which the table or horizontal slab rests[1].
This is surrounded by a tumulus consisting of large stones
with a filling of small ones, which lean inwards towards
the horizontal slab and almost reach it, so that the general
form of the monument is that of a truncated cone[2],
a probable prototype of the Nuraghi of Sardinia described
below.

Another similar monument on the plain of Gorra
has a rectangular sepulchral chamber approached by a
descending passage or dromos, and surrounded by a regular
circular enclosure of stones[3], an arrangement recurring in
the Talayots of the Balearic Isles and perhaps formerly
in the Nurhags though no traces now remain.

This plan also occurs at Teboursouk. The tombs are
of small proportions, one for instance at Teboursouk
measuring 4·25 m. in diameter from the exterior, so that
the limbs of the corpse must have been bent when it was
deposited in the small rectangular chamber, an early
example of a crouch burial[4].

When two or three burials occur in the same enclosure
the small rectangular tombs are side by side, and the
enclosure often tends to become oval in form, while still
remaining small[5]. One such at Dougga containing two
rectangular sarcophagi has a diameter of 6 m.[6]

To the S. W. of Dougga is another large group of two
or three hundred tombs with round, elliptical and square
enclosures[7]: at Kern el Kebch also all types occur, from
the simple slab to the twin tombs side by side with a
common dividing wall and a circular enclosure[8].

[1] Carton, *op. cit.* pp. 332–36.
[2] *op. cit.* pp. 338–9.
[3] *op. cit.* p. 341, fig. 143.
[4] *op. cit.* p. 348, fig. 149.
[5] *op. cit.* p. 349, fig. 152.
[6] *op. cit.* p. 361, fig. 174.
[7] *op. cit.* p. 362.
[8] *op. cit.* p. 365, fig. 179.

It is curious to notice how many of these dolmens, especially at Gorra and Bulla Regia, seem to assume the form of the neighbouring rocks, so that in the distance they are hardly to be distinguished from them.

At Bainum again about a hundred such tombs are preserved, scattered over an area of from ten to twelve acres[1], and at Djelfa the tombs are surrounded by circles of stones and sometimes even double circles[2].

Thus we have in North Africa a complete series of all the early forms, which we shall find reproduced and modified over an extended European area, probably peopled by tribes emanating from this vast continent. Even crouch burial which is so common a custom in Mycenean times would seem to have been practised here in far earlier ages[3].

The natural bridges to Europe are Sicily, Sardinia and Spain, where similar remains are found of tombs and houses.

About midway between the coast of Africa and Sicily lies the little island of *Pantelleria*[4], whose interesting prehistoric remains may be briefly noticed. The grim, barren nature of its volcanic coast and the entire absence of earth made it necessary for the handful of inhabitants who must have been tempted to settle there on their way from Africa to Sicily to modify somewhat the original type of tomb, though the form is practically the same as in North Africa.

The remains of the dead were here deposited in artificial mounds, called Sesi, scattered about in the lava, and though more modest in character than the Nuraghi or Talayots they are yet wonderful constructions for

[1] Rhind, *l.c.* p. 253.   [2] Rhind, *l.c.* p. 258.
[3] *vide* p. 7.
[4] Orsi, Pantelleria *Mon. Ant.* IX. p. 451 sqq.

men working in such an unyielding material without metal implements.

These tombs may be considered to be of the tholos type, though naturally somewhat rough in execution, and consist of a tapering mound 7 or 8 m. in height formed of unworked blocks of lava, the interstices being filled in with lava rubbish: the width at the base may be 10 m., at the top 5 m.

Within this mound or hillock is a number of small circular cells, each approached by a gallery, also of narrow dimensions. A typical tomb is No. 30 in Orsi's account: the mound is here elliptical, its dimensions being 8·70 × 8·40 × 2·40 m., the south-east gallery is 2·75 m. long by ·65 m. wide while the cell attached is 1·05 m. × 1·31 m. × 1·25 m. The "Sese Grande" though of nobler dimensions is of the same type[1].

In connection with a subsequent discussion we may notice here that the elliptical form occurs not only in some of the mounds but also in a Mursian house of the prehistoric epoch[2], while remains have been brought to light of two rectangular huts[3]. The bones found between the walls of these houses perhaps point to an age when the dead were actually interred in the house or quite near it as on other Neolithic sites, *e.g.* Spain[4], Dimini and Sesklo[5], Thoricus[6], Orchomenos[7], etc. This is a practice which did not entirely die out, for Semiramis the widow of Ninus, according to Diodorus Siculus[8], had her husband

---

[1] Orsi, Pantelleria *Mon. Ant.* IX. pp. 491–2, figs. 38, 39 and 40.

[2] *l.c.* p. 460, fig. 8.   [3] *l.c.* pp. 458–9, figs. 6 and 7.

[4] Siret, *Les premiers âges du métal dans le sud-est de l'Espagne,* pp. 95, 102, 174.

[5] Tsountas, Αἱ προϊστορικαὶ ἀκροπόλεις Διμηνίου καὶ Σέσκλου, pp. 131, 383.

[6] Ἐφ. Ἀρχ. 1895, p. 228.   [7] Bulle, *Orchomenos*, p. 67.

[8] Diod. Sic. II. 1.

interred in the enclosure of the palace, and in our own times Wagner was buried in his garden.

The above-mentioned constructions are of great interest as evidence for the early appearance of the elliptical and rectangular house in South Europe, side by side with the circular tomb.

In the neighbouring island of *Malta* at Hagiar Kim and Mnaidra[1] considerable remains have been found of sepulchral chambers ovoid in form which must have had roofs of corbelled vaulting and may have been surrounded with a mound. They are probably of Neolithic origin, though Caruana regards them as Phoenician[2]. The Tomb Caves which have been artificially worked with sharp metal tools certainly belong to a later period[3]. In the centre of the adjacent island of *Gozo* Neolithic remains of the same character are also standing[4].

The prehistoric inhabitants of *Sicily* belonged, according to Orsi, to the same Mediterranean stock which came from Africa and was diffused through all the islands and coasts of the Mediterranean. The Sicani, the older branch, were a Neolithic people and left no trace of metal; the Siculi were Aeneolithic but belonged to the same race. Many rock-hewn tombs of Neolithic period consisting of a rectangular chamber, sometimes with others communicating, have been found, especially in the south-east of the island[5].

The round form predominates in *Sardinia*, the soil of

---

[1] Caruana, *Megalithic antiquities of Hagiar Kim, Malta*, p. 3. *Archaeologia*, XXIX. pp. 227–240, pls. 23–28.

[2] Caruana, *l.c.* pp. 8, 9.

[3] *l.c.* p. 7.

[4] Fergusson, *Rude Stone Monuments*, p. 416.

[5] Orsi, *Atti del congresso internazionale di Scienze Storiche*, 1903, v. "Quattordici anni di ricerche archeologiche nel sud-est della Sicilia," p. 167.

which is covered with conical structures known as Nuraghi, built of layers of rough stones[1].

As far as it is possible to judge, in view of the enormous
masses of stone carried off by the peasants for building
purposes, these erections were in the form of truncated
cones, and were finished not with a dome but with a
terrace. The sloping walls are most carefully finished,
so that no block projects to spoil the regularity.

These buildings all contain one, two or even three
rooms, situated one above another, to which access is
given by means of a corridor in the wall. The lower
storey is generally about 5–7 m. in diameter, the upper
storey being about half the size, and the lower storey
often contains two or three cells or niches which are
lighted by a small fent in the wall. The entrance is
small and difficult, and a second often occurs before the
large chamber is reached[2].

The would-be vault is closed at the top by a large
slab, and again we do not find the perfected form of the
Mycenean tholos. The oval form is also present here[3].
The use of the Nuraghi remains unexplained, but they
would appear to have been abodes for the living, perhaps
modelled on dolmen prototypes[4].

The burial chambers of Sardinia were the so-called
Tombs of the Giants[5]. A typical tomb is that near

---

[1] Ferrero della Marmora, *Voyage en Sardaigne*, I. ii. 3. Mackenzie,
"The Dolmens, Tombs of the Giants and Nuraghi of Sardinia." *Papers
Br. Sch. Rome*, v. p. 89.

[2] Ferrero della Marmora, *op. cit.* I. ii. 3, figs. on p. 42.

[3] *op. cit.* I. ii. 3, p. 38.

[4] *op. cit.* I. ii. 4, pp. 117 sqq. Prof. Myres tells me that similar
modern constructions may be seen on the island to-day scattered about
in the fields: they are used as tool-houses. The inhabitants now live
in square dwellings.

[5] Mackenzie, *Ausonia*, 1909, pp. 18–48.

Pauli-Latino[1] standing in the vicinity of another tomb, and a partly destroyed Nurhag, and consisting of a semicircle of ten stones with the eleventh in the form of a stele having a very small square door at the bottom, which leads into a corridor 1½ m. wide and 7 m. long formed of two rows of upright stones with cross stones over to cover in the sepulchral chamber.

Judging then from present remains we might deduce that the domestic architecture of Sardinia was round and the sepulchral rectangular. Dr Mackenzie however mentions two dolmens of the earliest type found at Birori, near Macomer[2], which are of rounded elliptical shape, so that it is impossible to generalise, and indeed the tombs of the giants show a blending of the two forms.

Though the island of *Corsica* lies in such close proximity to Sardinia the architectural conditions are entirely different, for, according to Dr Mackenzie[3], no round huts existed here in prehistoric times. The same writer cites a village which he has seen in Corsica, where rectangular dwellings exist side by side with dolmen tombs of the usual rectangular type, found all over the Mediterranean[4]. Merimée's description of the Stazzone makes it clear that they belong to the usual dolmen type. The Stazzona del Taravo in the Taravo valley is one of the more simple, and consists of four stones, three forming three sides of a rectangle, and the fourth covering them and forming a roof[5]. The Stazzona del Diavolo in the Caurian valley consists of eight stones, enclosing a cell 3·15 m. long by 2·05 m. wide[6]. These massive stone structures recalled

---

[1] F. della Marmora, *op. cit.* I. ii. 2, pl. IV. 1 and 1 bis.

[2] *B.S.A.* XIV. "Cretan Palaces," IV. p. 346. *Papers Br. Sch. Rome*, V. p. 134, fig. 17.

[3] Mackenzie, *B.S.A.* XIV. p. 347.   [4] *ibid.* p. 347.

[5] Prosper Mérimée, *Notes d'un voyage en Corse*, pp. 16–18 and plate.

[6] *ibid.* p. 26 and plate.

to Merimée the dolmens of Brittany, but he was loath to admit any direct connection, for the Celtic hypothesis with regard to their origin was then in vogue. Now we can connect them with the dolmen builders of North Africa.

Of the two distinct classes of monuments in the *Balearic Isles* the Talayots or watch towers alone offer comparisons with regard to form[1]. For the funeral monuments, Navetas or Naus[2], are, as their name implies, in the form of an inverted boat, the walls having a distinct batter: in a woodcut of Ramis, an old traveller, a keel is actually pictured[3]. These tombs may perhaps be regarded as belonging to the transitional oval shape. The style of building in huge blocks with pillars supporting the roof is massive, and the isolated position of the monuments as well as the finding in them of human remains proves quite decisively that they were tombs, and prompts the inquiry as to what purpose the Talayots served[4].

These latter are in the form of round, slightly conical towers, built of rough or hewn blocks, the cubic measure of some of the blocks at the base being as much as 2 or even 3 metres. The largest Talayot is 16 m. in diameter and 14 m. in height[5], but the bulk are much smaller, the average height being about 6 m.

The majority of them enclose a single chamber, and from a height of about 2 m. each row of stones projects above the one below, apparently as with the Nuraghi of Sardinia; the vault is never finished, the chamber being finally closed with large slabs.

It is common to find Talayots with two storeys and a small spiral ramp in the thickness of the wall, leading from the lower chamber to the upper, of which the Talayot

---

[1] Cartailhac, *Monuments primitifs des Baléares*, pass.
[2] *ibid.* pp. 33–38, pls. 41–45.
[3] *ibid.* p. 33, fig. 22, pls. XLI and XLII, Les Tudons.
[4] *ibid.* pp. 23–33.   [5] *ibid.* p. 24, Morell in Majorca.

at Torre-Nova-di-Lozano[1] is perhaps the most perfect example. Such a spiral corridor is also found in the Nuraghi and in the so-called Towers of the Picts in Scotland[2].

Another curious feature, which is of interest for comparative purposes, is the use in some cases of a single pillar[3] and in others of two or three pillars composed of superimposed blocks for support. The single pillar would sometimes cover so large a space that the chamber was reduced, as at Hostal[4], to a corridor 1–2 m. wide.

The doorways which are on the level of the soil are of the ordinary size, not of the reduced proportions of the Navetas, a fact which points to their use as human dwellings; in no case is access given to a crypt, and the lack of human remains also argues against these buildings being of a funeral character.

They were perhaps special strongholds for times of danger: they would seem not to be ordinary dwelling houses since, if the argument from numbers is permissible, only two or three are found in a city.

A recent writer[5] regards them as having been built to clear the land in a measure of stones, and as having been used for housing pigs and sheep during raids. Are we to infer then that the Neolithic people put the safety of their animals before their own? or had such a sense of order as to erect monuments merely to use up loose rocks which were lying about?

The rectangular form occurs at Vey[6] in Majorca, but

---

[1] Cartailhac, *op. cit.* p. 27, fig. 20, pl. 35.
[2] Wilson, *Prehistoric Annals of Scotland*, II. pp. 101–2.
[3] Cartailhac, *l.c.* pl. 37.
[4] Cartailhac, *op. cit.* p. 27 and fig. 19.
[5] Guillemard, "On prehistoric buildings in Minorca," *Cambridge Antiquarian Society*, 1906, p. 465.
[6] Cartailhac, *op. cit.* p. 52.   Cape Corp Vey.

otherwise the building in the Balearic Isles is all in the round.

The remains of Neolithic culture in *Spain*[1], unearthed by the brothers Siret, are hardly adequate enough to allow of any general conclusion being drawn with regard to the prevalence of the round or rectangular form in primitive architecture on this site. A small civilised colony, probably attracted by the silver, settled over an area of about 65 km. along the coast of the Mediterranean[2].

In the very earliest settlement it is conjectured that the dwellings were made of boughs and twigs and clay, for only a layer of black earth remains, as at Tres Cabezos[3], to tell of this occupation. In the transition period walls of stone and mud of varying thickness were built: at Campos remains of a building were found of the form of a trapezium with inner and outer walls, the latter which had evidently been built later for purposes of fortification being flanked by turrets[4]. The primitive round form has not been found except in the turrets.

Inland, in the region of Granada, many tombs of the normal dolmen type were found by Gongora[5], of which the finest is that of Antequera[6], and the tendency in prehistoric Spain, as far as we can judge, seems to have been to the straight and rectangular.

In *Portugal* on the other hand round graves with dromos are found near Cintra and elsewhere, as well as monuments of the rectangular dolmen type, called

---

[1] Siret, *Les premiers âges du métal dans le sud-est de l'Espagne*, pass.
[2] Siret, *op. cit.* p. 252.
[3] *ibid.* p. 22.   [4] *ibid.* p. 53.
[5] D. Manuel de Gongora y Martinez, *Antigüedades prehistóricas de Andalucia*, pp. 80–104; plan of rectangular hut, p. 91.
[6] *Arch. Journ.* 1870, "Megalithic remains in the department of the Basses Pyrénées," p. 233 and fig. 6: Lord Talbot de Malahide.

Antas[1], with stones before them as in the Tombe dei Giganti.

The Neolithic grottoes in France sometimes known as allées couvertes, which closely resemble the Hünebeds of North Holland, conform to the same general type of sepulchral chamber with dromos, *e.g.* Fontvieille graves near Arles[2]; in some cases the dromos and burial cell are of the same width. The round type with false vault and dromos also occurs, *e.g.* Collorgnes and Fontenay le Marmion[3], and in Brittany we find both round and rectangular types.

Similar graves in England and Scotland (as far north as the Orkneys) and Ireland, as well as in North Germany, Denmark, the Netherlands and South Sweden[4], show how far-reaching this primitive Neolithic culture was, and how fixed the types for the early house and tomb.

A dwelling consisting of an underground chamber approached by a long covered passage is an exceedingly natural type to occur, providing as it does a shelter from extremes of heat and cold, for the passage keeps the temperature even more constant than it would be in the simple cave. The winter house of the Esquimaux is a living example: it consists of a large room built of planks with sleeping places around, approached by a long narrow underground passage[5].

The form is not confined to Europe but occurs also in Asia, even as far east as Japan, where burial mounds belonging to historic periods are common. In the neigh-

---

[1] Cambry, *Monuments de pierre en Portugal et en Espagne*, p. 199, quoted by De Marmora.

[2] Montelius, *Der Orient und Europa*, pp. 59–60, figs. 69–70.

[3] *ibid.* pp. 60–1, figs. 71 and 72.

[4] *ibid.* pp. 75–135.

[5] Rink, *Tales and traditions of Eskimo*, p. 8. Montelius, *op. cit.* pp. 43–44, figs. 43–45.

bourhood of Osaka[1], for instance, there are many widely scattered along the slopes of the mountains. They consist of stone chambers 15–20 ft high and 50–75 ft in diameter, approached by a long narrow passage or dromos and covered by mounds of earth, and date, according to Morse, about a hundred years back. The universality of the form then at different periods and in different parts of the globe is clear, whether it took its rise among the Neolithic peoples of the African continent as has been supposed, or had some still obscurer and remoter origin.

Our rapid survey of the western area of the Mediterranean basin tends to show that the type of dolmen cell surrounded by a tumulus, found throughout North Africa, spread to the islands and hence to the mainland of the European continent. Though there may be some exceptions, as in Spain and Corsica where the tendency, as far as present evidence goes, seems to have been rather to the rectangular, yet on the whole the round chamber approached by a dromos and surrounded by a conical tumulus is the more common form, and is the unmistakable prototype of the bee-hive tombs of Greece.

It is not possible to separate the style for the living from that for the dead among these early peoples: the two forms, viz. round and rectangular, occur interchangeably over this vast connected area, and at the very remotest date at which we have evidence there is no certain distinction.

The form adopted for the living and dead respectively seems to have been dependent on the whim of each little group of emigrants, who were probably influenced in their choice not only by climatic conditions but also by the materials and natural resources which they found around them.

[1] Morse, *Dolmens in Japan*, p. 5.

CHAPTER III

NEOLITHIC PERIOD IN EAST MEDITERRANEAN BASIN

IN the East Mediterranean area the case is different. Owing to the light materials, such as wood and brick, employed in *Egyptian* domestic architecture, and the precarious position of the houses quite close to the river, very little has survived to give us any complete idea of the early dwelling house: the various representations, however, in the tombs give a fairly adequate notion of the ground plan, which appears in all cases to be rectangular.

The house[1] stands in the midst of a court or garden, which is surrounded by a high crenellated wall, and must have presented the same barren exterior as the Moorish architecture in Spain to-day. The entrance court led to an open paved space sometimes with columns, on to which the various rooms opened, and at the further end of which was a reception room. Behind this was often a second court with trees, and the house further contained straight corridors with rooms on either side.

The house was normally two storeyed, but some of the bigger houses in Thebes had four or even five storeys. The streets were regular but exceedingly narrow.

The plan, then, somewhat resembles the later Greek plan, but the ground floor rooms were generally used for

---

[1] Wilkinson, *Manners and customs of the Ancient Egyptians*, I. v. 345–50.

storage, the upper for living rooms. The roofs were always flat.

The country houses were constructed on the same plan[1], and all through the military architecture we find the rectangular form prevailing[2].

With the tombs[3], both the pyramids and mastabas, it is likewise, though here we occasionally find a chamber of curved form recalling the tholos. At Abydos, for instance, there is a small pyramid from 5 m. to 6 m. high, built of crude brick in the form of a rough cupola[4]. So also in the Beni-Hassan tombs, though the general style is rectangular, we sometimes find the roof of the chamber in the form of a vault[5].

For the temples the rectangular form is used without exception.

Turning to *Phoenicia* we find that the tombs of Amrith resemble the Egyptian, and all show the rectangular plan. The descent to the tomb is by means of a long, vertical shaft or later by a staircase, and at the bottom are the doors leading into the various chambers, which were built as required, each to contain one corpse[6].

The necropolis of Tyre is disappointing, and the so-called tomb of Hiram[7] is certainly of later date, but in the necropolis of Sidon we find many tombs built in the same characteristic way, as also in Cyprus and Rhodes where Phoenician influence came.

In *Cyprus* the Neolithic period is almost entirely unrepresented[8]. No settlements or tombs have been

---

[1] Wilkinson, *op. cit.* I. v. 365.   [2] Wilkinson, *op. cit.* I. iii. 268.
[3] Perrot et Chipiez, *Histoire de l'Art dans l'Antiquité*, I. 3, pp. 168 sqq.
[4] *ibid.* p. 250.   [5] *ibid.* p. 256.
[6] Perrot et Chipiez, *op. cit.* III. iii. pp. 144 sqq.
[7] *ibid.* pp. 164 and 167, fig. 113.
[8] Myres and Richter, *Catalogue Cyprus Museum*, pp. 13, 14.

discovered and no distinct Neolithic pottery. The little building in the neighbourhood of Larnaka[1], consisting of two rooms with monoliths forming the roofs, is a remarkable megalithic structure, and the megalithic remains at old Paphos belong in all probability to Neolithic times[2].

Though *Caria* no longer holds the proud position in which she was placed by some former archaeologists (so Koehler and Dümmler)[3], who, struck by close religious analogies with Crete, wished to look upon her as the birthplace of the entire Mycenean civilisation, of which, as is evidenced by her pottery, she only felt the influence at quite a late date, some remains unearthed by Messrs Paton and Myres, which are interesting in connection with the history of early architectural forms in the East Mediterranean area may be mentioned.

These remains consist only of primitive tombs; of houses and towns there are none. The simple cist graves[4] of the dolmen type occur, resembling the Cycladic examples and consisting of four upright slabs and a cover, some only a metre long, others full length; side by side with this rectangular form occurs the round and sometimes oval form of the chambered tumulus with the last few courses projecting, the whole being closed in by slabs and covered with heaped-up stones. The dromos was generally filled

[1] Max Ohnefalsch Richter, "Ein altes Bauwerk bei Larnaka," *Arch. Zeitung*, 1881, p. 311, and pl. 18; cf. *Kypros, The Bible and Homer*, pl. CXXV. nos. 3 and 4. Professor Myres tells me that another megalithic structure in the island is kept covered by the peasants who consider it sacred.

[2] Ohnefalsch Richter, *Kypros, The Bible and Homer*, p. 352, pl. XVIII. 2. Guillemard, *Athenaeum*, April 14, 1888, p. 474, however considers them Roman, and Hogarth, *Devia Kypria*, pp. 47–52, concurs.

[3] The question discussed by Paton and Myres, *J.H.S.* XVI. pp. 264–70. Cf. Ridgeway, *Early Age of Greece*, p. 269.

[4] Paton and Myres, *l.c.* p. 243.

in with rubbish. Some of these tumuli had secondary chambers of rectangular form.

The large proportions of some of these graves have raised the question as to whether they were all roofed over. Paton considers this impossible in a circle of 50 m. diameter[1], and indeed it would imply a dome as vast as that of the Pantheon or St Peter's at Rome. The tomb of Agamemnon, which is the largest we know in complete preservation, has a diameter of only 48 ft. A mound may have been superimposed, as must have been the case with the shaft graves of Mycenae, and as we see in the tomb at Vulci[2] in Etruria, of which the original diameter must have been about 240 ft and whose mound with retaining wall was 115–120 ft in height.

The inward slope of the walls in the case of the larger Carian tombs must be a reminiscence of earlier use, and can only be regarded as a survival in a later age of the system which we find in the Mycenean tholoi, just as in Crete the stomion and dromos survive at Erganos, but are of such small proportions as to serve no purpose[3].

The tombs found by Mr Paton in the neighbourhood of Halicarnassus[4], on the site identified by Newton with Termera, show the same characteristics. The two large tumuli to the south-east of the Acropolis have circular walls about 30 ft in diameter, with stones piled above to form the tumulus. The walls of the sepulchral chamber curve inwards to allow of its being closed by slabs.

Near these tumuli were found circular enclosures, probably the remains of tumuli, containing sepulchral chambers, and rectangular enclosures, which only contained ostothekae in the shape of shallow circular cavities.

---

[1] Paton and Myres, *l.c.* p. 248 and p. 251, note 1.
[2] Dennis, *Cities and cemeteries of Etruria*, I. p. 452.
[3] *vide* p. 37.   [4] *J.H.S.* VIII. p. 66.

Another tomb showed the remains of sarcophagi, and there were besides two large rectangular enclosures containing rectangular tombs and circular ostothekae.

A finely built and excellently preserved tomb on another summit is of the tumulus form, with rectangular sepulchral chamber and dromos, and shows that the style of the Assarlik tombs continued to be in use at a much later period. These tombs are of comparatively late date; remains of iron weapons are found in all, the bodies have been cremated and the pottery is all of geometric design, but the old Neolithic forms are still persisting.

Three hours to the south-east of Halicarnassus Winter found similar graves, round and rectangular side by side in the same enclosure[1].

In the Eastern Mediterranean basin, then, the conditions are not so uniform. In Egypt and Phoenicia the rectangular form seems to have prevailed from the earliest times of which we have record, though it is naturally impossible to assert that the round form never existed in these countries.

On the coast of Asia Minor, which always seems to have felt Western influences more strongly than Eastern, we find survivals of the forms which prevailed in the West Mediterranean area, and which we shall study more particularly as they appear in the Mycenean age in Greece.

---

[1] Winter, "Vasen aus Karien," *Ath. Mitt.* XII. 225.

CHAPTER IV

LACUSTRINE DWELLINGS

AN interesting development in Central Europe, the existence of which in the Cyclades is perhaps implied by the island urns, is the rise of lacustrine villages, which began to make their appearance in the Stone Age and continued throughout the Bronze and Iron Ages. They even existed among the Dacians as late as the beginning of the 2nd century A.D., for they are twice represented on the column of Trajan[1].

In the early ages it was especially in the lakes on both sides of the Alps that they flourished, but Pfahlbauten existed all over Central Europe and even so far west as Ireland[2].

The growth of peat on the margins of lakes, by compelling the inhabitants to abandon their settlements, has preserved them for us, as well as the fact that they were built of combustible materials on wooden platforms, which subjected them to conflagrations and final desertion. Thus they have lain quiet for centuries below water with the implements of their former inhabitants buried beneath the peat.

Though many such settlements are found along the shores of lakes, some of them must have been artificial

---

[1] Cichorius, *Die Reliefs der Traiansäule*, Tafel xx. Bild xxv. Text II. pp. 122–28; Tafel XL. Bild LVII. Text II. pp. 261–3.

[2] Munro, *Lake dwellings of Europe*, p. 7.

island dwellings, *e.g.* Robenhausen[1], which is 2000 yards away from the nearest land and forms a quadrangle three acres in extent.   It would seem that, in general, all the refuse was thrown through holes in the platforms into the water beneath, where it gradually accumulated, until the intervening space was entirely filled up, when the platform had to be elevated and the same kind of construction erected at a higher level.

Herodotus' description of the dwellers on Lake Prasias, whom Megabazus could not conquer, tallies exactly with the deductions we should draw from existing remains with regard to the nature of these settlements.   He says (Hdt. v. 16) :—

ἰκρία ἐπὶ σταυρῶν ὑψηλῶν ἐζευγμένα ἐν μέσῃ ἕστηκε τῇ λίμνῃ ἔσοδον ἐκ τῆς ἠπείρου στεινὴν ἔχοντα μιῇ γεφύρῃ.   τοὺς δὲ σταυροὺς τοὺς ὑπεστεῶτας τοῖσι ἰκρίοισι τὸ μέν κου ἀρχαῖον ἔστησαν κοινῇ πάντες οἱ πολιῆται.   μετὰ δὲ νόμῳ χρεώμενοι ἱστᾶσι τοιῷδε.   κομίζοντες ἐξ οὔρεος, τῷ οὔνομά ἐστι Ὄρβηλος, κατὰ γυναῖκα ἑκάστην ὁ γαμέων τρεῖς σταυροὺς ὑπίστησι......οἰκεῦσι δὲ τοιοῦτον τρόπον, κρατέων ἕκαστος ἐπὶ τῶν ἰκρίων καλύβης τε ἐν ᾗ διαιτᾶται, καὶ θύρης καταπακτῆς διὰ τῶν ἰκρίων κάτω φερούσης ἐς τὴν λίμνην· τὰ δὲ νήπια παιδία δέουσι τοῦ ποδὸς σπάρτῳ μὴ κατακυλισθῇ δειμαίνοντες· τοῖσι δὲ ἵπποισι καὶ τοῖσι ὑποζυγίοισι παρέχουσι χόρτον ἰχθῦς· τῶν δὲ πλῆθός ἐστι τοσοῦτον ὥστε ὅταν τὴν θύρην τὴν καταπακτὴν ἀνακλίνῃ κατίει σχοίνῳ σπυρίδα κεινὴν ἐς τὴν λίμνην καὶ οὐ πολλόν τινα χρόνον ἐπισχὼν ἀνασπᾷ πλήρεα ἰχθύων.

Platforms supported upon tall piles stand in the middle of the lake, which are approached from the land by a single narrow bridge.   At the first the piles which bear up the platforms were fixed in their places by the whole body of the citizens, but since that time the custom which has prevailed about fixing them is this :—they are brought from a hill called Orbelus and every man drives in three for each wife that he marries . . . . . . and this is the way in which they live.   Each has his own hut, wherein he dwells, upon one of the platforms, and each has also a trap door giving access to the lake beneath; and their wont is

---

[1] Keller, *Lake dwellings of Switzerland*, pp. 41–63.

to tie their baby children by the foot with a string, to save them from rolling into the water. They feed their horses and their other beasts upon fish, which abound in the lake to such a degree that a man has only to open his trap door and to let down a basket by a rope into the water, and then to wait a very short time, when he draws it up quite full of them.

This account, formerly regarded as fanciful, has been proved correct in every detail by the discovery of the Swiss Lake dwellings, and we can no longer deny the possibility of such settlements having existed in Greece, even if we do not with Tsountas[1] see some connection with them in such a settlement as that on the island of Gha, which he considers to have had its origin in an allied system.

It is now conclusively established that races allied to the Swiss Lake dwellers built, perhaps at a slightly later date, similar settlements on dry land, of which may be mentioned, among many other interesting examples, the large flat mounds known as Terremare[2], scattered over the provinces of Parma Reggio and Modena, and formerly regarded as habitations of the dead.

Chierici's assumption of artificial basins filled by diverting the course of a running stream[3] accounted for the lacustrine type found away from lakes and rivers, before it was realised that the settlements could be entirely terrestrial, built by peoples conserving the lacustrine tradition with no further object than that of fortification.

The inhabitants may even have lived in tents or huts on their platforms, as well as in erected pile dwellings.

---

[1] Tsountas and Manatt, *Mycenean Age*, pp. 328–9 and Appendix B. Two-storey houses are also derived by him from pile dwellings, *ibid.* p. 249.

[2] Munro, *op. cit.* pp. 238 sqq.

[3] Chierici, *Le antichità preromane della provincia di Reggio nell' Emilia.*

Such pile structures occur not only in Italy but also in Hungary, Holland and Germany, showing both the strength of the lacustrine tradition and also the wide area over which it reigned. The Burgwälle[1] of North Germany, built in boggy places and sometimes actually over a former pile dwelling, though conforming to the same type, belong to a much more recent period.

The architectural evidence is scanty, but as far as it is possible to judge, the rectangular form prevailed in these lacustrine settlements. At Castione[2], which may be taken as typical, a rectangular space covering about two acres was chosen by the Terramaricoli for their site, a ditch was dug and the earth taken from it thrown up to make an embankment 6 ft high. To strengthen this dyke, log houses of rectangular form were constructed along its inner sides; rows of piles were planted in straight lines at regular intervals, and on these a platform of horizontal planks was laid upon which the huts were constructed.

Remains of some circular hearths, from 4 m.–6½ m. apart, have been discovered, but whether the actual huts were round or rectangular, there is no means of judging.

Wood was certainly largely used in their construction and probably straw and clay as well: they were thus of a highly inflammable nature and but slight traces of their form are left.

It is possible that here, as on other early sites, both the round and square forms were in use; in the case of the former we may suppose, calculating from the distance apart of the hearths, that the huts were some 18 ft or

[1] Virchow, *Zeit. für Ethn.* I. "Die Pfahlbauten des nördlichen Deutschlands," pp. 411 sqq.

[2] Pigorini, *Terramarà dell' età del bronzo situata in Castione dei Marchesi*, 1883, p. 44.

more in diameter, if placed quite close together like the Kurdistan huts[1] to-day, or somewhat less if, as probably was the case, spaces were left between them.

In some places, indeed, portions of clay have been found with a round impress; on the other hand at Schussenried[2], where the village was abandoned on account of the growth of the peat, and the evidence is clearer than is usually the case where a conflagration has brought the settlement to a sudden end, remains of a house were found of rectangular form 33 ft long by 23 ft broad, containing two rooms.

Scanty as are the remains of habitations belonging to this system, they are yet important as showing, though but in a very limited way, the architectural tendencies of at least one group of the Neolithic peoples, who spread over Europe after the Great Ice Age.

Again we find the curved and rectangular constructions side by side, with a tendency to prefer the rectangular, which is natural where the chief material employed is wood. Unfortunately, we have as yet no direct evidence for the part played by the development of this system in Greece itself, and can only look to the testimony of Herodotus until excavation has unearthed remains of such settlements, which were probably widespread.

[1] Bulle, *Orchomenos*, pl. XI. 1 and 2.
[2] Gross, *Matériaux*, XVII. p. 321, "Une hutte de l'époque de la pierre découverte à Schussenried."

CHAPTER V

THE NORDIC HOUSE

A SLIGHT reference must be made to the Nordic house, for, although its development belongs to historic times, it is useful for purposes of comparison, and more especially in connection with the part played by the central hearth in the Southern house. In the Northern house the hearth was of course for climatic reasons a permanent necessity.

In spite of the preponderance of the rectangular form in later times, the Nordic house was circular in origin, the earliest dwellings, as for example in Lapland[1], being of the tent form covered with wood or skins, a form which is soon developed by building a strong circular wall round the bottom on which the rounded roof rests. This type probably goes back to Neolithic times.

In the transition from round to rectangular we find both oval forms, *e.g.* Giant Graves in Gotland or the Black House in the Hebrides, and polygonal forms, *e.g.* some of the houses in Lapland[2].

This leads on to the rectangular plan which, whether due to a change of race or not, remains the established plan of the Nordic house.

In the tent and circular dwelling, the entrance was direct into the room, in the centre of which the hearth was placed: with the rectangular house we soon find

[1] Montelius, *Archiv für Anthrop.* XXIII. "Zür ältesten Geschichte des Wohnhauses in Europa, speciell im Norden," p. 451 and fig. 1. Cf. Schulz Minden, *Das germanische Haus*, p. 12, fig. 2; p. 33, fig. 9.

[2] *ibid.* p. 452, figs. 8, 9 and 10.

that a verandah is built[1], which becomes a vestibule by being built in on the four sides. The entrance is then changed to the side and the vestibule divided into two rooms, the second being entered from the principal room with the hearth. A similar construction is often built at the other end of the house, and then follow gradual additions and enlargements around the large room with the hearth, which remains the centre of the house.

The older round type did not, however, entirely die out, and round buildings exist in Sweden to-day, not only among the more primitive Lapps in the north but even in the south inhabited by Swedes, whilst in Öland and Gotland rectangular houses are found with rounded corners, which thus approach the oval ground plan[2].

Open hearths are still found in many parts: the chimney was quite a late development.

In spite of the glowing accounts in the Sagas of the great halls of kingly houses in the 9th, 10th and 11th centuries A.D., we are compelled to think of the Vikings' dwellings as of primitive form and materials, and as generally consisting of a large inner room with central hearth, the principal apartment (Ryggåsstuyor)[3].

Mr Lang's account of the Icelandic house[4] of the 11th century is interesting in this connection, and again shows the hearth the centre of the house. The hall is entered through a courtyard around which small rooms are built, and is supported by four rows of columns, of which the two inner rows are taller. The hearth is between them and sometimes in severe weather fire is kindled in a trench

---

[1] Montelius, *op. cit.* p. 453.
[2] *ibid.* p. 455.   [3] *ibid.* fig. 25.
[4] Andrew Lang, *Homer and his age*, p. 222. Cf. also *Odyssey*, Butcher and Lang, "The House of Odysseus," p. 422.

down the hall. The seats of honour for the lord and guests are near the hearth, as in the Homeric megaron.

The farmhouses of Schleswig belonging to the 16th, 17th and 18th centuries described by Mejborg may be taken as typical of the plan, which persisted for the Nordic house[1].

The building is divided into three parts: in the middle is a great hall or open courtyard (*A*) (as in Fig. 1 (*c*)) with a large chamber (*B*) at the further end, and around on the other two sides small rooms, stalls for pigs, oxen and horses, a place for the waggons and a barn.

Some (as in Fig. 1 (*a*)) have two smaller rooms opposite the entrance instead of the large chamber, and others have a second sitting room suitable for use in summer.

They are generally roofed over with a gable roof the ends of which are elaborately ornamented with wood carving, while windows letting in light from without are very numerous in the larger houses. Such a dwelling would present a very different appearance from that of the Greek house with its open courtyard and rooms lighted entirely from it: the ground plan however, as a glance at the plate will show, is similar.

The entrance is in some cases through a vestibule, in others the large door opens directly into the courtyard. The difference between rich and poor is especially noticeable in the interior. The general effect is gloomy, since but a weak light can penetrate through the window and door, and the walls and ceiling are blackened by the smoke which sometimes fills the room to such an extent that one cannot see one's hand before one's face. The kitchen is generally a separate room, but at the further end of the hall is a low-walled hearth where the kettles hang. The heavy carved post with hooks for lamps,

---

[1] Mejborg, *Das Bauernhaus im Herzogtum Schleswig*, pass.

etc., near the fire, against which the mother leans on winter evenings when all are gathered around the fire, offers a very close parallel to the Homeric columns around the hearth in the Palace of Alcinous, etc.

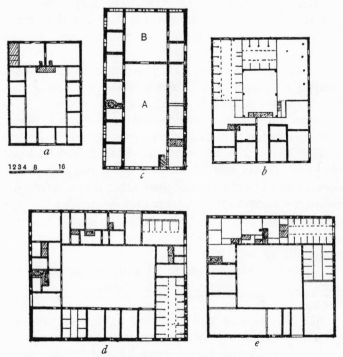

Fig. 1. Farmhouses of Schleswig.

Above are plans of some of the more typical farmhouses of Schleswig (Fig. 1). One sees to-day farmhouses of similar construction and disposition in the neighbourhood of Hamburg. Similar plans are found in Alsace[1], Hanover[2], etc.

[1] Henning, *Das deutsche Haus*, p. 21, fig. 10.
[2] *ibid.* p. 31, fig. 15.

The typical Nordic house, then, is rectangular in form and consists of a large common room with the hearth in the centre, around which the smaller rooms are grouped.

The possibility of this plan having exerted an influence on Greek building in its very early stages must be considered, it being assumed that the historical house conserves a type which goes back to the very earliest times.

In the North the hearth is the centre, in the extreme South the open court. This is a fundamental difference, which must not be lost from view, and which remains fixed all through the development of the Greek house, from the Cretan palaces of the Minoan age to the Hellenistic houses of the 2nd century. Indeed the courtyard plan with rooms opening on to a court and on the first floor on to a balcony has not died out, but is still common both on the mainland of Greece and in the islands. The Greek central hearth megaron of the mainland, abutting on to a courtyard, stands midway and perhaps owes something to both forms.

That it should first occur at Troy is another of the many unsolved problems in the early architecture of Greece.

The complicated and involved nature of the race questions renders any satisfactory and certain conclusion with regard to the part played by the Nordic house impossible, the Aryan controversy[1], which has raged for so many years, being as far from any definite settlement as ever.

But whichever of the various racial hypotheses we may accept, the plan of the Nordic house is fixed and definite: and as an established plan we may receive and study it until the time is ripe to explain its origin.

[1] *vide* Reinach, *L'origine des Aryens.*

CHAPTER VI

CRETAN TOMBS

Before we proceed to consider the earliest forms of the actual house of the living in Crete and on the mainland of Greece, a short digression may be made in order to take a rapid review of sepulchral architecture, which, by its perfectly developed and evidently well established form, implies houses for the living in the round at a very remote period. On the mainland of Greece positive evidence is not wanting with regard to these structures, but on the island of Crete no remains of any domestic building in the round have been found, so that the tombs are particularly important here as showing that the round form was not foreign to Cretan architecture, though the rectangular had become so fixed as a type by the time the earliest palaces were planned and built.

Three typical modes of burial[1] were prevalent and apparently contemporary, for objects of the same type were found in the three kinds of graves: but no explanation has as yet been given of their origin and history; possibly they bear witness to the customs of different tribes.

Of these three different modes the pit graves with the interment in a walled cavity at the side of the hole, and the shaft graves with the extended skeleton at the bottom, only concern us here in so far as they exhibit a rectangular

[1] Evans, *Prehistoric Tombs of Knossos*, I. pp. 1–21, types of sepulture.

form; the chamber tombs, on the other hand, have a direct bearing on prehistoric architecture.

The complete tholoi of Crete, which are of such great interest as a ritualistic survival of the probable primitive domestic plan, are as yet rare, and, with the exception of the tomb at Hagia Triada, never attained such perfection of form and proportion as the later tholoi on the mainland.

The tholos of Hagia Triada[1] is a huge burial vault 9 m. in diameter, surrounded by small rooms and containing, as far as can be estimated, about 200 burials, with 50 more in the rooms behind it. It is approached by a short narrow dromos. The early hypothesis that it was the grave of warriors, who had fallen in some great battle, has been abandoned since bones of women and children were found in it, in favour of the supposition that it was a family vault. The wall stands on one side only and to no great height, but there seems to be no foundation whatever for the theory that it was unroofed, especially in view of the mainland examples which are in some cases of even larger proportions. The Treasury of Atreus at Mycenae[2], the most perfect example in construction and decoration of this type, has the principal chamber about 50 ft in height and diameter and the circular vault of large hewn blocks is capped by a single stone. The Tomb of Clytemnestra[3] is similar in plan and those at Menidi[4] and Vaphio[5] are also of large proportions. It is clear, then, that the tomb at Hagia Triada may quite well have been completed in the same

[1] *Mem. del Institut Lombardo*, XXI. p. 249 and pl. VIII. figs. 18 and 19. Halbherr, *Hagia Triada*, Rendiconti XI. p. 445, report of Savignoni.

[2] Schliemann, *Mycenae*, pp. 42–49.

[3] *ibid.* pp. 118–120.

[4] Lolling, *Das Kuppelgrab bei Menidi*.

[5] Tsountas, 'Εφ. 'Αρχ. 1889, pp. 136 sqq.

way. It is probably not to be dated earlier than the middle of the Early Minoan period[1].

Another grave of noble proportions was the Royal tomb at Isopata[2] excavated by Dr Evans: it was unfortunately in a very denuded state, for the greater part of the upper masonry had been used for building purposes, and the vases found had been destroyed in the revolution, but the size and general construction proved it to be a tomb of some importance. The principal chamber was here rectangular, and measured 8 m. × 6·5 m., while the dromos was 24 m. long and ended in a fore-hall 6·75 m. × 1·50 m. The side walls of the chamber sloped inwards, while the end walls were vertical, and, though the bad state of repair of the tomb makes it impossible to decide what the exact form of the roof was, it is reasonable to think that it was composed in the usual way, with stone slabs to close in the vault.

Most of the remaining tholoi in Crete are of considerably smaller dimensions, but, though less perfect in form, they serve to show the strength and persistence of the tholos type, which was only abandoned very gradually and with great difficulty in face of the firm tradition.

One of the more interesting of these smaller tholoi, particularly noticeable on account of its contents, is that found near Anoja[3]: it was approached by a dromos 5 m. long but not high enough to allow a man to enter.

---

[1] So Burrows, *Discoveries in Crete*, p. 49, from primitive painted pottery and copper dagger blades found with bodies. Professor Ernest Gardner thinks not so early.

[2] *Archaeologia*, LIX. "Prehistoric Tombs of Knossos," Arthur Evans, pp. 525–29, pl. XCIII–XCVII. *Vide* also "Architectural details of Isopata tomb," Fyfe, *op. cit.* p. 551.

[3] Orsi, *Mon. Ant.* I. "Urne funebri Cretesi," pp. 203–4, and accompanying figs.

Within the chamber were found four small terracotta sarcophagi containing bones, but whether these had been burnt or not was not established by the discoverers. A funeral chamber without dromos[1] 2·30 m. in diameter containing a similar urn was found at Milatos to the south, and another urn of the same size and form was found in the neighbourhood of Pendamodi[2], though unfortunately no information is forthcoming as to its provenance.

These curious sarcophagi found in different parts of Crete but not elsewhere, manifestly from their shape and style of decoration belong to the same class and point to a uniformity of burial custom. Rectangular and oblong forms occur elsewhere as here, but the former is the commoner and is the forerunner of the rectangular chest of Homeric times, in which carpets, ornaments and valuables were kept.

The theory held by Tsountas that these Larnakes imitated the dwelling house of the living[3] has no real evidence to support it, and it seems much more likely that they served in the house as baths, perhaps even for a long period, before being turned to sepulchral use. The interesting discovery of a fragment of a terracotta bathing tub[4] with a handle of a similar nature at Tiryns would seem to confirm this suggestion.

With regard to the nature of the burial rite it is not likely that these sarcophagi were made for children, and they are too large for cinerary urns. Schliemann assumed a partial cremation[5], perhaps of clothes and flesh; otherwise the small proportions of the chests must have

[1] Orsi, *op. cit.* p. 208.

[2] *ibid.* p. 209.

[3] Tsountas, 'Εφ. 'Αρχ. 1891, p. 8. Tsountas and Manatt, *Mycenean age*, p. 137.

[4] Schliemann, *Tiryns*, p. 140; cf. pl. XXIV. *d* and *e*.

[5] Schliemann, *Mycenae*, p. 155.

necessitated burial in the crouched position[1], a mode which was prevalent on many early sites, even in cist graves.

One of the tombs at Muliana[2] which had been quite untouched contained two corpses, one buried on the floor, the other in a larnax, showing that custom was not absolutely fixed even in the same period.

These smaller tombs show the great tholos type undergoing gradual modification. Another tomb[3] at Muliana, which, though it had been re-used for some geometric burials, certainly belonged to a much earlier period, consisted of a rectangular chamber 2·42 m. × 1·82 m. enclosed by walls of unhewn stones, with the upper course built *en encorbeillement*: the top was closed by a single slab and the height was 1·60 m. Though the tholos form was still preserved, the dromos was missing, as also in the Panaghia tomb mentioned below as the final development.

At Hagios Theodorus[4] on the other hand the dromos is present, though it is only 3 m. long: the chamber measures 2 m. in diameter and has the usual vault with capping stone at the height of about 1·80 m. from the floor. The door is large enough to allow of a larnax being admitted.

The tombs at Erganos[5] represent, as it were, a transition stage between the tholos with stomion and dromos, such as the Isopata tomb, and the vaulted chamber of Panaghia, where the dromos is entirely absent and is only represented by a certain thickening of the front wall of the tomb.

---

[1] Evans, *op. cit.* fig. 4, and Xanthoudides, 'Εφ. 'Αρχ. 1904, pp. 6 sqq. and fig. 1.

[2] Xanthoudides, 'Εφ. 'Αρχ. 1904, pp. 38–9.

[3] Xanthoudides, *l.c.* pp. 23 sqq.

[4] Seager, *Trans. Univ. Penn.* 1906, II. pp. 129–32.

[5] Halbherr, *A.J.A.* 1901, pp. 270 sqq.

In these tombs the stomion and dromos are still present
but are of such small dimensions as to be entirely useless,
and can only have been made for traditional reasons. The
width of the stomion varies from 30–58 cm. and that of the
dromos is the same, so that the slabs which close the vault
must have been raised every time a body was introduced[1].

The tombs themselves, with circular ground plan and
tholos built *en encorbeillement*, are of exceedingly small
dimensions: one, in which six bodies were interred, was
1·30 m. in diameter and 80 m. in height[2], so that the only
possible mode of burial would have been to place the
skeletons with their legs towards the middle and their
backs against the wall. These were naturally poor
graves but are important as showing the persistence of this
type, even where the various component parts were built
in such a way as no longer to serve their original purpose.

At Panaghia the dromos has been frankly abandoned,
and the chamber is rectangular, with the four walls
inclining inwards, the final stage[3].

It is clear that the tendency towards rectangular
forms of building in Crete, which asserted itself at such
a remote period, in the realm of domestic architecture
modified little by little the type of tomb. A very
interesting piece of evidence in this connection has lately
come to light, for on a hill in the neighbourhood of
Koumasa Xanthoudides has found remains of an early
settlement of rectangular houses near some tholos tombs
with which they are probably contemporary[4]. Each of
these houses contains several rooms and in one is a stone
staircase leading to an upper storey.

About half an hour to the east of Koumasa near
H. Irene a similar settlement of rectangular dwellings

---

[1] Halbherr, *l.c.* p. 277.　　　[2] *ibid.* p. 272, fig. 6.
[3] *ibid.* p. 285, fig. 12.　　　[4] *Arch. Anz.* 1907, p. 108.

and tholos tombs were found side by side[1]. Here then
we have clear evidence of the round tomb and the
rectangular house side by side, the form of the tomb
probably representing a survival of the form of the earlier
house.

At the end of the summer of 1904 three tholos tombs
and one rectangular of E. M. period were found by
Xanthoudides[2] in the same neighbourhood containing
seals resembling those at Hagios Onouphrios and Hagia
Triada. The walls of the tholos were standing to the
height of $1-1\frac{1}{2}$ m. : the two larger were 10 m. in diameter
and the smaller about 4 m.

The scanty evidence which we have then for the
complete tholos suffices at least to prove that it was
established as a type in Crete, and that it struggled for
persistence, only gradually abandoning dromos and
stomion, and even then adhering to the round vaulted
plan, until at last the rectangular plan, so strongly
established for the houses of the living, creeps in also to
the realms of the dead.

The theory supported by Adler[3] and others that these
tholos tombs, modelled on the tent form, presuppose an
actual house of the living dug out in the hill-side, or in any
case a half subterranean earth hut, finds a curious parallel
in the account given by Vitruvius of the dwellings of the
Phrygians.

He says (Vitruv. II. I):

Phryges vero, qui campestribus locis sunt habitantes, propter
inopiam silvarum egentes materia eligunt tumulos naturales
eosque medios fossura distinentes et itinera perfodientes dilatant

---

[1] *Arch. Anz.* 1907, p. 108.

[2] Ἐφ. Ἀρχ. 1907, p. 145; Παναθήναια, 15. I. 05; Ἐπιστολαὶ ἐκ Κρήτης:
kindly sent me by Prof. Ernest Gardner through the courtesy of
M. Gennadius.

[3] *vide* p. 5.

spatia quantum natura loci patitur. Insuper autem stipites inter se religantes metas efficiunt, quas harundinibus et sarmentis tegentes exaggerant supra habitationes e terra maximos grumos. Ita hiemes calidissimas aestates frigidissimas efficiunt tectorum rationes.

The Phrygians, on the contrary, who live in plains, being without wood on account of the lack of forests choose natural hillocks, and piercing them in the middle and digging passages through, they enlarge the space as much as the nature of the place allows. Then above, binding stakes together, they make cones and covering them with reeds and twigs they heap up above these dwellings large clods of earth. Thus the disposition of the buildings assures very warm winters and very cool summers.

Such a dwelling with an approach like the dromos running into the hill-side, a pointed roof here made of stakes bound together with reeds and brushwood, and the whole covered with earth, closely resembles the tholos type, and makes the hypothesis of such a dwelling house in very early ages in Greece not impossible. It appears that similar constructions are found to-day in this district.

CHAPTER VII

ROUND, ELLIPTICAL AND RECTANGULAR FORMS

THE architectural evidence then shows the chambered tomb with dromos and tumulus spread over a very wide area in Neolithic times, an area which includes North Africa, Italy, Spain, France, Great Britain, and even Central Europe and Russia, and together with the craniological evidence and that derived from flora and fauna and artistic forms points to the conclusion of the existence of a common stock, diffused probably from North Africa through the Mediterranean in quaternary times[1].

The architectural forms, which we have briefly reviewed, predominating throughout the Mediterranean area during this epoch are for the most part approximately uniform, and include building in the round, oval and rectangular. The early history and development of these three styles of building will now be considered.

Curved and rectangular forms, as our survey of primitive constructions in prehistoric Europe serves to show, probably co-existed from time immemorial; it is in any case no easy matter to prove for certain which was the earlier form, however much presumptive evidence may point in favour of the former.

The circular is of course the natural shape: so the

---

[1] Sergi, *Mediterranean race*, p. 241. Cf. Hall, *The Ancient History of the Near East*, p. 32.

bird builds her nest and the beaver her home; nowhere in nature do we see a straight line; the natural materials, branches, reeds, etc., all bend in the wind and admit of bending, and primitive man would seem, when he first takes his twigs and his mud to erect for himself a shelter, to be generally inclined to the circular form, which with such materials is certainly the most easily made.   The boughs of trees are bent to the middle, smaller branches and twigs woven in horizontally, and the whole covered with mud, reeds or skins[1].   But a cursory glance will serve to show how common and widespread this natural form is.   To take an example in England, we have only to mention the hut circles of Dartmoor[2], consisting of the remains of a colony of such round huts, or the bee-hive huts of the Hebrides[3], some of which are quite modern.

Again the Antonine triumphal column at Rome gives us ample evidence of the prevalence of the round type of hut among the Germans[4].   To mention other examples, the "Kota" or round kitchens of the Finns, standing sometimes in close proximity to a rectangular house, are remnants of this type, and in France at the present day in the department of Lot round houses are built by the peasants[5].

But where hard materials, such as stone and timber, are forthcoming, the wattle and daub hut is easily abandoned and the rectangular form readily suggests itself, and may occur in quite an early stage of develop-

---

[1] Such huts are made in N. Italy to-day.

[2] Baring Gould, *Book of Dartmoor*, pp. 66–71.

[3] Wilson, *Prehistoric Annals of Scotland*, I. p. 121.

[4] Petersen, Domaszewski and Calderini, *Die Marcus Säule*, Taf. XIV., XXVIII., XXIX., XLIX., L. and LII.

[5] Montelius, "Die runde Hüttenform in Europa," *Archiv für Anthrop.* XXIII. p. 459.

ment as in Pantelleria[1], where examples built of lava blocks are found, though the circular form largely preponderates.

Formerly the round and rectangular were considered as the two exclusive types of early building in Greece, but the discovery by Xanthoudides of a farmhouse at Chamaizi, of distinctly elliptical ground plan, has raised

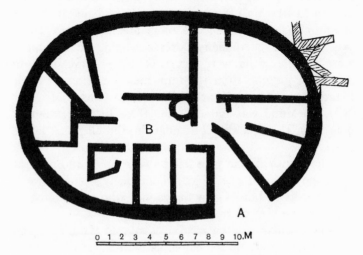

0 1 2 3 4 5 6 7 8 9 10.M

Fig. 2. Oval house at Chamaizi.

a discussion as to whether we are not to regard this as a transitional stage, which belongs essentially to the history of the complete development of the house, even though it may be represented but on few excavated sites.

This house was found near Chamaizi, about half an hour eastwards from Muliana, in 1903, but not published before 1906[2] (Fig. 2).

[1] *vide* p. 8.
[2] Xanthoudides, 'Εφ. 'Αρχ. 1906, pp. 118 sqq.

Though some damage had been done by the owner in digging foundations for new buildings, the ground plan was absolutely clear. The elliptical wall is preserved to a height of 1 m.–1½ m. all round, and encloses a space 22·20 m. × 14·50 m., divided by cross walls into large and small rooms. No traces of a door remain, but the entrance was apparently on the east side (*A*) into a rectangular space (*B*), which may have been uncovered and on to which all the rooms open, there being no direct communication between one room and another. There was probably a wooden staircase leading to an upper storey. The walls were made of stones embedded in clay, and judging from the implements and clay vessels found in the house, Xanthoudides dates it as E.M. iii or M.M. i. Metal was found in the three little rectangular houses on the east side, but none in the elliptical house itself.

The elliptical plan is in itself a reasonable and natural development, and one which would easily occur to races accustomed to building in the round, who yet desired to increase the size of their dwellings.

The circular vaulted form necessitated the height and breadth being about the same, as we may see in similar constructions built by savage tribes of the present day, *e.g.* the Mussgu huts[1] in Africa, where the height is actually a little greater. In general the narrower the vault, the more solid the construction, and indeed in such perfected buildings as the Mycenean tholoi[2] we find the same principle adhered to. Therefore a great height was necessary to roof a small room, and a round building could not exceed a certain size. The introduction of

[1] Barth, *Travels in North and Central Africa*, p. 601 (8 ft in diameter, 12 ft to top of cupola).

[2] Cf. proportions of Treasury of Atreus, *Mycenae*, p. 48.

niches into the wall as in the Nuraghi[1] of Sardinia gave added accommodation without however really increasing the size.

The floor space is then generally exceedingly limited in these primitive circular buildings, and the substitution of the oval for the round is a very palpable solution of this difficulty, while it affects but little the traditional construction. We have already seen several examples of prehistoric date in the Mediterranean area.

The development is one, then, which, on *a priori* grounds, is to be expected, and which now in view of the very abundant and unmistakable evidence on the site of Orchomenos excavated by Heinrich Bulle, and on some other prehistoric sites in a less complete form, is hardly any longer to be gainsaid for Greece.

This evidence is so exceedingly interesting and so vital to the question that it may be useful briefly to review it.

Apart from the myriad race problems which complicate to such a great extent the study of early architecture, and which the limited state of our knowledge at the present time makes it impossible to solve definitely, the site of *Orchomenos*[2] may be studied as showing a complete and consistent line of development from the round through the elliptical to the square and rectangular.

In the earliest layer the remains consist exclusively of circular buildings: the walls, which are built on the virgin rock, are strong and solid, and generally about one metre in thickness: within and without are large stones and the intermediate space is filled with smaller ones, the whole being levelled to carry the clay top. The interesting photograph, given by Mr Bulle in his publication, of huts in Kurdistan[3], shows a complete

[1] *vide* p. 11.   [2] Bulle, *Orchomenos*, pp. 1–68.
[3] *ibid*. Tafel XI. 2.

present day analogy, with the sole exception that the walls of the latter are very thin and consist of one layer only of clay bricks.

Some of these huts in the first layer were of quite diminutive proportions; in the smallest a man would just have been able to lie if he had put himself exactly in the middle. Such one-storyed round stone huts have not been found elsewhere in Greece hitherto: we may perhaps regard them as the true forerunners of the bee-hive tombs.

The next layer shows quite plainly and distinctly that the oval form has been adopted for the house: the walls are less thick than those of the circular layer but of similar construction and everywhere unmistakably elliptical in contour.

Some of these oval houses had rectangular corners, which would point to a transition stage: there is no definite proof that the rectangular house yet existed on the site.

The βόθροι or small holes in the floor of the huts of this layer for the deposition and apparent preservation of ashes is a curious feature, which points perhaps to its builders as superstitious folk, who regarded them as sacred.

The round buildings are dated by Bulle *circ.* 3000 B.C. and the third, or as he designates it the Old Mycenean layer, *circ.* 1700–1500 B.C.

Here many small rectangular houses occur, and in and between the houses very perfect examples of that characteristic Mycenean form of burial, the Höckergrab.

It is impossible to form any adequate idea of the normal ground plan in this layer, since no whole house really survives, but three distinct layers are visible, of which the second is the best built and the most crowded;

it was evidently an age of prosperity, and of great agricultural activity at Orchomenos, since much corn was found.

In the settlement there were probably common walls and courts, some of which, as in the case of the burnt houses, were paved with plaster slabs. The lower part of the walls was built of stone, and the upper probably of clay bricks. The fourth and top layer, of the late Mycenean epoch, does not present any architectural evidence of importance.

On this site, then, we have unmistakable evidence of the existence at a very early period of the oval house, and the three layers show the three styles in chronological sequence, whether they were built by different tribes or not.

In view of this very positive evidence at Orchomenos, it seems needlessly far-fetched to explain the farmhouse at Chamaizi as the adaptation of a rectangular plan to a circular (so Mackenzie[1]) : in fact it is to put the cart before the horse.

The round house, as we have seen, did not admit of much enlargement and was not divided into separate rooms, unless the hut urn of Amorgos shows such a division on the simplest lines[2]. It seems much more probable, as Noack[3] suggests, that the division into rooms depends originally upon the roof. The roof of the round hut was often supported in the middle by a pole or post like the tent; if the house was much enlarged, the rafters could not run to one point, and a principal beam was substituted along the principal axis and supported at both ends.

---

[1] *B.S.A.* xiv. "Cretan palaces," iv. pp. 415–21.

[2] Dümmler, *Ath. Mitt.* xi. p. 18; also *Kleine Schriften*, iii. p. 49, fig. 32.

[3] *Ovalhaus und Palast in Kreta*, pp. 55–56 and fig. 6.

In the oval house then, the rafters would run at right angles to this beam in the middle and would radiate at each end.

Walls running up to the rafters would greatly strengthen the fabric and would form the natural division into rooms. That some of the end walls do not so radiate but follow the line of the principal axis, only shows the tendency towards the rectangular form, which was so generally adopted afterwards for buildings both in Crete and Greece.

A few other interesting sites in connection with this question may be briefly mentioned: though not so absolutely clear as Orchomenos, where we have perfect skeleton ground plans of elliptical houses, they yet serve to strengthen the hypothesis of the general development from the circular to the rectangular through the transitional elliptical form, which persisted when regular rectangular houses were already being built.

In the course of Dörpfeld's excavations at Olympia in 1907[1] it became clear from the pottery and remains that there was a prehistoric layer between the Heraeum and the Pelopion: in the following year the walls of six dwelling houses were unearthed, the ground plan of four of which could be easily made out. Dörpfeld gives no plan of the buildings but describes them as having curved ends which in two cases are cut off from the chief room which is rectangular by a cross wall.

Two other buildings of this period had been discovered 25 years before but not recognised as prehistoric. One of these to the south of the Metroon, which was long thought to be the foundation of the great altar of Zeus, is of the regular elliptical shape with which we are now familiar on various prehistoric sites, and adds confirmation

---

[1] Dörpfeld, *Ath. Mitt.* 1908, XXXIII. pp. 188 sqq.

to the ever increasing evidence for the oval house as a transitional form.

The oval house at Rini in Thessaly (*vide infra*) is another very clear case of elliptical ground plan.

On the island of *Paros*[1] Tsountas has found remains of a prehistoric settlement, much of which had already been washed into the sea, and which consisted of houses and tombs. The acropolis was fortified by two series of walls of slightly different date, within which the lower parts of the walls of four buildings were preserved to a height of about ·60 m.

They were built, according to the usual prehistoric system, of stones embedded in clay, with the foundations slightly wider than the upper part, and the floors were of small flat stones or beaten earth. Three of the rooms were rectangular, but the fourth, in the building to the north, had two of its corners rounded: whether or not it was connected with the rectangular room beside it and formed as it were a prodomos, it is not now possible to say: in any case there was no direct exit to the passage, which runs alongside of both. That the building of elliptical walls persisted is clearly shown on this site, by the bow-shaped piece of wall which was later built over these rooms[2].

About 20 m. to the north of these remains, was found a fragment of wall belonging to a building with rounded corners[3], a transition from oval to rectangular. It was straight for 4 m. and then began to curve. Here then we have distinct remains of the transitional oval style.

Of the roofs of these primitive dwellings we know nothing: they cannot however have been very heavy to judge from the thickness of the walls, and were probably,

[1] Tsountas, 'Εφ. 'Αρχ. 1898, pp. 168 sqq.
[2] 'Εφ. 'Αρχ. 1898, p. 170, fig. 9.   [3] *ibid.* p. 171.

on the evidence of the triangular piece of clay with marks of reeds, made of reeds or branches daubed with clay or plaster in the customary manner[1]. The four stones found with the hollow mark caused by the pivot are evidence for at least one door to each room.

Further testimony of a similar nature is forthcoming in the neighbouring island of *Syros*[2], where a prehistoric settlement was unearthed by Tsountas in the following year. The acropolis was likewise surrounded by two fortification walls, the inner of which was very strongly built and furnished with curved towers at a distance of from 4 m.–8 m. apart. The gateway is cleverly contrived in the outer wall by building one part of it slightly back, so that the entrance faced east instead of being in the direct line of the wall, and would be quite invisible from a distance.

Such fortification walls which are also found in *Siphnos*[3] may be compared with those at Phylakopi in Melos of the second period of occupation and were evidently long in use on the islands in the Neolithic age.

The houses within the walls of the Acropolis in Syros, which are of exactly the same style in plan and materials as those in Paros, show in the same way a blending of the rectangular and elliptical forms. Two are entirely rectangular, while the other three have three straight sides and one curved (Fig. 3).

The houses marked *A* and *B* in Fig. 3 show a primitive form of prodomos with a curved wall, through which the inner rectangular room was entered.

On the second acropolis no remains of houses were found: it was probably only used as a refuge in case of unexpected danger, and was left unfinished.

---

[1] See p. 60. [2] Tsountas, 'Εφ. 'Αρχ. 1899, pp. 115 sqq.
[3] *ibid.* p. 130 and fig. 38.

The earliest Cycladic houses are then rectangular, with some indications of a round form in previous use: of the earlier Neolithic period we have unfortunately no evidence here. The cist tombs which exist alongside of the houses are of rectangular type like them.

Fig. 3. Houses in Syros.

The square form is then well established in the Cyclades in the early Minoan age, but the scanty remains excavation has brought to light point to an earlier round form, the existence of which is confirmed by the island urns now to be described.

The hut urns of Melos[1] and Amorgos[2] are both, on the evidence of the stone of which they are made, of island fabric and appear to represent huts standing on pile platforms (Fig. 4, *a* and *b*).

a.   Melos Urn.

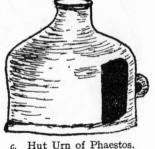

b.   Amorgos Urn.   *c.*   Hut Urn of Phaestos.

Fig. 4   Hut Urns.

The Melian urn was thought by Sir John Lubbock to represent a building of the lacustrine type[3], and was accordingly published by him as a model of a Swiss lake dwelling: this view has however been disputed by many

---

[1] Lubbock, *Prehistoric Times*, p. 48, fig. 78.
[2] Dümmler, *Kl. Schr.* III. p. 49, fig. 32.   [3] Also by Pigorini.

critics. Tsountas regards these models as representing complete cities[1]. He recalls the fact that Tiryns, Orchomenos and Amyclae are all situated in marshes, which he thinks were chosen for sites as being in themselves a protection. It is perhaps pressing the evidence too far to derive the two-storied Mycenean villa represented in the miniature models from Knossos from such a type of house (so Tsountas[2]), but the possibility of lacustrine dwellings having existed in this part of Europe can no longer be overlooked.

The Melian urn seems to represent a little colony of round huts on a rectangular platform, constructed upon four piles of logs: the seven huts are arranged in rows of three, around three sides of a square courtyard, on the fourth side of which stands a thatched porch leading into it.

The lid of the urn is unfortunately missing, so that the shape of the roofs can only be inferred, but the huts represented were probably of clay, with the round roof finished in the usual primitive manner.

These little lacustrine dwellings, if such they be, must have been known to the Greek islands in prehistoric times, and show an interesting combination of the circular and rectangular styles, the round huts being arranged on the sides of a square courtyard.

The Amorgos urn is not quite such a clear example, but taken in conjunction with the Melian, it may safely be regarded as representing a building of the same type, in this case however only a single hut. The four piles are connected by cross beams, supporting the platform on which the hut stands, which in this case is complete with its conical roof in which are holes, perhaps smoke outlets.

---

[1] Tsountas, Μυκῆναι καὶ Μυκηναῖος Πολιτισμός, p. 222.

[2] Tsountas and Manatt, *Mycenean age*, p. 249.

This hut is particularly interesting as showing the primitive division of a circular hut into two parts by means of a partition wall. Both urns are ornamented with the double spiral so characteristic of the Bronze Age.

The dwelling, resembling the urn in ground plan, which has been found in Amorgos, is of much later date and probably belongs to the 7th century[1].

The little votive terracotta, ·068 m. high and ·07 m. in diameter, found at Phaestos[2], is also of interest in this connection (Fig. 4 c). It has been said to represent a round hut standing on a round platform: its vertical walls support a conical roof, which ends in a slightly projecting horizontal disc. In the side is an opening reaching to the roof, with supports about half way up, apparently for the bar which closed it. If it is a house model[3] it would be of particular importance as showing the round type of house, so widely spread in primitive times, but probably replaced in Crete at a very remote date by the rectangular form.

But it is not only in the islands that we have evidence of the style and development of prehistoric building: the settlement at Orchomenos[4] in Boeotia has already been mentioned and *Thessaly* has also yielded important remains bearing out the same conclusions, though not illustrating so strikingly the complete development from round to rectangular.

The Stone Age settlements in Thessaly, where the

---

[1] Tsountas and Manatt, *op. cit.* p. 261.

[2] *Mon. Ant.* XII. p. 128, fig. 55.

[3] Prof. J. L. Myres suggests that it may be a lamp-shade such as he has often seen in Greek bazaars, about ·15 m. high and the same breadth. Its size makes it possible that it may have been a cover for a lamp set in a kernos like that figured in *B.S.A.* XII. p. 7.

[4] *vide* p. 45.

Neolithic culture lasted on till very late times, are extremely numerous[1]. Tsountas writes that he knows of sixty-three, and doubtless many more would be discovered if Thessaly were exhaustively excavated. The ἀκροπόλεις are either conical or rectangular with flattened top, the former generally being burial places and the latter settlements, of which the two most important for the history of the house are those of Dimini and Sesklo.

The acropolis of *Dimini* lies in the plain of Volo already known for its tombs. It is surrounded by no less than six walls, somewhat irregularly built, in some parts from 10 m.–15 m. apart, in others with not a metre between them, so that the passage became so narrow that two men could not stand abreast.

This is the same system of fortification as on the islands but somewhat more elaborated, as necessitated by the site, which rose not more than 16 m. above the plain and was quite unprotected naturally.

The entrances, which were very narrow (·85 m.–1·10 m.), were cut in a straight line through the successive walls, so that the acropolis could be divided into sections in times of stress, each of which could be completely cut off by shutting the gate and gangway. The cattle would probably be driven in and left in the spaces between the walls, while the inhabitants living around would shelter themselves behind them, just as Polydamas advised the Trojans to do in later times. Hector's reply on that occasion shows that, in the case of Troy at least, the space was very limited, when all were within the city walls.

> Πουλυδάμα, σὺ μὲν οὐκέτ᾽ ἐμοὶ φίλα ταῦτ᾽ ἀγορεύεις,
> ὃς κέλεαι κατὰ ἄστυ ἀλήμεναι αὖτις ἰόντας.
> ἦ οὔ πω κεκόρησθε ἐελμένοι ἔνδοθι πύργων;[2]

---

[1] Tsountas, Αἱ προϊστορικαὶ ἀκροπόλεις Διμηνίου. καὶ Σέσκλου, pass. Cf. Hall, *History of Near East*, p. 32.

[2] *Il.* XVIII. 285–7.

Polydamas, no longer to my liking dost thou speak now, in that thou biddest us go back and be pent within the town.   Have ye not had your fill already of being pent behind the towers?

The acropolis must thus have been well-nigh impregnable: an enemy entering one of these narrow passages would have had no chance of escape, and each part would have had to be attacked and stormed separately.   Some such catastrophe seems indeed to have occurred in the earliest period when only three walls existed, but these were quickly rebuilt and three new ones added in the same style, so that the acropolis has a long continuous history throughout the Neolithic period.

Since the walls are only on an average from ·80 m.–1 m. thick and less in the upper part, Tsountas concludes that there would have been insufficient room for armed warriors to stand, and the weakness of the foundations seems to preclude the possibility of the walls being very high, so that he is led to the conclusion that the defenders fought from behind the walls, the outside height of which probably never exceeded 3 m.   The natural upward slope of the hill would make it easy for the defenders to see the enemy, and in other places earth and stones would be piled up inside the wall.   These walls, unlike that of Syros, have no towers, though there are a few buttresses to strengthen them.   The walls are of clay and small stones, as in so many buildings of the Neolithic Age, when stone was only occasionally used, as at Magasa.

The chief interest of this site for the architectural student however lies in the two megara, which at this remote date show in embryo all the essential features of the later mainland palace form, and the subsequent Hellenic house and temple.

One (Fig. 5 *a*) lies within the first circuit wall[1], and

[1] Tsountas, *op. cit.* pp. 50–52, fig. 9.

consists of three parts called by Tsountas the prodomos
(*A*), doma (*B*) and thalamos (*C*). The roof was supported
by the two antae and two posts or columns, holes for
which remain in the floor of the prodomos towards the
middle and a little behind the antae. Through the prodomos the larger room was entered. It is in the shape
of a trapezium 6·35 m. long by 4·20 m.–5·50 m. wide, and
in the centre is a round hearth, whose inner diameter is
·75 m.

Two holes on each side, which contained bones of
goats and sheep, are supposed by Tsountas to have been
sockets for supporting columns, and suggest the later
Homeric arrangement of four columns round the central
hearth.

The second room entered from the first is more irregular,
for the curved circuit wall forms one side, and one of the
walls is shorter in consequence.

Here are also remains of what seems to be a circular
oven, as well as a polygonal structure which served either
as a hearth or a storage place for dried fruit.

The second megaron (Fig. 5 *b*) is situated between
the second and third fortification walls and consists, like
the first, of three parts, *A*, *B* and *C*: it is however more
irregular, and does not recall so closely the later plan.
The hearth here is square and stands, not in the centre
of the large room, but against its end wall: beside it is
a small rectangular hearth[1].

It seems probable that in many cases where we find
two hearths, one was reserved for heating and lighting
purposes and the other for cooking, as in Thessaly at the
present day.

Two holes, presumably for supporting pillars, are
near the doorway leading into the second room, where

[1] Tsountas, *op. cit.* pp. 60–62, fig. 11.

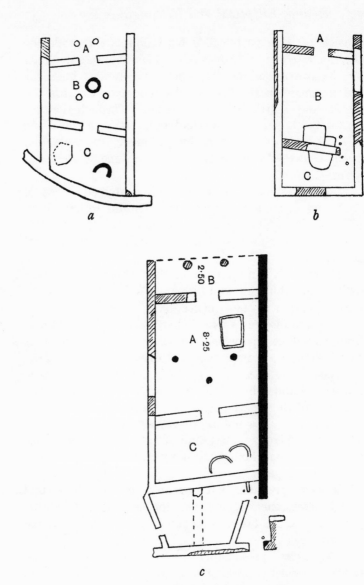

Fig. 5.   Houses at Dimini and Sesklo.

holes for pillars are also found, as well as a hearth built up against the cross wall.

These two megara are synchronous, but the first is much more symmetrical than the second, which would seem to have been somewhat carelessly built.

But while at Dimini the round huts and elliptical buildings have already been completely superseded by the rectangular, in the neighbourhood of Sesklo there are distinct remains of three or four round huts of early Neolithic period. The walls have disappeared but the floors and some fragments of pottery remain, as well as pits which must have been used either for stores or rubbish. One of these huts[1] is exceedingly interesting as showing a primitive prodomos with the round plan: the second room, which is 2·80 m. in diameter, is entered from the first by an opening 1.40 m. across.

The acropolis is fortified only on its south and most exposed side, but otherwise the style of building is exactly the same as at Dimini: the houses are rectangular, or approximately so, with the threefold division, and in some of the later ones we even find an unconnected room behind, such as we know as the opisthodomos in the later temple plan.

One large building of the Neolithic Age must be described in detail[2]: it consists of two parts, each with prodomos and two rooms, but the little northern building, though with a common party wall, has no connection with the other (Fig. 5 c).

The principal room (A) of the larger building, which is 8·25 m. deep, is entered through a prodomos (B) 2·50 m. deep, containing no trace of holes for supporting columns though such must have existed: within there are three holes for posts towards the centre, but the hearth, which

---

[1] Tsountas, *op. cit.* p. 116, fig. 25.   [2] *ibid.* pp. 88 sqq., fig. 18.

is four-sided and of irregular form, stands to the left of the entrance door.

Another irregularity is noticeable in the lie of the walls, which either through sinkage or carelessness in construction are not at right angles to each other. The further room (*C*) contained remains of two circular hearths, perhaps used for cooking. This house, which is the best of the later period, must have belonged to the chief of the little community. The walls are well built and about ·60 m. thick, and stones with holes caused by the revolution of a pivot testify as at Dimini to the existence of doors between the rooms.

A little to the west of this large building was another, which, if rightly restored by Tsountas, consisted of two rooms with prodomos and opisthodomos with access from each: the circular hearth was here in the second room[1].

Another interesting question is raised with regard to primitive architecture by the discovery at Sesklo of some pieces of clay bearing the impress of reeds, and indicating in some cases the lie of the roof, which must have been sloping[2]. In its simplest form it would probably have but one slope; this would develop into two and give the simple gable roof which we find in Mycenean times for the common dwelling house. Later the flat roof which belongs to a warm climate where rain is rare, and which we find everywhere in the south, seems to have almost ousted the old gable form in Greece, except for sacred buildings, though as late as Homeric times we find both still existing.

Another prehistoric site which must not be left unmentioned is that at *Zerelia* near Almyro in Phthiotis where a Neolithic layer 6 m.–8 m. deep, representing

[1] Tsountas, *op. cit.* p. 99, fig. 22.
[2] *ibid.* p. 80, figs. 13–16, cf. supra p. 50.

according to stratification eight settlements, was discovered[1]. The finders date the 8th layer, which contained
cist graves of the usual type with five slabs, at 1200 B.C.,
and consider that the first layer may go back to *circ.* 3000
B.C., for the oldest painted pottery resembled that found
at Chaeronea by Soteriades and at Dimini and Sesklo
by Tsountas.

In general the settlements are represented by layers
of reddish earth, the remains of huts of mud brick
destroyed by fire, but no indications of plan remain.

At the south-east corner of the mound, however, remains of a well-preserved building of the second settlement
were unearthed, with walls ·65 m. thick standing to a
height of ·80 m.[2] No complete plan can be given since
the building was not entirely excavated, but enough has
been laid bare to show clearly that it was rectangular.

The excavations of Messrs Wace and Thompson[3] have
revealed house plans of equal interest on several other
prehistoric sites in Thessaly.

At Rakhmani in North Thessaly where the deposit at
its highest point was 8·10 m. deep the walls of two houses
of the same general plan belonging respectively to the
Chalceolithic and the Bronze Age were unearthed. They
both show a curved end wall. House P (Fig. 6 *a*) which
is later and better preserved contains a hearth or oven
such as we have already seen at Dimini and Sesklo
(pp. 57, 59, cf. fig. 5) and the burnt patch near the platform of beaten earth in House Q (Fig. 6 *b*) probably
indicates a similar hearth there. It is difficult to ascertain
the position of the door in each house but it seems most
probable that it was at the straight narrow end in both.

[1] *Ath. Mitt.* XXXIII. 1908, pp. 289 sqq.; *B.S.A.* XIV. pp. 197 sqq.
[2] *B.S.A.* XIV. p. 202.
[3] Wace and Thompson, *Prehistoric Thessaly*, pass.

The walls which were of sun-dried brick about ·30 m. thick probably rested on a course of stones which survives.

At Tsangli in Central Thessaly four houses were discovered of square type, three of them (Houses P, Q

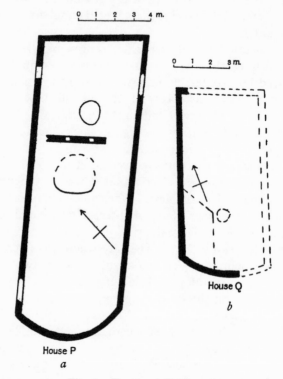

House Q

b

House P

a

Fig. 6.   Houses at Rakhmani.

and R) superposed (Fig. 7, *a* and *b*). It is interesting to notice in these houses the internal buttresses which Wace and Thompson suggest served to support the roof beams. Across House T (Fig. 7 *a*) were four thick posts, the charred ends of which were found embedded in the

earth: they may have served to support the main roof
beam as well as to form a partition.

The house at Rini (Fig. 8) is of particular interest as

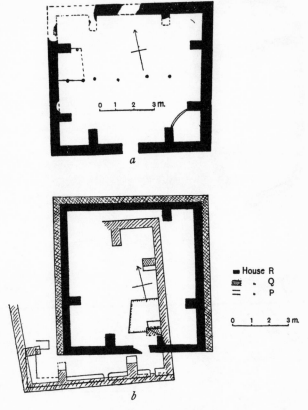

Fig. 7. Houses at Tsangli.

showing once more in a very perfect way the existence
of the elliptical house. Its walls which were of small
rough stones were standing to a height of ·60 m. and it
consisted of three rooms, the central of rectangular plan

while the two end rooms were semi-circular.   No entrance
was found to the northern room, but it is possible that the
floor of the house was at a higher level.

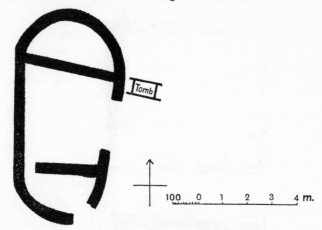

Fig. 8.   House at Rini.

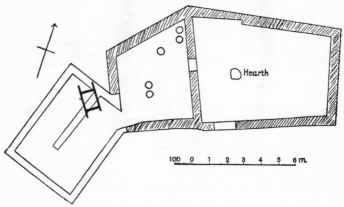

Fig. 9.   House at Lianokladhi.

In the third and uppermost layer at Lianokladhi in
the Spercheus valley a large house was discovered consisting of two distinct parts (Fig. 9), and the discoverers

suggest that it was either a combination of two houses
or else a single house to which rooms have been added.
The west portion which is probably the addition is of
regular rectangular form, while the east and principal
portion though its walls are straight is irregularly built:
the foundations too differ, those of the eastern portion
being small stones set in mud while the foundation of
the western portion consists of a single layer of larger
stones; the upper part was in both cases of wattle and
daub. The hearth is distinctly visible in the larger room,
the smaller was probably a store room to judge from the
πίθοι found there.

In the north of Greece then we find round, elliptical,
square and rectangular houses, and it is not possible with
the present evidence to point to any one type as universal
in this region.

The large megara at Dimini and Sesklo bearing as
they do a strong resemblance to the later "Mycenean"
megara of the mainland have been regarded by Tsountas[1]
as their forerunners. Mackenzie[2] however lays less stress
on their importance and derives both from a common
prototype.

The prehistoric remains then in Boeotia and Thessaly
point to a preference for the rectangular, though traces
of the use of the round are not lacking.

Again at *Thoricus* in Attica traces were found of an
old race who used clay vessels and buried their dead in
πίθοι within the houses[3]. Though the hope of unearthing
a Mycenean palace like those at Tiryns and Mycenae
was not realised, the site is of great interest as showing
walls, which must have formed part of rectangular

[1] Δ. Σ. pp. 390 sqq.
[2] *B.S.A.* XIV. pp. 343 sqq.
[3] Staïs, 'Εφ. 'Αρχ. 1895, pp. 221 sqq.; Πρακτικά, 1895, p. 12.

R. G. H.

dwellings, side by side with a bee-hive tomb of the usual form.

Again on the island of *Aegina*, between the temple and the 7th century house containing Corinthian pottery, at a slightly lower level remains came to light of a building of the prehistoric period[1], whose walls were composed of small stones and clay. The plan was again rectangular, and the house consisted of nine small rooms communicating by means of doorways. The dead had been buried beneath as on so many prehistoric sites.

Fig. 10.   Neolithic house at Magasa.

Turning now to the island of Crete we have a piece of curious evidence: the rectangular dwelling house found at *Magasa*[2] is significant, not only as being a very early example of this plan in Crete, but also as showing the use of stone for building purposes in the Neolithic period (Fig. 10).

The house stands but twelve yards away from a rock shelter, and was probably constructed when it was found that the simpler dwelling did not provide adequate

[1] Staïs, 'Εφ. 'Αρχ. 1895, pp. 244 sqq., fig. 3.
[2] *B.S.A.* xi. p. 263.

accommodation. The pottery found in the house and in the rock shelter proves quite conclusively that they are of the same period, and it is interesting to notice the quick progress from a primitive artificial dwelling, which is only a slight advancement on the troglodytic stage, to a square built stone house. Though but a single course of undressed limestone blocks is now left *in situ*, the outline of the ground plan is quite distinct. It is L shaped, the greatest width being about 6 m., but the scanty remains of walls do not enable us to make any deductions as to interior arrangement, or even to say with certainty where the entrance was.

Of the Neolithic layer at *Phaestos*[1] only two walls remain forming an angle: they are composed of little stones bound together with mud.

Such evidence then as is forthcoming with regard to the prehistoric house, and it becomes every year more complete, does not point clearly in favour of either the curved or rectangular style as the earliest[2].

This being understood, the general conclusion may be drawn that the circular form tended to prevail in the Mediterranean area in the earliest times, the rectangular in Egypt and the East. For Central Europe the evidence is scanty, but in the North we meet the rectangular form again, preceded however by the circular.

At a very remote date the rectangular style was adopted in Crete and continued to be preferred throughout its history, and it is a very reasonable hypothesis that this architecture influenced that of the mainland of Greece, where after the prehistoric period we find the rectangular style universally adopted.

[1] Pernier, *Mon. Ant.* XII. 22.

[2] For an interesting discussion of the subject *vide* Ernst Pyl, *Ath. Mitt.* XXX. pp. 331–74.

The normal type consisted of a square court, usually facing south, with stalls around it for the animals and a living room or rooms at the north end (Fig. 11).

In the centre of the court was an altar to Zeus Herkeios, and in the room at its upper end a circular hearth (ἑστία) where the cooking was done.

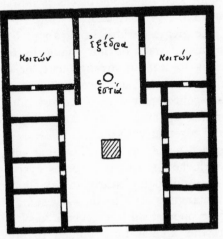

Fig. 11. Imaginary plan of simple square house.

The description by Galen, a Roman writer of the 2nd century A.D., of the ordinary country house of his time is interesting in this connection. In his *De Antidot.* I. 3 he says:—

κατὰ τοὺς ἀγροὺς ἅπαντας παρ᾽ ἡμῖν οἶκοι γίγνονται μεγάλοι, τὴν μὲν ἑστίαν, ἐφ᾽ ἧς καίουσι τὸ πῦρ, ἐν μέσοις ἑαυτῶν ἔχοντες, οὐ πολὺ δὲ αὐτῆς ἀπέχουσιν αἱ τῶν ὑποζυγίων στάσεις, ἤτοι κατ᾽ ἀμφότερα τὰ μέρη, δεξιόν τε καὶ ἀριστερόν, ἢ πάντως γε κατὰ θάτερον. εἰσὶ δὲ κρίβανοι συνεζευγμένοι ταῖς ἑστίαις κατὰ τὸ πρόσω μέρος ἑαυτῶν ὃ πρὸς τὴν θύραν βλέπει τοῦ παντὸς οἴκου, τοιοῦτοι μὲν οὖν ἅπαντες οἱ κατὰ τοὺς ἀγροὺς οἶκοι κατασκευάζονται κἂν εὐτελεῖς ὦσιν. οἱ δ᾽ ἐπιμελέστεροι αὐτῶν κατασκευαζόμενοι κατὰ τὸν ἔνδον τοῖχον ἔχουσι τὴν κατ᾽ ἀντικρυ τῇ θύρᾳ τεταγμένην ἐξέδραν. ἑκατέρωθεν δ᾽ αὐτῆς κοιτῶνα, καθ᾽ ὃν ἄνωθέν ἐστιν ὑπερῷα οἰκήματα καθάπερ καὶ κατὰ

πολλὰ τῶν πανδοχείων ἐν κύκλῳ κατὰ τρεῖς τοίχους τοῦ οἴκου τοῦ μεγάλου,
πολλάκις δὲ καὶ κατὰ τέτταρας.

In all the country near us are large houses with the hearth
on which they burn the fire in the middle, and not far from it
the stalls for the beasts of burden, either on both sides, right and
left, or at least on one side. There are ovens attached to the
hearths in the further part of them, which faces the door of the
whole house. Such are all the houses which they build in the
country even if they are poor. The richer ones have the sitting
room opposite the door along the inner wall, and on both sides
of it a bedroom above which are first floor rooms, just as in many
of the inns along three walls of the great house and often along
four.

Though Galen is here describing a Pergamene house,
he himself says that he has seen many similar buildings
in the district round Naples: in fact this type of peasant
house with a courtyard surrounded by small rooms, which
underlies the plan of the Greek house throughout its
development, is a very natural form to occur, and seems
to have been prevalent in all periods. An imaginary
plan is given (Fig. 11).

Though no specific mention is made of the altar in
the courtyard, the house of the swineherd Eumaeus
appears to conform to the same type of primitive
dwelling, which recalls also the Nordic plan already
described.

It consists of a hut, which would provide shelter for
the swineherd, behind an open court, where he could keep
his animals. The whole he had fenced round with stones
and a hedge.

Homer describes it thus:—

Τὸν δ' ἄρ' ἐνὶ προδόμῳ εὗρ' ἥμενον, ἔνθα οἱ αὐλὴ
ὑψηλὴ δέδμητο, περισκέπτῳ ἐνὶ χώρῳ,
καλή τε μεγάλη τε, περίδρομος· ἥν ῥα συβώτης
αὐτὸς δείμαθ' ὕεσσιν ἀποιχομένοιο ἄνακτος,

νόσφιν δεσποίνης καὶ Λαέρταο γέροντος,
ῥυτοῖσιν λάεσσι, καὶ ἐθρίγκωσεν ἀχέρδῳ.
σταυροὺς δ' ἐκτὸς ἔλασσε διαμπερὲς ἔνθα καὶ ἔνθα,
πυκνοὺς καὶ θαμέας, τὸ μέλαν δρυὸς ἀμφικεάσσας·
ἔντοσθεν δ' αὐλῆς συφεοὺς δυοκαίδεκα ποίει
πλησίον ἀλλήλων, εὐνὰς συσίν   .   .   .

ἀλλ' ἔπεο κλίσιην δ' ἴομεν, γέρον, ὄφρα καὶ αὐτὸς
σίτου καὶ οἴνοιο κορεσσάμενος κατὰ θυμὸν
εἴπῃς ὁππόθεν ἐσσί.   (*Od.* XIV. 15.)

And he found him sitting at the front entry of the house where his courtyard was builded high in a place with wide prospect: a great court it was and a fair, with free range round it. This the swineherd had builded by himself for the swine of his lord who was afar, and his mistress and the old man Laertes knew not of it. With stones dragged thither had he builded it and coped it with a fence of white thorn. And he had split an oak to the dark core and without he had driven stakes the whole length thereof on either side set thick and close. And within the courtyard he made twelve styes hard by one another to be beds for the swine.

.   .   .   .   .   .

But come with me, let us to the inner steading, old man, that when thy heart is satisfied with bread and wine, thou mayest declare whence thou art.

Thus we see the rectangular type in quite primitive domestic architecture. The circular style came to be regarded as ritualistic, for besides its use for tombs it survived in some cases for temples: the choragic monument of Lysicrates, a semi-religious dedication, is also of circular form. In domestic architecture it is never found in later times, except in the tholos[1] of the Homeric courtyard (*Od.* XXII. 442, 466), whose construction and object are unknown.

An interesting survival of the round type is the

[1] *vide* p. 208.

prytaneum[1] found in the agora of all independent Greek
towns: in this building the presidents (πρυτάνεις) dined
daily at the public cost and offered sacrifices: here the
standard weights and measures were kept, and on certain
occasions it was used as a law court. But its essential
feature was the hearth on which the fire was kept burning
night and day, the fire of the state which had been trans-
formed from a practical necessity to a sacred symbol,
and was always carried by the colonies from their mother
city to their new settlement.

The building was consecrated to Hestia, a statue of
whom, according to Pausanias, stood within the prytaneum
at Athens, and possibly also in other cities.

At Athens there was a second round building called
the tholos or skias, which seems to have served the same
purposes as the prytaneum.

Pyl[2] would trace the form back to the primitive hearth
or altar, which being round, would be closed in for
protection by a round wall: such a hypothesis is strengthened by the fact that the tholos at Epidaurus is referred
to in the inscription as the θυμέλη = altar or place of
sacrifice[3]. The conical roof however closely resembles
those of the Mycenean tholoi, and these buildings are
probably survivals of this traditional form.

Vitruvius classes the round temples as monopteral
and peripteral (Vitruv. IV. 8), and alludes to their sacrificial use, but gives no explanation of their origin.

The Vesta temples in Italy, also dedicated to the
goddess of the hearth, share their form with the Greek
prytaneum, and preserve a primitive tradition[4].

[1] Frazer, *Paus.* I. 18. 3 note.
[2] Pyl, *Die griechischen Rundbauten im Zusammenhange mit dem
Götter- und Heroencultus*, p. 88.
[3] Staïs, Ἐφ. Ἀρχ. 1892, p. 69, ll. 106 and 143 of inscription.
[4] Pyl, *op. cit.* pp. 106 sqq.

Hitherto we have been unable to draw any fixed line of demarcation between prehistoric sepulchral and domestic architecture: with the Cretan discoveries, however, we may begin to study the house and the palace quite apart, their development from the earliest times in Crete and their influence on mainland building.

CHAPTER VIII

EARLY MINOAN SETTLEMENTS IN CRETE

IT is at once clear in Crete that the rectangular form, which we already found occurring in the Neolithic period at Magasa[1], has been once for all adopted for the house, not necessarily through any foreign influence, Eastern or otherwise, but as a simple natural development, since it was found to be the best and most commodious form for the purpose required and with the materials which were to hand.

A brittle material like gypsum in particular, which was so largely used in building the Cretan palaces, would have lent itself but ill to the circular form.

Accepting Dr Evans' chronology of things Cretan[2], which is deduced principally from the thickness of the layers of deposit, we may roughly date the Neolithic period in Crete as the period before 3000 B.C. The Neolithic layer, which is 6·43 m. thick, contains remains of pottery and stone implements and goes back according to the discoverer to about 10,000 B.C.[3] Here we may trace the progress of primitive development in Crete, but even on the virgin soil the remains are not of a strictly

---

[1] *vide* p. 66.   [2] *B.S.A.* 1903, p. 25.

[3] Ridgeway thinks evidence insufficient to make any computation. Cf. "Minos the destroyer rather than the creator of the so-called Minoan Culture of Knossos," p. 4. Reprint from *Proceedings of Br. Acad.* vol. IV.

archaic character, polished pottery being found, and this fact has led to the inference that the original inhabitants were emigrants from North Africa or some other spot in the Mediterranean area, who had already attained to a certain stage of progress before their arrival in Crete.

Aristotle, comparing the Lacedemonian constitution with the Cretan to which it owes much, says of Crete that the island seems to be intended by nature for dominion in Hellas on account of its situation, "for it extends right across the sea around which nearly all the Hellenes are settled, and while one end is not far from the Peloponnese, the other almost reaches to the region of Asia about Triopium and Rhodes[1]." Its advantageous position must have been recognised in the earliest times.

No doubt the earliest Cretans at Knossos lived in wattle and daub huts, like many other Neolithic peoples, and the disintegration of these primitive dwellings has gone to make up the Neolithic layer.

At Magasa in East Crete, as we have seen, though the pottery is less advanced, the stone house of square plan is already constructed, side by side with the more primitive cave shelter of the usual type, where the cave forms a natural roof and the hollow is built in by a wall, a type intermediate between the primitive troglodytic dwelling and the artificially constructed house.

Further evidence of prehistoric dwelling in the island is furnished by the grotto at *Miamu*[2], near Gortyna, excavated by Taramelli. This cave had been used for burial at a later period, but below was found a layer of black greasy earth about 1·80 m. deep, which proved that the dwelling must have been used for some centuries. Besides the remains of fireplaces at different levels, bones of animals and pottery made without the wheel but

---

[1] Arist. *Pol.* II. 7. 2.   [2] Taramelli, *A.J.A.* 1897, p. 287.

showing some development gave evidence of the habitation of the cave in Neolithic times.

We may consider that the transition to metal took place about 3000 B.C. as quite a natural step in progress, and not through the invasion of a new race, for old traditions with regard to shape, etc., remained.

Crete had no Copper Age like Cyprus[1], which was perhaps the centre from which the use of metal spread all over Europe[2]: she obtained the harder alloy, probably at first by commerce, and then made it for herself.

From the opening of the Bronze Age or Early Minoan period in Crete, we have continuous and abundant evidence of domestic architectural forms, both for the palace and the house.

An exceedingly early settlement belonging to the Early Minoan period, before the older palaces came into being, is that at *Vasiliki* unearthed by Mr Seager[3], who traces among his remains four periods, the last being that which immediately preceded that of the fine Kamares ware at Knossos.

The first settlement, which dated from the middle of the E. M. period, must have consisted of the usual wattle and daub huts, for no remains of walls occurred before the second period.

The main building, which to judge from the débris must have had several storeys, was constructed in the third period: its plan is rectangular, as was also that of the lower building, but it is on a different axis (Fig. 12).

A doubt even exists as to whether this suite of 23 rooms belongs to one single building. In any case they

[1] Much, *Die Kupferzeit in Europa*, pp. 34–36.

[2] Myres, *Science Progress*, vol. v. p. 347, *Cyprus Mus. Cat.* p. 17. Mosso, *Dawn of Mediterranean civilisation*, pp. 299 sqq., regards this opinion as false.

[3] *Trans. Univ. Penn.* I. 219 sqq. and II. 111 sqq.

were destroyed in the fourth period, though the site was still inhabited by people living in poor huts built over the ruins. The two houses of M. M. period excavated on the east slope are well constructed, and preserve the rectangular tradition.

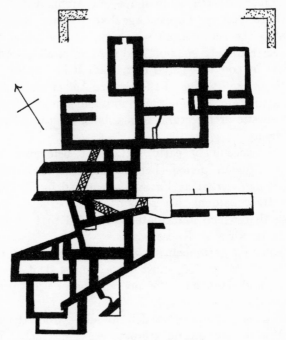

Fig. 12.   Houses at Vasiliki.

The excavations of Mr Seager on the island of Pseira[1], which lies about two miles off the coast of Crete opposite the plain of Kavousi, have brought to light remains of a Mycenean settlement on a tongue of land to the east. The masonry of the top layer was of heavy squared

[1] Seager, *Pseira*, pass.   *A.J.A.* 1908, p. 94; *Antiq. Crét.* II. pl. 15, 16 and 17.

blocks of stone in the style usually associated with L. M. i
and beneath were walls of lighter, smaller stones of
M. M. i period: unlike Gournia and Vasiliki no bricks
seem to have been used. The site was occupied as early
as E. M. ii and was apparently deserted after the end of
L. M. i; the best preserved houses belong to this latter

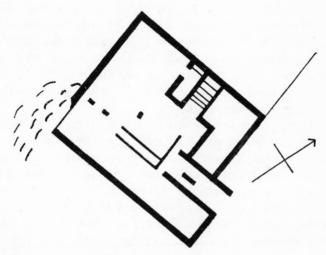

Fig. 13.   House in Pseira.

period. Of these the most interesting, as reproducing
many characteristic features of Knossian architecture,
is the house figured in I. 5 on Mr Seager's plan (see
Fig. 13).

A narrow passage leads into a vestibule from which
through a triple doorway with the two stone bases for the
wooden door posts still remaining one enters the megaron.
In one corner is a small rectangular construction with
remains of plaster on the floor and an outlet hole: this
was probably a bath. Behind it a stone stairway leads

from the megaron to an upper floor where the principal living rooms must have been.

House A (H. 10 in Seager's plan) and House B (H. 12) were both large houses probably belonging to wealthy citizens, to judge from the rich nature of the finds. The other houses are of the usual type of the small Minoan dwelling.

Mokhlos[1], an island lying about 200 yds from the shore off the north coast of Crete towards the east side and perhaps connected with it in early times, as the corresponding Minoan walls on the mainland seem to show, was inhabited from the beginning of the E. M. period to the beginning of the M. M., when all the settlements of East Crete fell.

It was later re-occupied for a short time in M. M. iii and finally destroyed by a conflagration in L. M. i.

The later Roman settlement destroyed to a large extent the Minoan walls, and consequently but few complete houses remain. Fragments of pottery show clearly that the site was inhabited in E. M. i, but the earliest walls belong to E. M. ii and iii. They are probably only dividing walls and are very small and poorly built.

Another building, which seemed to be a single house, had a stout wall of large roughly hewn stones, and crude bricks had been used in the construction and had been fired in the conflagration which destroyed the house.

The best preserved houses are those along the water front: their outer walls are strong and massive, and the remains of column bases in the rooms seem to indicate that there were upper storeys.

One house in particular, built shortly before the destruction of the settlement, showed very clearly the

[1] *A.J.A.* 1909, III. p. 273; *Antiq. Crét.* II. pl. 1, 2 and 3.

style of building and materials then in vogue[1] (Fig. 14).
The portico on the south side with central column to
support an upper storey led into the megaron (*A*), which
was of irregular shape, with a large column base in the
centre and a recessed seat in the wall in true Cretan style.
The influence of the palace architecture is also clear in

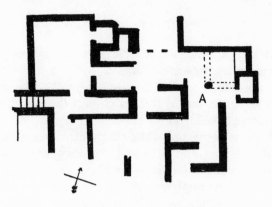

Fig. 14.   House at Mokhlos.

the triple doorway, which is not often found on small
sites, as well as in the open court. The walls are of
brick clay with small stones, and much wood is used in
the construction.

Leaving the somewhat scanty remains of the E. M.
period, we now pass to the great periods of Cretan architectural development.

[1] *A.J.A.* 1909, III. pp. 293 sqq., fig. 14.

CHAPTER IX

CRETAN PALACES

WITH the opening of the M. M. period we have abundant remains on the two great sites of Knossos and Phaestos, which must have shared between them the hegemony of the island, for it was at this epoch that the earlier palaces on both spots were built.

It seems very probable that both sites were very carefully cleared and prepared, for they were no doubt continuously inhabited from the Neolithic period onwards, yet the architectural remains of the E. M. period, when the art of building as we have seen had already made considerable progress, are quite insignificant. The thick hard layer of lime mixed with clay and pebbles at Phaestos[1], which the excavators had to break up with explosives, was no doubt part of this preparation.

The state of political and social safety in which the peoples of this civilisation lived is clearly shown by the fact that neither building, in contrast to those later palaces on the mainland, possesses fortification walls. They must nevertheless from without have presented a somewhat fortress-like appearance with their massive walls rising one above another, plain and barren, with nothing to indicate the intricacy of design, or the marvellous wealth of decoration lavished on the interior.

---

[1] Mosso, *Palaces of Crete and their builders*, p. 20. Cf. *Mon. Antic.* XII. p. 24.

In this respect the palace of Phaestos is certainly the simpler, for the decoration is less ornate in character and commoner materials are used for the fabric, but speaking generally the style and plan of the two buildings are very similar. To both access is given by means of a corridor and propylaea, both are grouped around a great open courtyard on the east, and in both a series of large and small rooms, corridors, magazines, shrines and a theatre form conspicuous features of the design.

Let us take a glance more in detail at the ground plans of the respective palaces before proceeding to a closer comparison: it is clear that they must have had a long tradition behind them to allow of the building being so elaborate and perfected.

To the south-east and south-west of the great palace of Knossos[1] were discovered in 1902 remains of an earlier palace[2] with abundant supplies of painted pottery of the M. M. period.

It is not possible to make out the plan of this earlier building, but the lines of orientation seem to coincide for the most part with those of the later palace.

The remains consist of chambers and cells of simple construction, built of rubble masonry, and were probably used as basements in the later building. It would seem that this earlier palace was planned and built about the beginning of the M. M. period and destroyed at the end of M. M. ii.

The history of the great palace seems to have been long and to have lasted from M. M. iii to the beginning of L. M. iii, when Knossos fell and the great Cretan civilisation gradually broke up and was transferred to the mainland capitals.

During this period, the period between the 12th and

[1] *B.S.A.* vi.–xi. pass.   [2] *B.S.A.* ix. pp. 17 sqq.

18th dynasties in Egypt, extending, according to the system of Egyptian chronology adopted, over a shorter term of a few hundred years or a longer increased by one Sothis period (*circ.* 1460 years)[1], there must have been various upheavals caused either by internal revolution or foreign invasion, for the palace at Knossos was twice destroyed by fire, and Phaestos and some of the smaller towns met with a similar fate. Aristotle[2] says of the Cretans that they have a habit of setting up a chief: "they get together a party among the common people and gather their friends and then quarrel and fight with one another." If such a state of things prevailed in the Minoan period, it would account for the many disasters, which yet were not followed by any change of conditions to point to conquest by a new race.

The Kamares pottery which has been found in such large quantities on the site is the principal evidence for the early chronology, whilst the fact that no geometric pottery has come to light, though it is found in other parts of the island, shows that the palace was not in use in the latest period of the Mycenean age. The generally accepted date for the fall of Knossos is about 1450 B.C.[3]

We turn now to the ground plan[4] of the palace (Fig. 15) which was entered on the south-west from the large west court by a spacious portico (*A*), leading to a large double entrance, which opened on to a fine corridor (*B*), called "the corridor of the procession." This probably took a turn to the left and followed the south terrace

---

[1] *vide* Burrows, *Discoveries in Crete*, c. v. and appendix A; also *Brit. Sch. Arch. in Egypt Historical Studies*, II. pp. 1–22.

[2] Arist. *Pol.* II. 10.

[3] Evans, *B.S.A.* x. p. 2, about 1500 B.C. Reisch, *Mitt. d. Anthrop. Gesell. Wien*, 1904, p. 16, and Dörpfeld, *Ath. Mitt.* xxx. p. 292, prefer a later date.

[4] *B.S.A.* VI.–XI. pass.

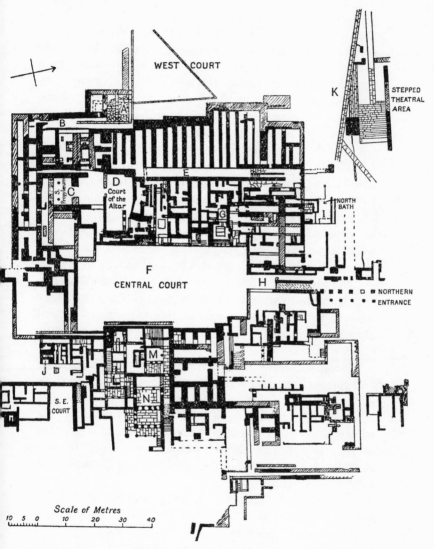

WEST COURT

K

STEPPED
THEATRAL
AREA

A

B

S. Propylaeum

C

D
Court
of the
Altar

E

G

I

NORTH
BATH

F
CENTRAL COURT

H

□ ⬛ NORTHERN
⬛ ENTRANCE

M

J

N

S. E.
COURT

Scale of Metres
10 5 0   10   20   30   40

Fig. 15. Palace at Knossos.

wall to the south propylaeum (C), of which one anta, the door opening and threshold remain. Within are two column bases and the remains of a paved floor. The propylaeum gives on to a large space (D) bounded by a straight limestone wall to the north, but otherwise very irregular in shape. Its floor is of the pale clay of the Neolithic stratum, but it seems probable that it was originally paved like the other two courts.

It is here that Dr Evans restores an upper storey[1] containing a reception hall of the nature of the great hall at Phaestos, and perhaps, to judge from the fallen frescoes, the most handsome room of the whole palace. Like the hall at Phaestos this may have been approached by a broad stairway, and the three columns across the width probably rested on the two bases and the pier of the wall beneath, which are still in position.

The present remains in this part, which would on this hypothesis have served as foundations, indicate that there were three rooms at the side of this hall, viz. a central chamber with annexe, and a room over the room of the chariot tablets.

Along its west side another corridor was discovered and further west still some rooms, from which a corridor with several turns led to the "long gallery[2]," a spacious passage-way running from north to south across the palace (E). Opening on to it on its west side is a series of 17 smaller "galleries," which are shown by the abundance of the πίθοι discovered in them to have been used for magazines.

Supplies were probably brought into the palace by way of the great west court and the south-west portico: here was ample space for traders to wait with their goods and for business of all sorts to be transacted, and access

---

[1] *B.S.A.* VII. pp. 21–26, fig. 8. [2] *l.c.* VI. p. 19.

was easy to the store rooms of the "long gallery," though more complicated than at Phaestos where communication was direct and not as here through subterranean rooms.

The long gallery is connected by means of a corridor at its north end with a series of rooms lying between it and the central paved area (*F*), including a suite of rooms which from the low seats are thought to have been set aside for women. Though rigorous exclusion of women was not a feature of Mycenean civilisation, if we may judge from the miniature frescoes[1], yet it is quite likely that certain apartments would be set aside for their special use.

To the south of this suite of rooms and opening on to the great central court is the state apartment (*G*) known as the Throne Room[2]. It is entered by four descending steps which give access to an antechamber 6 m. square, surrounded by stone benches, doubtless intended for those waiting for royal audiences. This vestibule leads into the principal room, which is also surrounded with gypsum benches, except in the middle of the north side, where stands a fine gypsum throne with its back in the shape of an oak leaf. On the opposite side are steps leading down to a stone tank, which may have had some ceremonial use. The floor of the room is paved with gypsum slabs, which had been decorated, as had also the benches, with red and white pigment.

On the north a wide walled gangway (*H*) gives access to the central court, where was, if not the principal, at least the most fortified entrance, for it was the chief means of access from the city and sea port. This passage ran alongside of the great northern portico and piazza[3],

---

[1] *B.S.A.* VI. p. 46.   [2] *l.c.* VI. p. 35 and fig. 8.
[3] *l.c.* VI. p. 45.

and to the east of it another series of magazines was discovered, containing pottery of a poor character, perhaps in use by servants or workmen attached to the palace. This would seem to have been the industrial and domestic quarter, and also probably included the stables.

Another interesting discovery near the northern portico was that of a bath room (*I*), which belonged to the original structure, as was proved by the fact that the tank had been filled up and later walls built over it, as well as by the style of the fresco pieces found within.

A double staircase and parapet led down into the square basin of the bath (2·56 m. × 2·45 m.), which was 2 m. deep and lined with large gypsum slabs covering walls of fine ashlar masonry: the floor was of gypsum slabs.

In the south-east quarter of the palace, next the queen's megaron, a similar bath room (*J*) was found, but the basin here was very shallow and Evans[1] suggests that it was used, as was also probably the similar basin in the throne room, for washing the feet. A similar room with a shallow basin has also been discovered in the south part of the palace at Phaestos[2], belonging to the later structure: there is as yet no evidence of a bath room in the earlier. This bath, in contrast to that at Knossos and like that at Tiryns, would seem to have been lined with wood. Phaestos has the added convenience of a room with a bench of gesso around, open to the air on one side so that bathers could sun themselves there after the bath. This little room is also interesting on account of the curious decoration of the bench in vertical bands, which may very well have been the origin of the later triglyph and metope of the Doric style[3].

[1] *B.S.A.* VII. p. 63.
[2] *Mon. Ant.* XII. pp. 44–5 and fig. 12.
[3] *ibid.* p. 47, fig. 13.

In view of the otherwise elaborate and perfected drainage and sanitary arrangements of the palace, it is curious that no signs are present of any arrangement for filling and emptying the baths. Rain water would provide but a precarious supply, and if these rooms really were bath rooms, which is not as yet definitely proved, water must have been carried and emptied by hand. This would, however, present no difficulty, since labour would be even more plentiful than in the east to-day, and bands of slaves would always be at hand to perform all such offices.

But to return to the palace plan. A little to the north of the north-west angle of the building an irregular paved area (K) was found, with tiers of stone steps, 18 on the east and six on the south, decreasing on the west side to three. This was described by the excavators as a stepped theatral area[1], and will be alluded to again later.

The east slope is occupied by various rooms and corridors, and three large halls, the queen's megaron (L), the hall of the colonnades (M), and the hall of the double axes (N)[2].

Of these the largest is the hall of the double axes (N), which is reached from the central court by descending a staircase and passing down the east corridor alongside of the hall of the colonnades (M), which is not in direct communication with the hall of the double axes.

As the plan of the latter is characteristic, it may perhaps be described in detail. The hall was divided into three parts: its west end, which was open to the air, was formed of a wall of limestone blocks, all marked with the sign of the double axe, which gave its name to this hall: the rest of the building, which was covered, had walls of

---

[1] *B.S.A.* IX. pp. 99 sqq. Cf. p. 105.   [2] *l.c.* VII. p. 110.

rubble with a layer of gypsum in the usual manner. The covered part of the hall was divided into two parts by square column bases, which evidently supported a storey or storeys above. Without is a paved portico with column bases indicating a colonnade. This is the largest hall in the palace and measures 8 m. wide by 24·4 m. long, reckoning from the outer edge of the portico, or 10 m. from the columns to the inner side of the portico.

The queen's megaron (L) and the hall of the colonnades (M) are similar halls.

On the south side of the hall of the double axes a short paved passage with a turn at both ends leads to the queen's megaron[1], a hall and suite of apartments in a very secluded position with every arrangement for privacy and comfort. This quarter has been regarded as set aside for the queen and her waiting women, hence its name.

There is evidence that there were at least three storeys in this part of the building[2]: two are still standing, a third would be on the level of the court, and a fourth has even been proposed on the level of the upper storey on the west side of the palace, but there is no evidence for this supposition.

In connection with the chronology of the palace it is interesting to notice the deep walled pits discovered in the north-west quarter in 1903[3], which give sufficient evidence of an earlier building, having no apparent connection with the later palace. Indeed they seem to have been the cause of some trouble to the later builders, who have sometimes carried their foundations down 25 ft to the original floor level.

---

[1] *B.S.A.* VIII. pp. 46 sqq.   [2] *l.c.* VIII. p. 60.

[3] *l.c.* IX. 22.

The ground plan of the palace, speaking generally, shows unity of design. The various halls, rooms and corridors are grouped around the great central court, whilst their walls for the most part run at right angles to one another. The north and south propylaea, the great southern terrace, the open courts on the west and north, and the long gallery with its series of magazines, are all prominent features of the plan.

Noack[1] has thrown further light on the systematic nature of the design by showing how the whole vast building is not put together at random, as a cursory glance might indicate, but laid out with special reference to the open court. He finds a number of parallel axes drawn through the great east court connecting the chief rooms, so that walls and rooms far removed from one another lie in the same straight line. Such a connection is clearly no chance one, but forms part of the architect's idea in laying out the building: there is order hidden in the apparent chaos.

A close examination, however, reveals many irregularities of construction. For example the walls surrounding the paved courts of the palace show frequent angles and returns, a characteristic feature of Mycenean building, which may according to Bosanquet have had its origin in the division of inner apartments, each being considered separately[2].

Again the long gallery, one of the most regular pieces of building in the palace, only attains half its width at its south end till it reaches the third magazine, while at its

---

[1] Noack, *Ovalhaus und Palast in Kreta*, p. 51.

[2] Bosanquet, *B.S.A.* IX. p. 278. But it occurs at Troy where there is no internal division, *Troja*, 1893, p. 42. Noack discusses the question *Ath. Mitt.* XIX. pp. 425–31. Dörpfeld in Schliemann, *Tiryns*, p. 315, and *Ath. Mitt.* XIX. p. 384.

north end there is a flight of steps half the width of the
gallery leading to a higher level, and a little further on
it is abruptly terminated by a cross wall.

One cannot help being struck by the intricacy of the
palace, even more so when one walks down its narrow
corridors than when one examines its ground plan on
paper: it is indeed a veritable labyrinth.

It is true that there are several large corridors, but
speaking generally communication, not only between
one part of the palace and another but also between
adjacent rooms, is difficult and involved, and the whole
system of narrow corridors, dog-leg passages and small
rooms is most bewildering.

The magnitude of the ground plan is also very striking:
the long gallery is 3·4 m. wide in its widest part and 60 m.
long, and the great southern terrace is about the same
length. The huge central court which is no less than
200 ft long by about 90 ft wide, and the numerous halls,
rooms and corridors surrounding it, must have formed
altogether a most imposing structure.

A word may be said here about the drainage system,
which is remarkably thorough and perfect. The drinking
water supply is brought through terra-cotta pipes [1]
composed of sections, with a well-made cemented joint
and stop-ridges to hold them together. Such pipes were
found below the floor in the corridor of the draught-
board, and smaller clay pipes socketed into one another
in a room near the south propylaeum, outside the north
tower and in the court of the sanctuary. The rain
water was probably used for other purposes, whether
stored in the so-called bath rooms or not, and accordingly
we find runnels for draining it off in the central court,
theatral area, etc., and the floors of the light wells are

[1] *B.S.A.* VIII. p. 13.

made gently sloping for the same purpose, as also the platform before the state entrance at Phaestos.

The sanitary arrangements are equally perfect, the drains communicating directly with the sewer.

The runnels and spouts for oil in the eastern quarter of the palace, where it was prepared and stored, show equal skill in this branch.

The position of the ancient city of *Phaestos* is exactly described by Homer, in the narrative of Nestor to Telemachus of how Menelaus came back from Troy, and was overtaken by a storm after losing his pilot Phrontis:—

> ἔστι δέ τις λισσὴ αἰπεῖά τε εἰς ἅλα πέτρη
> ἐσχατιῇ Γόρτυνος ἐν ἠεροειδέϊ πόντῳ
> ἔνθα Νότος μέγα κῦμα ποτὶ σκαιὸν ῥίον ὠθεῖ
> ἐς Φαιστόν, μικρὸς δὲ λίθος μέγα κῦμ' ἀποέργει.

Now there is a certain cliff, smooth and sheer towards the sea, on the border of Gortyn, in the misty deep, where the southwest wind drives a great wave against the left headland, towards Phaestos, and a little rock keeps back the mighty water[1].

The site, which was explored by the Italian school in 1900-1[2], is interesting in its physical features, since it consists of three peaks forming a chain and following the course of the river Geropotamos from west to east.

The first acropolis ends in a sharp peak and yielded no remains; on the second acropolis remains were found of a private house rectangular in plan[3], containing Kamares ware. On the third and most easterly the palace was discovered.

Though the architectural remains are scanty, it is clear that there was an earlier building on the site, erected at about the same period as the earlier palace at Knossos,

---

[1] *Od.* III. 293–6.
[2] Pernier, *Mon. Ant.* XII. pp. 33–84.
[3] *ibid.* p. 15, fig. 2.

and probably destroyed by some catastrophe at the end
of the M. M. period. In the west quarter of the palace,
south of the galleries, remains of a Neolithic settlement
already referred to[1] were found, including bones and
pottery.

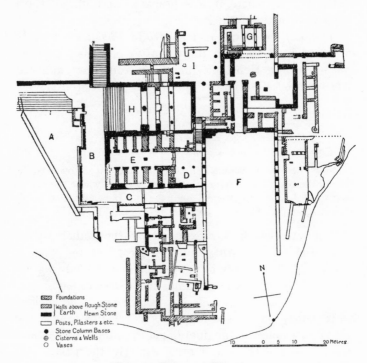

Fig. 16. Palace at Phaestos.

The later palace (Fig. 16) is generally supposed to date
from L. M. i. Unlike Knossos this site was inhabited,
after the fire and final destruction of the palace, right up
to Byzantine times.

[1] p. 67.

On the west is a large paved courtyard (*A*) with remains of a propylaeum at its south-west end, bounded on its east side by a wall, and on its north by a huge flight of steps. The court is crossed from north-east to south-west by a footpath at a slightly lower level, formed of polygonal blocks of limestone fitted together, and in the north-east corner of the courtyard are what appear to be the remains of an altar. The propylaeum, courtyard and altar are on the lowest level and probably belong to the earlier palace: they were incorporated in the later palace while other remains of the earlier period were levelled and covered.

This area probably corresponds to the stepped theatral area at Knossos, though simpler in type and probably earlier in date[1]. From the steps the spectators would enjoy a splendid panorama of the mountains to the south, while witnessing religious or other functions taking place in the court.

Ascending the steps at the north end of the courtyard to the principal level, we find on the right a large rectangular vestibule (*B*) 36 m. in length.

The great central corridor of the palace (*C*) opens out on the south end of the vestibule, and divides the palace into two distinct parts: to the north are the more important rooms, conspicuous by their size and solidity of construction, while to the south are many small rooms and corridors.

The central corridor was crossed at about a third of its length by a doorway, and just beyond this was an opening in the north, and probably also in the south wall, giving access to the interior of the palace.

At the end of this great corridor an opening on the left leads into a large rectangular apartment (*D*) (9·75 m.

[1] *vide* p. 87.

× 8·45 m.), called by the Italian excavators the men's megaron[1]. On the east where it faces on to the great open court there are remains of four square pilasters and the base of one elliptical column: the arrangement of two supporting columns along the major axis of the megaron is peculiar, and recalls early Neolithic constructions, *e.g.* tomb at Antequera[2] near Malaga.

On the north of this apartment is an entrance to a square room and also a staircase to a third and higher level.

To the west is the internal corridor (E) with magazines on both sides, similar to those at Knossos. The finds show distinctly that these were used as treasure houses of the lords of Phaestos. Moreover they are protected by a strong outer wall, and can only be entered from the megaron or the central corridor.

The great open court (F) on the east is 46·50 m. × 22·30 m., and is bounded at its north end by a massive wall with the familiar setbacks of Mycenean times.

An opening in the middle, with half columns on either side, leads to the rooms in the north-east quarter of the palace, which were probably family living rooms and included the megaron delle donne (G).

The principal entrance to the palace is thought to have been on the south side of this great court, though no traces now remain. Five square bases, with smaller ones between, are all that remain of a great portico on the east.

But the tremendous slope on the south and east sides of the palace almost precludes the idea of a principal entrance here, and makes the west side, as at Knossos, seem more probable.

We have left for final consideration the most interesting

[1] *Mon. Ant.* XII. p. 50, fig. 14.   [2] *vide* p. 15.

apartment of the palace.   To the north of the magazines
near the entrance first described, a large staircase leads
to an apartment (*H*) on the third level, which is shown
by its scale, height, position and the materials of its
construction to be the most important room of all, and
is in communication by means of a staircase with the
so-called men's megaron[1].   The steps lead to an open
landing with two antae projecting from the walls and a
column in the middle facing the vestibule proper.   Two
great doors opposite give access to the interior, which
consists of a room of the same proportions as the vestibule :
behind it are three columns and at the back a light well
of the usual construction, its floor composed of hard
cement with bevelled edges.   The arrangement of three
columns across the hall before the light well is peculiar,
and unique on this site : the spaces between the columns
thus face the entrances and correspond with them.

It has been now generally acknowledged that Mackenzie[2] is right in describing this stately building as the
state entrance to the later palace, and that it is to be
regarded as a pure Cretan development from the simpler
form of entrance door.

It has in common with the earlier entrances a corridor
leading to it, and the front divided by a column into
two parts.   The staircase and light well make it imposing
and majestic, but the actual principles of construction are
similar.   Such a development may have arisen naturally
from the increasing love of elegance and display, or

---

[1] *Mon. Ant.* XII. pp. 70 sqq.

[2] Mackenzie, *B.S.A.* XI. pp. 187 sqq.   Dörpfeld, *Ath. Mitt.* XXX.
pp. 285 sqq., regards this building as a "megaron" of Achaean type.
In *Mitt.* XXXII. p. 580 he agrees with Mackenzie that it is a state
entrance but still regards it as being of Achaean plan with "Cretan"
modifications.   Noack, *Ovalhaus und Palast in Kreta,* pp. 4 sqq.,
regards it as typically Cretan.

perhaps as Noack[1] suggests some ceremony was carried on in the light well, which would be covered with a canopy and adorned with carpets for the occasion.

The hall which Evans[2] restores on the first storey at Knossos, on the evidence of the remains of walls below, is similar in so far as it is approached by steps, the front is divided into two by one column, the chief room is entered by two doors from the vestibule, and behind stand three columns. These columns, however, appear in the restoration to stand in the middle of the room, which is thus longer in proportion than the corresponding room at Phaestos, and the light well is lacking. Rooms of a similar shape as those at Knossos at the side of this apartment, might easily be restored at Phaestos over the present remains.

Finally to the north is yet a fourth and higher level, containing a vast peristyle (*I*) with columns[3].

Traces of a Neolithic layer have been found, but the evidence here is not so complete as at Knossos.

The palace, which is built on uneven ground, contains, as we have seen, no less than four different levels, viz. the theatral area (*A*), the central courtyard (*F*), the great hall (*H*) and the peristyle (*I*).

The architect not only made use of the materials he found to hand, viz. limestone, gesso, a coarse reddish clay and cypresses, but even procured marble of coloured grain not found in the island, and spared no pains to make his erection elegant as well as solid.

The house signs on the Phaestos disc[4], though exceedingly curious, do not add much to our knowledge

---

[1] *Ovalhaus und Palast in Kreta*, p. 13.
[2] *B.S.A.* VII. pp. 21–26.   [3] *ibid.* p. 75.
[4] Evans, *Scripta Minoa*, figs. 128 and 129 (reproduced also *Antiquités Crétoises*, Pl. 48 and 49).

of Minoan architecture. The disc has been pronounced on the evidence of the characters non-Cretan, and the house hieroglyph[1] is certainly identical with secondary forms of the Egyptian hieroglyph for palace. In addition, however, we have two very interesting signs which may represent two huts on piles[2], and further strengthen the evidence afforded by the Melos and Amorgos urns for this peculiar type of dwelling in the south.

The most interesting sign of all is the pagoda-like building[3], which has a most foreign appearance.

It has been explained that the reason is simply that the drawing is defective, and that this sign represents a rectangular building with a carinated roof. It will be noticed that the roof timbers do not curve. The beams project quite in the manner of the Lycian rock-cut tombs[4].

Together with the palaces we may mention the two lordly villas of Knossos and Hagia Triada, which are as it were dependencies of Knossos and Phaestos respectively, and which are so intimately connected in construction, plan and arrangement.

---

[1] Evans, *op. cit.* p. 197, No. 41.   [2] *ibid.* p. 198, No. 43.
[3] *ibid.* p. 24, fig. 11*b*, 2nd diagram.
[4] Perrot and Chipiez, *op. cit.* v. 9, figs. 261, 264–6.

R. G. H.

7

The *Royal Villa at Knossos*[1] was discovered on the slope to the east of the palace site, and seems to have belonged to the later palace period. There are no signs of its having been destroyed by fire, but it was evidently plundered and left to decay.

The house was built on the side of the hill and had

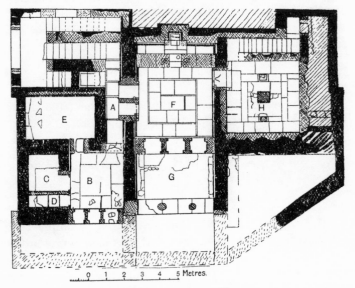

Fig. 17. Royal villa at Knossos.

three or possibly four storeys, the ground floor probably being reached by a staircase from the floor above (Fig. 17).

The stateliness of this house, its elaborate construction and its magnificent pottery, seem to indicate clearly that it was a dependency of the palace.

The ground floor is very spacious in construction with its large halls and elaborate staircases. The corridor (*A*),

[1] *B.S.A.* IX. 1902, p. 130.

which was first struck in excavating, leads at its east
end into a passage hall (*B*) with seven exits: on the
south side of this hall are two small chambers (*C* and *D*)
while on the west it opens on to a large rectangular
apartment (*E*).

To the north of corridor (*A*) is the most interesting
room of all, as well as the largest and most important (*FG*).
This megaron is divided into two parts by three doorways evidently arranged in such a manner that the doors
could be thrown back and fitted into the piers, when the
whole room was required for use, an idea which we find
in the Japanese house to-day. When the doors were
closed, there were two absolutely separate apartments.
The eastern apartment (*G*) was of simple character,
rectangular in form with two columns at its eastern end.
The west apartment (*F*) is more elaborate and highly
interesting: it is a rectangular area (4 m. × 4·55 m.)
paved with gypsum, and at its western end a double
balustrade running out from antae in the side walls, with
three ascending steps at the opening in the middle, crosses
the whole width of the megaron.

Behind this balustrade is a narrow rectangular space,
and in the middle of the west wall a square niche with
remains of a gypsum throne. It is impossible to help
noticing the very striking resemblance of this arrangement
to that of the later Roman basilica, with its apse
containing the magistrate's seat and the screen for
division.

Some have sought the origin of this in the στοὰ βασίλειος
of the Archon Basileus[1] in the agora at Athens, but while
the ground plan of that building remains as conjectural
as it is, it would not seem safe to point any connection
here between Minoan building and that of later classical

[1] *B.S.A.* IX. p. 148. Cf. Lange, *Haus und Halle*, pp. 60 sqq.

times.   On the north side of this interesting hall is a
square pillar room (*H*).

The royal villa of Hagia Triada[1], which must have
been the residence of the heir apparent or of some great
functionary of the palace, is situated on a hill between
Phaestos and the sea: the architect has built round the
hill on the west and north sides, leaving the summit

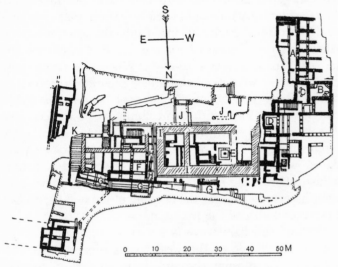

Fig. 18.   Royal villa at Hagia Triada.

free (Fig. 18).   The older and larger villa was probably
built in M. M. iii, while the later villa belongs to the end
of the late Minoan period.   On the west slope is a long
corridor (*A*) with magazines and two large rooms, one
of which was a workshop (*B*), and the other a repository
for vases (*C*).   The north-west corner is the finest part,
containing the megaron (*D*) and its dependencies, with

[1] *Mon. Art.* XIII. pp. 5–15; *Rendiconti,* XI. 433 sqq; *Mem. r.
Ist. Lomb.* XXI. 238–40.

a staircase to the higher level. Round the corner is a
complex of rooms over which the later palace was built:
among them is an interesting square room (*E*) with pave-
ment and sloping floor and the remains of a square
pilaster, which Halbherr[1] considers to have been a sanctuary of a similar nature to the pillar rooms at Knossos
and in the Royal Villa.

On the north side is the women's megaron (*F*) and
rooms communicating, three of them with benches. A
fine ramp and stairway (*G*), running along the north wing,
give access to the palace.

The fire which destroyed the villa seems to have raged
principally in the magazines and men's quarters.

The second edifice, which was much smaller, was built
on the north slope, which was divided into two by a
dromos-like passage way (*H*): on the west a great
terrace (*I*) with walls of finely squared ashlar was constructed, to the south of which are imperfect remains
of a few rooms (*J*). The grand staircase (*K*), however,
proves that the villa, if smaller, attained perhaps even a
higher level of elegance than the earlier.

The parallelism of the main designs of the two great
palaces, in that they are built around a large open inner
court, which determines their main axes, though it does
not prevent parts being enlarged in various directions,
may further be followed in all the different details of
construction.

It is true that speaking generally Phaestos is built
on broader, simpler lines: the great open staircases with
steps 13½ m. wide, 70 cm. broad and 12 cm. high find
no parallel in Knossos, and can only be compared with
those of some of the Egyptian temples; the great terrace
is between 7 m. and 8 m. wide at its widest part, and the

[1] *Mem. r. I. L.* p. 238.

corridor leading from it to the east court 5 m., like the similar corridor existing in the north part.

There are also more straight lines and fewer setbacks; *e.g.* in the open court, in contrast to Knossos, we only find setbacks at the north end.

This orderliness of plan is all the more surprising when one considers the difficulties presented to the architect by the varying levels of the site, difficulties which have only been full of suggestion to him for the beautification of his building.

In Knossos, which covers a larger area, there is a greater and more confused mass of rooms and narrow passages. The proportions of the east court are certainly a little greater, but otherwise no individual room is as large or passage as broad.

The magazines are longer but at the same time narrower, the great staircases are wanting and there are numerous setbacks in courts and corridors. There are also more small state apartments such as the throne room, queen's megaron, hall of the double axes, hall of the colonnades, etc.

On the other hand the disposition of rooms is similar; in the north is the domestic quarter, the inner court is on the east, and the magazines and great hall (restored by Evans at Knossos over the court of the Altar) lie on the west.

With regard to the proportions of the state rooms, as for example those mentioned above at Knossos, and the great hall and the megaron delle donne at Phaestos, the breadth is much greater than the length, a noticeable feature of Cretan building, which has analogies in Egypt, *e.g.* twelfth dynasty houses at Kahun[1], but not on the

---

[1] *Zentralblatt der Bauverwaltung*, XIII. 517 and 521.   Petrie, *Kahun Gurob and Hawara*, pp. 23, 24 and pl. xv.   Cf. Noack, *Homerische Paläste*, pp. 27 sqq.

mainland of Greece. The light wells are also of the same proportions and the idea is clearly elemental in the architecture of both palaces.

The magazines, whether used as store rooms for valuables and documents or, as Mosso suggests from the strength and perfection of their building, for private banks[1] to which separate owners only had access, form an exception, being long in proportion to their width: some magazines at Knossos are as much as 20 m. long by 3 m. broad. These store houses however cannot be regarded as rooms.

This wonderful Cretan race who knew so well the art of living and carried elegance and beauty into the veriest commonplace details of existence, never shrank into the dark, the morbid, the mysterious; theirs was the healthy life which finds an outlet for all faculties physical, intellectual and emotional, and the ease and luxury around them did not, as far as we can now judge, lull them into Oriental apathy.

We are astonished to see the almost incredible athletic capacities of the commoner women[2], as they sport with the bull in a manner which makes the modern corrida de toros, as one witnesses it in Spain to-day, but a travesty, a sport which is no sport, where the toreador has all the odds in his favour and the bull is but a persecuted victim utterly at his mercy.

In their architecture we find the same free healthy ideas, and among the most striking is the love of air and light; the great open spaces, the staircases, the terraces, the regular system of lighting stairs and corridors by means of wells, reveal this in the general plan, and in the individual rooms one is struck by the fondness for colon-

---

[1] Mosso, *Palaces of Crete and their builders*, p. 128.
[2] *B.S.A.* VII. pp. 94 sqq.

nades, by the recurrence of rows of pilasters with spaces between forming a series of doorways, and the number of doors in the same room. Privacy was evidently no part of the scheme, the Cretan lived too fast and too intensely to feel the need of solitude, and there is hardly one room in the whole palace scheme which is entirely cut off. Large and small rooms have common party walls, and many even communicate directly with each other.

The question of columns in Cretan architecture is interesting. With regard to the shape, the square pilaster frequently occurs, as in the great east court at Phaestos or the hall of the double axes at Knossos; the circular form is everywhere found, and even the elliptical occurs in the megaron degli uomini at Phaestos on the side of the east court. The favourite arrangement seems to be the single standing column dividing the front into two parts, and giving in the case of a room two entrances[1].

An alternative is the three column arrangement giving four passage ways, *e.g.* hall of the double axes.

Three columns across the breadth of the room occur in the hall of the colonnades, the propylaeum at Phaestos, and the restored hall at Knossos.

Examples of the two column arrangement, as on the mainland, are not lacking, but the odd number is characteristically Cretan. The south propylaeum at Knossos for instance has only two column bases remaining, but as these are placed toward the side walls it is possible that a third stood between them, and in the great hall above Evans restores the one and three column arrangement, as in the corresponding hall at Phaestos.

The two column arrangement occurs in the megaron delle donne at Phaestos. We also find the single standing

[1] Cf. Noack, *Homerische Paläste*, pp. 9 sqq.

column in the corridor between the magazines, in the corridor to the North etc., and frequent groups of three, *e.g.* colonnade outside hall of the double axes, etc.

Whether this be an essential feature of Cretan architecture or not, it is a striking arrangement without analogy in the great palaces of the mainland, or in Chaldaea or Egypt.

The arrangement of the propylaeum[1] is not stereotyped but varies according to the disposition of the part of the building where it occurs. It generally consists of an open passage-way between the outside wall and that of the rooms, terminating in a vestibule, behind which is a wall with doors, *e.g.* south propylaeum at Knossos. The later propylaeum at Phaestos, if it be such, differs entirely in proportions and arrangement, and, even if it is to be regarded as a development from the earlier form, has become almost as it were a separate building, for it seems to lead to no important apartment, and the only egress from it is by a staircase at the back.

There seems no doubt that the stepped areas found both at Knossos and Phaestos represent some sort of early theatre, though of quite different construction from that of later Greece. The building was, however, admirably adapted to its use for dances, wrestling matches, etc., for it provided an excellent view for spectators, and acoustic properties were probably quite a secondary consideration. Otherwise in view of the perfect tholos tombs constructed by them, there seems no reason why the Myceneans should not with equal ease have built a circular theatre. The stepped area at Knossos[2] consists of a paved rectangle, 10 m. × 13 m., divided in the middle by a paved footway 1·50 m. wide: on the east and south sides were two flights of stairs,

---

[1] Noack, *Ovalhaus und Palast in Kreta*, p. 8.　　[2] *vide* p. 87.

that on the east composed of 18 tiers, that on the south
of about six, and between them a square bastion of good
limestone masonry, which Evans designates the Royal
Box. On the steps outside the spectators must have
sat or stood, for they do not lead to any great building.
The importance of the theatre is shown by the fact that
it is connected directly by means of causeways with the
north and west entrances of the palace.

The similar area at Phaestos[1] differs from that at
Knossos in that it has a large paved platform behind the
steps, which gave additional accommodation.

The existence of windows, clearly shown by the
enamelled models of houses and the frescoes, has been
proved beyond a doubt in several parts of the palace,
e.g. between the light well of the hall of the double axes
and the east-west corridor, in the wall to the north of
the light well of the queen's megaron, in the south-east
house, etc.[2]

In the room of the plaster couch and the court of the
distaffs were double windows with two side posts and
one centre post: apparently the whole of the upper wall
rested on these posts which were of wood, of which the
carbonised remains were found: the masonry had consequently collapsed.

The size of these windows, sometimes two or three
metres across, is very noticeable and is peculiar to Crete.

Another point of comparison is the lighting system
which is common to the two palaces[3]: it consists of an
opening or shaft at the further end of the hall, by means
of which the hall and the adjoining corridors and staircases
were lighted, and which must have been designed to this

[1] *vide* p. 93.
[2] *B.S.A.* VIII. p. 40, fig. 21; *ibid.* p. 64; *B.S.A.* IX. p. 4 and fig. 2
[3] Cf. Noack, *Ovalhaus und Palast in Kreta*, p. 61.

end. That it was open to the air and exposed to the
weather is clear from the fact that the floor is slightly
sloping, and often connects with a drain, and is made
of a hard cement which would withstand exposure far
better than the perishable gypsum slabs used in covered
places for walls and flooring. Such a light well, for
instance, at the end of the hall of the double axes, has
walls of good solid masonry[1], whilst within the walls are
made of rubble coated with gypsum slabs. The light
wells are of good proportions, that for instance lighting
the columnar hall and storey above measures 5·40 m. ×
3·30 m.[2] This system which is peculiar to Crete is natural
and effective, and gives a much pleasanter light than a
direct light from overhead: on the mainland the megara
with their central hearths were of course lighted by a
lantern above, where an opening was necessary as an
outlet for the smoke.

Religion, which in other lands is often responsible for
the best and grandest architectural forms, would seem in
Crete to have been almost of a private character and its
rites confined to private sanctuaries. In absolute contrast to the magnificent temples of the same epoch at
Thebes with their colossal avenues and colonnades, we
find the Cretan worshipping his goddess in a shrine only
one and a half metres square[3], which recalls the Mihrab
or prayer niche of the Mohammedan such as one sees in
the mosque at Cordova, though even this is considerably
larger than the Mycenean sanctuary.

The tiny shrine at Knossos was divided into three
parts or ledges, one above the other, and on the third
against the end wall horns of consecration, a double axe
in steatite, semi-anthropomorphic images of the dove

[1] *B.S.A.* VIII. p. 36.
[2] *B.S.A.* VII. pp. 109–10.   [3] *ibid.* VIII. pp. 95 sqq.

goddess and other objects of cult were found[1], and may still be seen in position. The simplicity of such a "holy of holies" is in strange contrast to the extreme complication of the profane architecture.

The terracotta remains of a miniature sanctuary[2] found in the north-east quarter of the palace showed three columns without any tapering, surmounted by square capitals, on each of which rested two round beam ends: the doves seated upon them seem to point to the worship of the dove goddess and the objects probably belonged to an earlier shrine. The cult of the Cretan Zeus, whose symbol was the double axe and who, according to tradition, was born in the cave of Dicte, reared on Ida and buried in Joukta, was evidently of the same intimate character, and the west central region of the palace with its three altar bases in the central and west courts and the court of the altar respectively, and its frequent sign of the double axe, would appear to have some special connection with this worship. In this region we find two small adjoining rooms[3], in the middle of each of which stands a pillar composed of a series of blocks engraved with mystic sign. Evans has recognised in these pillars an aniconic image of the god[4], and scenes of such worship are clearly depicted on the vase from Cyprus[5] and the sarcophagus of Hagia Triada[6]. Such a baetylic form of religion is a natural advance on tree worship, and may even be seen to-day in Macedonia, where the pillar is anointed with oil[7] just as Jacob's at Bethel. The striking Semitic analogy leads on to a further consideration, as

[1] *B.S.A.* VIII. p. 99, fig. 56.   [2] *ibid.* VIII. p. 28 and fig. 14.
[3] *ibid.* IX. pp. 35 sqq.
[4] Evans, *Mycenean Tree and Pillar Cult*, p. 13.
[5] A. S. Murray, *Excavations in Cyprus*, p. 73, fig. 127.
[6] Figured *Antiquités Crétoises*, pl. 44, 45.
[7] Evans, *op. cit.* p. 102 and fig. 69.

to whether such a pillar may not have on occasions a structural function in the building. It is said that Solomon "reared up the pillars before the temple, one on the right hand, and the other on the left; and called the name of that on the right hand Jachin [he shall establish], and the name of that on the left Boaz [in it is strength]" 2 Chron. iii. 17.

Whether these were "pillars of the house" or not is not clear, but it seems quite possible that at Knossos these pillars served such a function in supporting the upper storey columns, at any rate in the later palace history.

The pillar room of the south-east house[1] with its rich decoration and sacrificial vessels was clearly never anything but a domestic sanctuary, as also that in the Royal Villa and others occurring in several private houses at Knossos and Phylakopi, where we find again two contiguous chambers as in the palace.

The two monolithic limestone pillars[2], on the other hand, in the basement near the south-east house appear to have served a purely structural purpose in supporting the roof.

These Minoan sanctuaries are all of diminutive proportions, the room in the north-east house for instance being about 3 m. square, and that in the Royal Villa 4·15 m. × 4 m. with the pillar ·52 m. square, and are built of gypsum blocks well finished in the interior.

Such is the scanty evidence for Minoan religious architecture: there remains for consideration the interesting little temple fresco[3] found in one of the rooms to the north of the east court, representing animated crowds outside the building, doubtless on some festal day.   The sanctuary

[1] *B.S.A.* IX. pp. 7–9.   [2] *ibid.* IX. p. 18 and fig. 7.
[3] Evans, *op. cit.* figs. 18 and 66; cf. *B.S.A.* VI. p. 46.

which is apparently built of stone in its lower courses, and wood and stucco above, is divided into three parts, of which the middle stands higher than the others, and is again of small proportions if we may judge from the seated figure at the side of the temple, whose head is on a level with the capital of the side column. The columns, which according to Evans are clearly shown to be aniconic images by the horns of consecration at their bases, are of characteristic Mycenean form, tapering downwards.

The foregoing is a rough analysis of the resemblances in plan of the great Cretan palaces, which create as it were a canon for architectural form in the island in its highest development. As we have seen, the tradition behind such perfected buildings must have been long and consistent, and we can only regard them as a final form, a culmination of all that was finest and noblest in preceding eras. It is a matter of some surprise that their influence on mainland structures was not more pronounced, but the type there grew up under such multifarious influences that it is with great difficulty that the exact rôle played in its history by any one style can be traced.

CHAPTER X

MAINLAND PALACES

THE excavations in Crete have set all doubts at rest with regard to the origin of this wonderful culture previously called Mycenean, and the mainland palaces at Mycenae, Tiryns and Arne can now only be regarded as a faint reflection of its glory and brilliance, which came into being at a time when it had reached its highest point of development and was already threatened with destruction.

We have seen that the sites of Knossos and Phaestos were inhabited from the very opening of the Neolithic period, and that the earlier palaces were erected in M. M. i, some few hundred years after the opening of the Bronze Age: on the mainland, on the contrary, the early Bronze Age is almost entirely unrepresented, and the earliest finds belong to L. M. i, *i.e.* towards the end of the Bronze Age.

The mainland palaces were constructed in the succeeding period (L. M. ii), the "Palace" period of Crete.

This period, though apparently the most flourishing in Cretan history, was already in its love of ostentation, its lack of thoroughness and its gradual loss of the true artistic sense, decadent.

It was the time of the re-modelling of the palace at Knossos and the completion of the palace at Phaestos: at the end of the period sudden destruction and annihilation came upon them both.

It was a time too of outward expansion and political prosperity, for the great King Minos[1] reigned. Under his thalassocracy piracy, which had been everywhere rife, was gradually but firmly suppressed until it became almost a thing unknown, and unwalled coast villages and towns like Palaikastro, Zakro, etc., existed in perfect security and were only abandoned when Crete lost command of the sea.

The relations of Minos with Egypt were very close, and the Keftiu[2] represented on the wall-paintings of Thebes, who bear vases of characteristic Cretan form in their hands, have been identified with the men of the great maritime empire of Knossos, and prove a close contact in an age of prosperity and peace.

With the mainland of Greece, however, the relations of Minos were not so peaceful, and, whatever may be the true explanation of the Minotaur legend, there can be no doubt that it rested upon some tribute exacted by the king "who walked with God."

Plutarch[3] tells us that the Cretans themselves denied the truth of the legend, and only allowed that the labyrinth was a prison from which it was impossible to escape. One is led at once to think of the walled dungeons in the Northern quarter at Knossos[4]. The death of Minos took place by violence in Sicily, according to Herodotus (VII. 170):—

λέγεται γὰρ Μίνων κατὰ ζήτησιν Δαιδάλου ἀπικόμενον ἐς Σικανίην τὴν νῦν Σικελίην καλευμένην ἀποθανεῖν βιαίῳ θανάτῳ.

[1] On Minos cf. Ridgeway's Tract, "Minos the destroyer rather than the creator of the so-called Minoan Culture of Knossos," where the tradition for two kings called Minos is discussed, pp. 14–17.

[2] H. R. Hall, "Keftiu and the Peoples of the Sea," *B.S.A.* VIII. pp. 157 sqq.

[3] Plutarch, *Theseus.*   [4] *B.S.A.* IX. p. 22 and fig. 12.

The history of these early times, which has such an important bearing on the architecture, is shrouded in mystery, and we can only feel our way in the dark and hope for the discovery of some bi-lingual inscription, which will aid in reading the language, though the tablets hitherto found do not promise to be historical records[1].

In Crete, as we have seen, the architecture and pottery point to a continuity of race from the Neolithic period onwards, though exterior influences were at times strong and invasions not unknown: the evidence of cranial types points in the same direction, the dolichocephalic or true Mediterranean type always prevailing[2].

The brachycephalic type only begins to find its way in towards the close of the Neolithic period.

On architectural evidence Mackenzie[3] has conclusively proved that the ethnic change in Crete, postulated by Dörpfeld[4], is imaginary, and Sergi[5] even goes so far as to suggest that the Achaeans may have been part of the same race which inhabited Greece from the Neolithic period, and that "Achaean" is simply a new name.

But these are all moot points and serve to show the uncertainty prevailing with regard to racial questions, which bear so largely on the architecture. In any case the architecture itself makes it clear that in Crete no great racial change took place, at least before the final destruction; in the days of Homer the population was very mixed[6]. There remains however the question as to how Minos lost his power, and by whose instrumentality the great palaces at Knossos, Phaestos and Hagia Triada

---

[1] Evans, *Scripta Minoa*, pp. 20, 21.
[2] Mosso, *Dawn of Mediterranean civilisation*, pp. 409 sqq.
[3] Mackenzie, "Cretan Palaces, III," *B.S.A.* XIII. p. 423.
[4] Dörpfeld, *Ath. Mitt.* 1905, p. 257.
[5] Sergi, *Europa*, pp. 606-7.   [6] *Od.* XIX. 170 sqq.

were razed to the ground, at the beginning of the L. M. iii period.

Some have seen in this a great internal revolution[1], but it seems more probable that the invasion was from the mainland where Minos had already been at war, and, if Sergi[2] be correct, an invasion of the "Achaeo-Pelasgians" of the same original Mediterranean stock as the Cretans themselves. Not only were the palaces completely destroyed, the sites only being partially re-occupied afterwards, but many of the provincial and coast towns also fell. The men who re-occupied the sites afterwards continued to use not only pottery and domestic objects of pre-cataclysmic forms, but also the linear Minoan script. This fact also lends support to the theory that they were of the same original stock as the Cretans themselves.

Henceforth we must follow the development of the architecture on the mainland, which had become prosperous and important during the late Minoan period, but where the different conditions make the solution of the problem of the origin and development of the palace plan difficult.

Crete through her commercial intercourse had doubtless come under the influence of various nations, and more especially under that of Egypt: there is certainly something Oriental in the maze of small rooms and passages side by side with the great staircases, courtyards and corridors. At the same time the originality of the race never admitted of a slavish copying, and any ideas that the Cretans adopted they made their own. Thus the architecture always remains Cretan, an individual style not found elsewhere; resemblances and analogies may be traced but never imitation.

[1] Mosso, *Palaces of Crete and their builders*, p. 163.
[2] Sergi, *op. cit.* p. 608.

On the mainland the case is not so simple, for the very geographical position of Greece made a direct influence from the North inevitable. To Crete, on the other hand, Mycenean building does not seem to have owed much: presumably the flow of emigration from the South northwards did not continue to any very large extent after the first settling of the Mediterranean race, while the flow from the Northern lands into Greece must have been more or less continuous.

The Mediterranean stock of the mainland had the same fine instinct for building which the Cretans possessed, but not the same opportunity of undisturbed development.

Whatever racial relation the Achaeans may have borne to them, it is clear that they continued for several centuries to trouble the peace of the Mediterranean basin until they finally attacked Troy *circ.* 1200 B.C.

The growth of the power of the Phoenicians, after the downfall of Minos, also contributed to bring to an end the former state of security, and led to the building of great walled cities of which Troy, which seems indeed always to have been surrounded by a wall, furnishes an example.

In this connection the palaces of the mainland stand in striking contrast to those of Crete, which had no fortification wall.

The palace of Tiryns[1], for instance, stands on an eminence rising 59 ft above the plain and is entirely surrounded by a massive wall, 23–26 ft in thickness. The upper citadel walls attain in some parts a thickness of 57 ft, and are fortified by towers and pierced by galleries and chambers. The curious construction in the south wall, regarded by Dörpfeld[2] as a simple series of

[1] Schliemann, *Tiryns*, pass.
[2] In Schliemann, *Tiryns*, pp. 319–23.

store chambers, may possibly have been built to the same end.

In any case it is well hidden and protected, the gallery contracting to a loop-hole only 4 in. across at one end and being completely closed in at the other.

The walls of Mycenae, which may have been built a little subsequently to those of Tiryns, are from 10–23 ft thick, but in two places attain a thickness of 46 ft[1].

But a cursory glance at the ground plan of these mainland palaces reveals political and social conditions utterly different from those prevailing in Crete. Protection and defence have been the first consideration of their architects, the palaces are real fortresses.

The approaches carry out the same idea. At Tiryns after penetrating the outer wall one finds one's self in a passage some 60 m. long between massive walls, at the very end of which is the propylaeum leading into the large forecourt. Here the enemy would have the right side exposed, according to the strategical principle of those times, and would have but a small chance of entering if the position were well guarded. Vitruvius writing on this point says :—

Curandumque maxime videtur ut non facilis aditus sit ad oppugnandum murum sed ita circumdandum ad loca praecipitia et excogitandum uti portarum itinera non sint directa sed scaeva. Namque cum ita factum fuerit tum dextrum latus accedentibus, quod scuto non erit tectum, proximus erit muro (*de Archit.* I. 5).

And it seems that special care should be taken that the entrance is not easy for attacking the wall but in consequence the circuit must be traced near the steep places and care must be taken that the roads to the gates are not in their direction but on their left. By this arrangement the right side of the invaders which will not be covered by the shield will be nearest the wall.

[1] Schuchardt, *Schliemann's Excavations*, p. 138.

The little west postern gate at the bottom of the hill was a veritable death trap for an enemy, who would have found himself enclosed in a long narrow ascending passage, where any long resistance to attack would have been impossible: the inhabitants no doubt used this stairway as a convenient means of communication with the lower city.

At Mycenae the two entrances to the citadel are also constructed with a view to defence, being approached by a passage (in one case only 10 ft broad) between wall and tower, so that the enemy would be absolutely exposed. Within the Lion Gate at Mycenae there is no long passage as at Tiryns, but two sentry boxes are there, probably for a daily guard. At Arne[1] we find similar precautions in the shape of towers, massive walls and gateways, as well as in the interior of the palace.

The purpose of towers in fortification is also explained by Vitruvius (I. 5):

Item turres sunt proiciendae in exteriorem partem, uti cum ad murum hostis impetu velit adpropinquare a turribus dextra ac sinistra lateribus apertis telis vulneretur.

Furthermore the towers should be projected towards the exterior part of the wall, so that if the enemy wishes to approach the wall with a rush he is wounded with darts by the fact of the towers with their open flanks being on his right and left.

The outline of the walls presents a series of zig-zags both inside and out, a system which we find also at Mycenae, Tiryns and Troy, and which may have originated in a desire to break the monotony of surface[2], or may have been part of some older system of fortification, which later became stylised in Mycenean building and even found its way into interiors[3].

[1] *B.C.H.* XVIII. p. 273.
[2] Dörpfeld, *Ath. Mitt.* XIX. p. 384   [3] *vide* p. 89

The Homeric description of the building of the wall about the Achaean ships shows how practised in the art this race was, and how very quickly they could construct such defences in case of war.

> ποτὶ δ' αὐτὸν τεῖχος ἔδειμαν
> πύργους θ' ὑψηλοὺς, εἶλαρ νηῶν τε καὶ αὐτῶν.
> ἐν δ' αὐτοῖσι πύλας ἐνεποίεον εὖ ἀραρυίας
> ὄφρα δι' αὐτάων ἱππηλασίη ὁδὸς εἴη.
> ἔκτοσθεν δὲ βαθεῖαν ἐπ' αὐτῷ τάφρον ὄρυξαν
> εὐρεῖαν μεγάλην, ἐν δὲ σκόλοπας κατέπηξαν.

Il. VII. 436.

And thereto built they a wall and lofty towers, a bulwark for their ships and for themselves. In the midst thereof made they gates well compacted, that through them might be a way for chariot driving. And without they dug a deep fosse beside it, broad and great, and planted a palisade therein.

Here is a wall, which though roughly and hastily constructed, exemplifies the embryonic system underlying the fortifications of any city of this age.

Another striking general difference is the added simplicity of plan of the mainland palaces, indicating a race less refined and not so luxury-loving as the Cretans, though the art forms and decoration are similar, and the rich treasure of the city, called by Homer πολύχρυσος[1], finds no counterpart in Crete.

A more detailed comparison of the three principal mainland palaces of Tiryns, Mycenae and Arne with the palace of Crete may more advantageously be made after a brief review of their respective ground plans.

The principal entrance to the *palace at Tiryns*[2], as we have seen, is by means of a wide passage on the east between the citadel wall and the palace wall to the left of the entrance gate (Fig. 19) (*A*).

[1] *Il.* XI. 46.   [2] Schliemann, *Tiryns*, pass.

At a distance of about 50 ft down are some folding gates, and further on a forecourt with colonnade (*B*) is reached.   On its west side a propylaeum (*C*) of the type so common in Mycenean and afterwards in classical times, leads into a large open courtyard (*D*) surrounded by chambers.

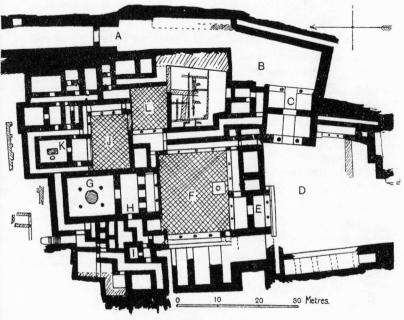

Fig. 19.   Palace at Tiryns.

A smaller propylaeum (*E*) on the north side gives on to another courtyard (*F*) of regular, rectangular shape, surrounded by porticoes. This can also be reached direct from the greater propylaeum by means of a narrow passage.

The portico on the north side of the courtyard, with its two columns, leads by means of three doorways into a vestibule of the same proportions, which leads by a doorway, facing the middle entrance of the portico, to the megaron (*G*) with its circular hearth and four columns.

In the west wall of the vestibule is an opening (*H*) which leads to the bath room (*I*), which is of about the same proportions as those discovered in the Cretan palaces. The floor is composed of one huge slab of limestone 13 ft × 10 ft and over 2 ft thick: the holes round the base have led to the conclusion that the basin was lined with wood, like that at Phaestos. The two holes in the north wall are supposed to have been destined to hold jars of oil for anointing (cf. the regular Homeric practice of anointing with olive oil immediately after the bath (*Od.* XXIII. 154, etc.)).

From this room a narrow corridor winds, with many zig-zags, to the east side of the megaron, where we find identically the same plan reproduced on a smaller scale. There is a courtyard (*J*) surrounded by porticoes with the megaron (*K*) on its north side. This is entered by means of a vestibule but there is no portico, probably on account of its diminished size, which may also account for the absence of supporting columns round the square hearth in the centre.

On three sides of this smaller megaron runs a corridor, communicating on both sides with the vestibule and leading to various apartments between it and the enclosure wall. This smaller megaron can also be reached by means of a passage leading direct from the greater propylaeum.

To the south-east of the court of the smaller set of apartments is another open court (*L*) of about the same size, and to the south of this again are more walls and chambers.

The large megaron is distinguished both by its position

and construction as the most important part of the
building. Not only is it the largest covered room with
the thickest walls, but it also stands on the highest and
most secluded part of the citadel.

There is evidence of a building belonging to an earlier
epoch, especially in the north-west quarter of the palace,
where remains of rubble walls and fragments of rough
monochrome pottery have been found, but the remains
are not sufficient to warrant any conclusion as to its
plan.

Palace at Mycenae[1]. The excavations of the Greek
Archaeological Society under the superintendence of
Tsountas in 1886 brought to light at Mycenae the
foundations of a palace whose ground plan is similar to
the ground plans of the palaces at Tiryns and Troy
(Fig. 20). The Homeric epithet wide-wayed (εὐρυάγυια
Μυκήνη), which is also used of Troy, does not apparently
imply roads of great width, for in Mycenae streets of
$1\frac{1}{2}$ m. wide were found on the acropolis.

The walls of the early Doric temple (*A*) (probably of
the 6th cent. B.C.) were found to rest on the south side
on a layer of débris about 10 ft deep, within which were
discovered ancient walls of two periods.

The better built walls, constructed of large blocks
of stone, some of which are dressed, enclose the remains
of the palace, which was approached by a road winding
up from the grave circle to a staircase on the south side (*B*).
On mounting this one entered, probably through a gateway
of which no traces remain, the courtyard (*C*), which is
38 ft wide and paved with concrete.

The principal apartment (*D*) of the palace lies on the
right of this courtyard, and is rectangular in plan with
two columns of wood on stone bases indicated between

[1] Schliemann, *Mycenae*, pass.

the antae.   The first vestibule led by means of an entrance
with a stone threshold into the second, which opened on
to the spacious megaron 28 ft × 42 ft.   The roof of this
apartment was supported on four wooden columns,
according to the usual mainland plan, and remains of
the hearth have been found in the centre.

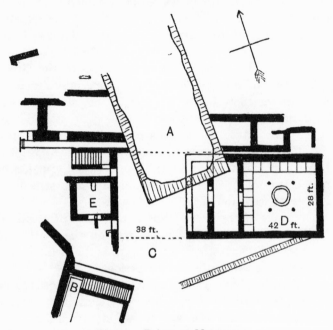

Fig, 20.   Palace at Mycenae.

On the west side of the courtyard is a similar smaller
structure (*E*) facing north, consisting of a main apartment
with two vestibules, but the entrances are not on the
main axis of the megaron.   To the north of this room a
passage leads to the western part of the palace, of which
nothing now remains.

Palace at Gha[1]. The island of Gha in the plain of
Copaïs in Boeotia was fortified in Mycenean times with
a massive enclosure wall, resembling strongly in character
the fortification wall of the citadel at Tiryns. The wall
contained four gateways, two of which were fortified, and
on the north side close up to it stood the palace. The
fortified area is far greater than the acropolis either at
Tiryns or Mycenae. The pottery indicates that the
architectural remains belong to L. M. ii and iii, though
they may be somewhat earlier[2].

So far as we can judge from the remains, the palace
(Fig. 21) was composed of two wings at right angles to each
other, one of which is built in the thickness of the fortification wall and follows its general direction from west to east.

Near the middle of the north wing on its south side
is the entrance (*A*), with a large corridor on the left and
right: the right bends at the corner at right angles and
is continued down the east wing with two projecting
angles in its length. The north wing is 80 m. long, and
the east wing rather shorter.

With the exception of two rooms (*B* and *C*), one at
each extremity of this long corridor, none of the apartments is entered directly from it, but the rooms open into
other corridors parallel to the first set, an added precaution
for purposes of defence.

The strength and massiveness of the walls, the curious
arrangement of rooms and corridors, and the towers,
one at the end of each wing on a slightly lower level and
without access to the palace, seem to show that special
care was taken to make this palace impregnable: the time
of its habitation was comparatively short.

In the north wing, which includes three sets of apart-

---

[1] *B.C.H.* xviii. pp. 271 sqq.
[2] So Wace and Thompson, *Prehistoric Thessaly*, p. 193.

ments, no less than three of the rooms (D, E, F) are entered through a vestibule, a repetition of the plan of many of the houses of the sixth city at Troy.

The east wing is divided into two distinct sets of apartments, and we find the same system of rooms entered through vestibules. The principal axes vary, some rooms

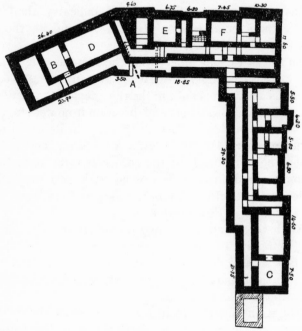

Fig. 21.   Palace at Gha (Arne).

being entered from the side, and others opening directly on to the corridor. No mention is made of the hearth, but we presume that it existed in its normal position in the centre of the closed megaron.

In comparison with the other Mycenean palaces with which we are familiar, which generally form a rough

quadrilateral and include open courts, the palace at Gha
with its two wings is unique.   It has been suggested that
the lie of the ground, which slopes considerably between
the wings, necessitated this plan, but there seems no reason
why the terrace which was specially constructed for the
palace could not have been made wider.   As it is, each
wing forms, as it were, a separate dwelling, and points to
the favourite early method of enlargement by repetition.
Within each wing not only is each room isolated, but
each group of rooms, and between the north and east
wings are three parallel corridors.

The rooms are small, and the absence of any remains
of staircases would seem to show that the palace contained
but one storey.

The essential features, however, are the same as those
of other palaces of the same epoch.   The palace is contained in an enclosure with one entrance, and the principal
rooms are entered through a vestibule, and communicate
with each other by means of narrow corridors with
frequent setbacks.   The largest room which covers an
area of 82 sq. m. is considerably smaller than the megara
of Mycenae and Tiryns, which measure more than
100 sq. m.

The comparison with Tiryns and Mycenae may be
carried on to the style and materials of building.   We
find the same Cyclopean walls with clay mortar, the same
plaster floors sometimes strengthened with small stones,
in one vestibule flags as at Mycenae, and the stone
thresholds showing the marks of doors.

The walls were covered with plaster and decorated
with frescoes, but the palace was destroyed by fire and
very little of this work remains.   There is also some
evidence of a drainage system similar to that at Tiryns[1].

[1] Schliemann, *Tiryns*, p. 204.

Bronze hinges are the only trace of metal, except the lead used for rivets.

In the middle of the island are remains of fortifications and habitations, which must have been occupied by the retainers of the palace, for from the style of the building they evidently belong to the same period.

Mycenean remains on the Acropolis at Athens[1]. The remains of walls of the Mycenean epoch at Athens do not enable us to form any idea of the houses of which they must have formed a part: they are evidence, however, for the habitation of the acropolis in Mycenean times.

Some other interesting remains of this epoch are two square, stone bases such as we frequently find in Mycenean palaces, rounded in order to carry the customary wooden columns, and a piece of wall of the same date near by. These all stand within the walls of the early temple of Athena, and it is possible that they are the remains of the ancient palace of Erechtheus, where Athena took up her abode. Its position on the acropolis which was well fortified also corresponds with that of the palaces at Tiryns, Mycenae and elsewhere.

Such then are the ground plans of the three principal palaces representative of L. M. culture on the mainland: in detail they present some striking differences from those of the M. M. and L. M. periods in Crete.

There are of course many resemblances. We find the same love of columns and porticoes, the same style of building, in any case in the outer walls, with salient and re-entrant angles, open courtyards are always present though of smaller proportions, and the rooms open off them as is sometimes the case in Crete. The bath room is also an interesting point of comparison.

[1] Harrison, *Primitive Athens*, pp. 14–15 and cf. Dörpfeld, *Ath. Mitt.* XI. pp. 162 sqq.

But the interior disposition is in many points absolutely different.   The characteristic galleries for the storage
of valuables are entirely lacking, the system of lighting
by means of wells is not in use, the mighty staircases and broad inner corridors do not occur.   Further,
important points in the buildings are not connected by
means of straight lines drawn along the major or minor
axis of the inner court, as Noack[1] has shown to be the
case in Crete, though the corridors run parallel with the
principal axis, and with regard to the rooms we find quite
a different system prevailing.

We noticed in Crete the number of exits and entrances,
how one room often communicated directly with another,
and large and small rooms had common party walls, so
that there was no privacy or seclusion.

On the mainland this is far from being the case.   The
principal rooms open on to the courtyard from which
alone they are entered: if there is any other doorway it
leads into the vestibule, the megaron itself being always
isolated.   It is thus impossible to cross it; at Tiryns and
Arne one has to pass by means of an outside corridor
right round it, for its walls never form a common partition.

The proportions of the room itself are also different,
for instead of the breadth being greater than the length
we find everywhere the long narrow room.   In the centre
of this is built the hearth, sometimes surrounded by four
columns, which helped to support the roof.   The more
rigorous nature of the Greek climate necessitated this
permanent provision for artificial warmth, a provision
which is entirely lacking in Crete, where the portable
brazier[2] must have been requisitioned as in the Aegean
to-day, or the footwarmer as in China.   The climate in
Crete, if we may judge by the costume of men and women,

[1] *vide* p. 89.   [2] *B.S.A.* VII. p. 24.

must have been considerably warmer in Minoan times than now.

The propylaea, which preserve the old proportions of width greater than depth, are isolated, another striking contrast to the Cretan plan, where they are built into the palace. The form of propylaeum found on the mainland is that which survives into later Greek times, and is also in contrast to the Cretan. A wall with folding doors divides it into two parts, of which the inner is a little deeper at Tiryns, and before and behind stand two columns as a support to the architrave beams. The propylaea at Athens show the same tradition preserved, just as the temple in antis of classic times preserves the traditional form of the Mycenean megaron[1].

Another interesting point of difference which has been specially emphasised by Noack[2] is the column arrangement. The one and three column system, so much in vogue in Crete, is not found on the mainland, either in the megara or in the propylaea. Two columns with one doorway, as in the case of the propylaea, or two columns with three doorways, as in the larger megaron at Tiryns, is the prevailing arrangement.

In spite of these differences in detail, however, it is quite clear that the palaces of Crete and the mainland belong to one and the same civilisation and were constructed by people of a common stock. External influences, invasions, climate and separation are sufficient to account for the dissimilarities, without presupposing an entire difference of race.

At the same time the problem of the isolated megaron with central hearth of the mainland is puzzling and invites conjecture.

[1] Noack, *Jahrbuch*, XI. p. 236.
[2] *Homerische Paläste*, p. 9.

Mackenzie[1] would regard the megaron with central hearth at Phylakopi as proving the southern connection of the Mycenean central hearth, and would consider the Mycenean megaron as a simple transformation of the "Aegeo-Pelasgian." He would see in it no different type, but a natural adaptation when the hearth was introduced, necessitating the isolation of the hall, in order to prevent air currents spreading the smoke and making the room uninhabitable.

This final form he traces in its development from the one-roomed hut through three phases; first the fire was made in the centre of the one-roomed hut, secondly the necessity for enlargement was met in the primitive way by multiplication and a front room was added to which the hearth was removed, finally the hearth was fixed in the centre and the back room dropped, and this remained the final plan. One is tempted to ask why the hearth was transferred from the back room if so many difficulties were thereby created. The line of argument is ingenious and interesting, but somewhat far-fetched. The changed proportions of the megaron are accounted for by him on the hypothesis that added room was needed when the hearth was introduced, or that the light well of Cretan plan was roofed in and thrown into the room.

Noack's[2] view is more reasonable and convincing. He realises that the isolated megaron is wholly foreign to the Cretan system, and suggests that the isolated rooms of mainland type, which are already found in the second city at Troy in E. M. ii, ousted the system of several rooms communicating, which previously prevailed in the

[1] Mackenzie, "Cretan palaces IV," *B.S.A.* xiv. pp. 368 sqq. Evans, *B.S.A.* vii. p. 24, suggests that the Cretan house was a more southern type where a permanent fire was unnecessary.

[2] Noack, *Ovalhaus und Palast in Kreta*, pp. 43, 44.

Aegean zone, and that Cretan influence was not strong
enough to change this.   The culture stream from North
to South along the Danube valley and across the Balkan
peninsula to Troy must have brought with it this type of
house[1].

Dörpfeld[2], on the other hand, finds two distinct styles
of building in Crete itself, the earlier which has no con-

Fig. 22.   Mycenean megaron.

nection with the mainland and which he calls Carian-
Lycian, and the later introduced by the Achaean invaders
from the mainland, who ousted the old Cretans and built
the new palaces, partly after their own plan and partly
in imitation of the earlier.   Though he has now admitted
Mackenzie's view that the large building in the later
palace at Phaestos is a state entrance and no megaron[3],

---

[1] Houses in Balkan peninsula, Meitzen, *Wanderungen, Anbau u.
Agrarrechi der Völker Europas*, III. p. 471, figs. XI. XII *a* and *b*.   Cf.
§ 140, "Das nordische und das altgriechische Haus."

[2] Dörpfeld, *Ath. Mitt.* 1905, p. 257.

[3] Dörpfeld, *Ath. Mitt.* XXXII. p. 580.

this does not affect his general thesis of Achaean partici-
pation in later Cretan building. We shall return to this
question in the next chapter.

The external appearance of a Mycenean palace may
be gathered in part from Tiryns as we see it to-day. The
sober, massive, surrounding wall was its most conspicuous
feature, and possibly a few gables and roofs showed above,
as in the palace of Odysseus. By inference from extant
remains Professor Middleton[1] made a restoration of the
Mycenean megaron, which is given opposite (Fig. 22).

As we have seen the columns were of wood, and the
walls, which were stone at the foundations and crude
brick above, were probably covered with wood with
bronze repoussé work or other ornamentation attached.

[1] *J.H.S.* VII. p. 162.

CHAPTER XI

CENTRAL HEARTH IN MELOS AND CRETE

THE question of the central hearth, which is so vital in the history of the development of Cretan and Mycenean architecture and the external influences playing upon it, has been further complicated by the discovery at Palaikastro[1] in Crete and at Phylakopi[2] in Melos of a plan identical with that of the Mycenean palaces of the mainland. Mackenzie would regard the Hagia Triada[3] villa as conforming to the same type, though there is apparently no trace of any hearth. Furthermore it has been ascertained by Evans[4] and Noack[5] that there was a third cross wall: it was almost destroyed and was not shown on the original plan. It is inserted on Noack's plan[6]. This fine terrace was probably built as a foundation for the later villa and is certainly not a megaron of mainland type.

The houses at Palaikastro belong to the M. M. period and the palace at Phylakopi to the L. M. period according to Mackenzie[7]; Dörpfeld however considers that the palace at Phylakopi is roughly contemporary with the later palace at Knossos[8].

There seems but little doubt that this cannot be an

---

[1] *vide* p. 143.

[2] *J.H.S. Supplementary Papers*, No. 4, p. 56, fig. 49.

[3] *vide* p. 100 and *B.S.A.* XIII. p. 220.

[4] *J.H.S.* XXXII. p. 281, note 7.

[5] *Ovalhaus und Palast in Kreta*, p. 27, note 24.   [6] *op. cit.* p. 30.

[7] *J.H.S. Supplementary Papers*, No. 4, p. 267.

[8] *Ath. Mitt.* XXXII. p. 595.

original Cretan plan arising spontaneously, but that some connection with the mainland must be assumed. The people of Greece must have been driven out to the islands, or else they came on expeditions and were perhaps themselves responsible for the sack of Knossos: in any case their connection is clear with the type of palace in question, for the one important isolated room is certainly not Southern, as far as present evidence goes. Moreover intercommunication and consequent interacting influence are proved in the case of Crete, by such importations as the "Palace Style"[1] vases and the Vaphio[2] cups, whose direct relationship with Cretan art cannot be disputed.

The *palace at Phylakopi*[3], belonging to Period III (L. M. ii), was discovered near the eastward limit of the town (Fig. 23). It faces on to a large open space or courtyard (*A*) and is entered on the south. The rectangular megaron (*B*) with its square hearth in the centre is approached through a single vestibule. On the right of it is a series of rooms separated from the main megaron by a corridor (*C*), while to the north is a large room which has been conjectured to be the bath room (*D*). On the west side of the megaron runs a long corridor (*E*) similar to that on the east.

The palace is of simple plan, but the striking resemblance of the essential features with Tiryns cannot fail to be noticed, and the unity of type can with safety be assumed. Here there are no columns round the hearth (cf. smaller megaron at Tiryns), but in several of the houses at Palaikastro, described under Minoan houses, we have the actual four column arrangement. We also find the isolated megaron in a house of the re-occupation period at Gournia[4].

---

[1] *J.H.S.* xxiv. pp. 317 sqq. pl. xiii, vase of "Palace style" found in tomb at Mycenae restored by Mr Marshall.

[2] 'Εφ. 'Αρχ. 1889, pp. 136 sqq. Cf. also *J.H.S.* xxiv. pl. xi.

[3] *op. cit.* pp. 55–58.   [4] *vide* p. 146.

Evans[1] mentions that in one of the small rooms into
which the large megaron of the Little Palace at Knossos
was broken up in the re-occupation period there is a

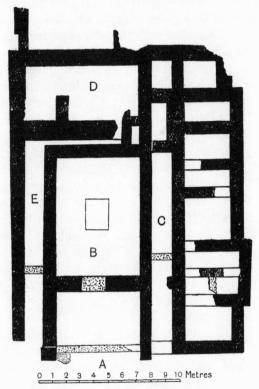

Fig. 23.   Palace at Phylakopi.

stone fireplace set up in one corner.   He regards this as
a mainland innovation.

Are these isolated plans the missing links between
Minoan and Mycenean architecture?   We must wait for
further discovery to ascertain their true position.

[1] *J.H.S.* 1912, vol. XXXII. p. 281, footnote 7.

CHAPTER XII

PALACES AT TROY

THE well preserved remains of buildings on the site of the second or "burnt" city of Troy[1], which must have flourished about the middle of the early Minoan period (*circ.* 2500) or a little later according to Dörpfeld, of identically the same plan and arrangement as the later megara of the middle of the late Minoan period (*circ.* 1500 B.C.) on the mainland of Greece, cannot fail to point to the North rather than to the South for the origin of the peculiar Mycenean arrangement unknown to Crete in its best and early periods.

If we accept Mackenzie's hypothesis of the Southern origin of the later Greek plan[2] and of its subsequent modification to suit a climate where a permanent central hearth was imperative, we are bound to regard this change as having taken place before, and some time before, Troy II was built, *i.e.* before 2500 B.C., a period when remains in Crete are but scanty, and neither of the great palaces has been begun.

Surely this date is too early in itself to warrant such an assumption, especially as there is no proof of direct contact between Crete and Troy, and any influence must have passed along over the north of the Balkan peninsula

---

[1] Dörpfeld, *Troja und Ilion*; Dörpfeld, *Troja*, 1893; Schliemann, *Troja*.　　　　[2] *vide* p. 129.

and across the Hellespont. The plan too in the second city at Troy is quite clear and definite, and must have a long history behind it.

A comparison with the mainland palaces of Mycenae, Tiryns and Arne, will show that it is much more natural and in accordance with facts, either to find the origin of the later Greek plan here[1] or to trace both back to a common plan arising in the Danube valley or farther north.

In Troy II are isolated megara side by side opening on to a courtyard, which lies in front of them, and which is entered by a propylaeum of identically the same form as in Greece, and like the Greek propylaea, standing free opposite the megaron.

At Troy, as indeed at Mycenae, there are common party walls, but not for the principal rooms.

The absence of columns both in the second and sixth city is in contrast with the Greek palaces, where we always find two columns between the antae, but is natural for a less advanced form: the remains seem to indicate that the roof, which must have been flat and without support, consisted of great beams of wood stretching from side to side and covered with clay.

The megaron of the sixth or Homeric city is but evidence of the continuance of a plan already firmly established in the E. M. period. A more detailed comparison of the ground plans, which will now be given, with those of the mainland will only serve to demonstrate that the style of building conforms absolutely to one and the same type.

The second city at Troy, formerly considered to be the Homeric city but now pronounced early Minoan, contains a most interesting example of a palace[2] of the true mainland Mycenean type, such as persisted in the

[1] Dörpfeld, *Troja und Ilion*, pp. 81–95; Schliemann, *Troja*, pp. 75–87.
[2] Leaf, *Troy: a study in Homeric geography*, p. 21.

later prodomos temple. Like Tiryns, Mycenae and Arne, it is strongly fortified with massive walls and towers.

Passing within the three outer walls of successive periods, we come upon this palace situated in the middle of the citadel (Fig. 24). A gateway (*A*), as at Tiryns, leads into an open courtyard (*B*), through which the

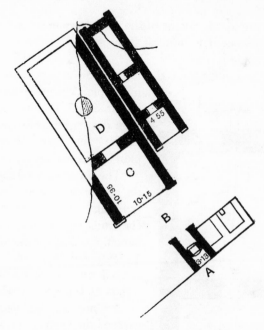

Fig. 24. Palace at Troy (second city).

building (*CD*) is approached. The gateway is of simple type with outer and inner vestibule. In contrast to Tiryns the outer vestibule is the deeper, while the inner vestibule is less in length than breadth, a combination of Cretan and mainland proportions. Access is given to the great rectangular megaron (*D*) with its circular hearth through a vestibule (*C*) about half its depth.

On the right and left of this megaron there are two similar buildings, shorter and narrower than the principal megaron, and with two ante-chambers instead of one. The building on the north side, which was ruined by the great trench, has a small hall like an opisthodomos behind, and Dörpfeld would restore a similar hall behind the other buildings of the same period[1].

The remaining rooms of the palace are in such a ruined condition that it is difficult in most cases to re-construct a ground plan.

Of the building on the left of the principal megaron in the plan the north end only is remaining, the rest having been destroyed in excavating, so that the complete ground plan is conjectural.

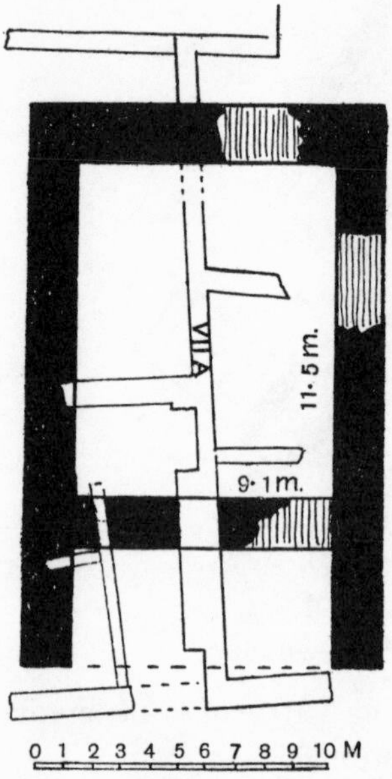

Fig. 25. Palace at Troy (sixth city).

The sixth city at Troy with its circuit wall and its large buildings has been proved by the finds of pottery, etc., to have flourished during the late Minoan period, and is regarded by Dr Dörpfeld[2] and others as the Troy of Homer.

Among the buildings unearthed the most complete was on the extreme west of the city[3]. Its ground plan is very simple and closely resembles that of the Greek temple in antis of later times (Fig. 25).

The vestibule leads into a stately hall of regular

[1] Dörpfeld, *op. cit.* pp. 85, 86.   [2] *op. cit.* pp. 601 sqq.
[3] Dörpfeld, *op. cit.* p. 151 and fig. 56.

rectangular form, whose length is 11·5 m. and breadth
9·1 m.

Some walls brought to light within this hall and at
first conjectured to be foundations for an inner row of
columns, have been since proved to belong to the fifth
city[1] and stand in no relation to the later building.

The proportions of the shallow rectangular vestibule
are noticeable, and resemble those of the vestibules at
Tiryns and Mycenae, rather than those of the palace of
the second city. No remains of columns or foundations
for column bases have been found between the antae:
these may have been destroyed when some later structure
was erected, but it seems more probable that the building
was of the same type as those of the second city, which
were entirely without columns.

It is possible that these are the remains of some
early temple, but Dörpfeld[2] is inclined to regard the
building as a dwelling house or megaron. It is true
that there are no actual remains of a circular hearth:
a layer of ashes, however, is distinctly visible in the
middle of the chamber.

On the east side of the city was unearthed a building
similar in plan[3] but probably with a row of columns along
its main axis. Other buildings near the megaron were
excavated by Dörpfeld: they seem to conform in general
to the same type but are very incomplete. Leaf[4] draws
attention to the fact that some of the houses at Troy
are arranged on a radial plan, with passages between
them running to the centre of the fortress. We have
already noticed such a system of converging passages
on the acropolis of Dimini[5], and some of the houses[6]

---

[1] Dörpfeld, *Troja*, 1893, p. 19.   [2] *op. cit.* p. 152.
[3] Dörpfeld, *Troja und Ilion*, p. 165; cf. Leaf, *Troy*, p. 99, note 1.
[4] *Troy*, p. 97.   [5] *vide* p. 55.
[6] Αἱ προϊστορικαὶ ἀκροπόλεις Διμηνίου καὶ Σέσκλου, pl. 11. 24, 26–28.

there actually show a similar disposition to those at Troy.

The points of dissimilarity with Cretan architecture are the same as already noticed on the mainland. The propylaeum leads into the open irregular courtyard, on to which the megara open. Too little remains to make any comparison of the general system, but in the second city, although the megara are built so close together, each has its own wall, showing the insistence on the independence and total isolation of the single room, which at this remote date must surely imply a tradition going back to the origin of the plan, and is absolutely the contrary of what we find prevailing in Crete.

With regard to the proportions of the megara as compared with those of the mainland Mycenean palaces, the large megaron of Troy II, which has only one vestibule, has the inner room with the hearth exactly two-thirds of the whole building, while in the sixth city the vestibule is much shallower in proportion, the inner room being nearly three times as long as the vestibule: in the case of the little megaron at Tiryns where the vestibule is nearly square, the inner room is only half as long again.

The smaller megaron at Troy II, which has two vestibules of equal size, also has the inner room about half as long again as one of them. At Mycenae, on the other hand, where the megaron is approached through two shallow vestibules of equal size, the inner room is four times the depth of each vestibule, at Tiryns only between two and three.

The proportions then are varied, but in general the megaron tends to become wider in proportion to its length and the vestibule shallower. We see a similar development in the earliest Doric temples.

Again at Troy the entrance is through one doorway

in the middle of the cross wall (at the side in the case of the smaller megaron), as also in the smaller megaron at Tiryns; in the larger megaron at Tiryns we find three passage-ways behind the two front columns into the second vestibule, and one in the middle of the cross wall into the actual inner room. Mycenae has only one door-way in the middle of the cross wall, both into the vestibule and into the megaron itself, as has also the propylaeum at Tiryns.

It is also noticeable that the materials employed in the sixth city at Troy are far superior to those used in Greece. There is no rubble or crude brick work, all the walls are built of well dressed blocks of stone and carefully finished.

These, however, are only differences of detail: the general plan, disposition and arrangement are strikingly similar and assure close relationship. The problem of the origin of the Trojan plan is one among a myriad other archaeological problems which await solution, and when solved it will remove some of the greatest difficulties in the way of a rational explication of the Greek historic house and its connection with the Homeric.

CHAPTER XIII

MINOAN HOUSES

WE have traced the course of the primitive architecture of the common dwelling, as far as is possible from
the scanty evidence to hand, until the opening of the
Bronze Age. We will now take up the thread again and
follow its development through the great period of
Cretan history and subsequent Mycenean culture.

The evidence for the private house is singularly
complete since several whole cities like Gournia[1], Palaikastro[2], Phylakopi[3], whose history is long, have been
excavated and studied during recent years: they show
that the houses were for the most part small and crowded
together, with little open space between them, and the
streets narrow, rough, and of such varying levels that
wheeled traffic would have been impossible.

The circular and oval house, as has already been
mentioned[4], had long disappeared, except for sepulchral
uses, in Crete by the early Minoan period.

The methods of construction and details of plan were
already fairly advanced: the houses contained several
storeys and were divided into separate rooms, the walls,

---

[1] *vide* p. 145.   [2] *vide* p. 143.
[3] *vide* p. 155.   [4] *vide* p. 33.

which were rectangular, were of rubble or stone in the lower part and in the upper of sun-baked bricks. The floors were sometimes merely of beaten earth, in other cases they were plastered over or formed of flagstones.

Again the mixture of types occurs which has been already noticed in the palaces, the earlier Aegean system of communicating rooms side by side with the isolated living room of the type where the hearth was the central point of the house. We have found this blending as early as Troy II and it is particularly clear in Melos.

It was the age of chieftains and kings, and accordingly we often find the dwelling houses clustered round the palace or citadel.

Small independent towns seem to have flourished for the most part in the earlier and later periods of the L. M. age, and not in the great "Palace" period when the Knossian dynasty was so mighty: accordingly towns like Kato Zakro, Gournia and Palaikastro, which were all flourishing at the opening of the late Minoan period, fell in the succeeding period and were not re-occupied, and that only partially, until L. M. iii after the fall of Knossos.

We will first then take a brief review of the houses in Crete itself, at Palaikastro, Gournia, Kato Zakro, Knossos and Goulas.

The excavations at *Palaikastro*[1] have opened up a number of buildings which, on the evidence of the pottery, belonged to the M. M. and L. M. periods. The town, which lies 13 miles to the north-east of Praesos and eight miles to the north of Zakro, was laid out in regular blocks, intersected by streets lined with houses: these streets are from 1·40 m.–2·50 m. wide.

---

[1] *B.S.A.* VIII. p. 286, IX. p. 274 and X. p. 192.

The houses face the street in rows and often have a staircase opposite the entrance door, but otherwise they are very irregular in construction. The fronts show many setbacks, such as are so familiar in Minoan building, and the walls of the various rooms run at different angles.

Several of the houses, however, the more important as we may assume, exhibit more design in construction, though the walls still run at various angles.

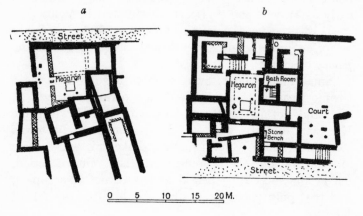

Fig. 26. Houses at Palaikastro.

For example in Block δ (Fig. 26 *a*) we find remains of a megaron of an earlier house, with a second house built on the same site at a slightly higher level[1]. It consists of a room about 16 ft square with four pillars at the corners of a square space which is unpaved and probably represents the hearth. In any case there was a lantern above, by means of which the megaron was lighted. At its north end between it and the street was another room, which could only be entered by way of

[1] *B.S.A.* IX. p. 293.

the megaron, which was itself entered at the side from another court by two doorways with ashlar jambs.

In a house on the cliff in the quarter west of the ridge is a megaron with four columns supporting the roof[1] (Fig. 26, *b*). The bathroom in this house is similar in plan to those of the palace at Knossos[2].

In Block ε an interesting house built over remains of a M. M. house and destroyed by fire in L. M. ii shows very clearly the structure of the roofs[3]: they were made of clay laid upon the reeds which formed the ceiling, and rendered watertight by seaweed in the upper layers, as in the simpler dwellings in Crete to-day.

Gournia[4], on the isthmus of Hierapetra, is another interesting example of a small seaside town of Minoan times. It is unwalled and the general planning is very clear, though the separate houses are not perfect enough to throw so much light on the architecture as those of some of the other towns. The streets, which are paved with stones, are about 5 ft wide and ascend to the different levels by means of steps; the houses are built along them with their doorways flush with the street, and are entered through a vestibule from which the cellar steps often descend to the basement.

There were upper storeys supported by means of wooden columns of which the bases are still visible, and staircases led to them from the ground floor rooms.

The two houses of the early period (M. M. iii) are incomplete but well built, and speaking generally the building is better in the first and third periods. But the remains belong for the most part to the town period

---

[1] *B.S.A.* viii. pp. 310–12, and ix. pp. 278 and 287.
[2] *B.S.A.* viii. p. 312, fig. 25.   [3] *B.S.A.* x. pp. 204–5.
[4] Hawes, *Gournia, Vasiliki and other prehistoric sites on the isthmus of Hierapetra, Crete*, pass.

(L. M. i), and consist of a multitude of rooms, which often have two entrances, and paved courts: limestone thresholds are found and remains of round stone sockets to take the round wooden supporting columns for the upper storeys, which have superseded the earlier rectangular columns. One of the most interesting houses of this period (*Fd*)[1], which contained a carpenter's kit among other finds, had two entrances, and consisted of two good-sized rooms connected by a corridor with a possible outer court.

The so-called "Palace" (Fig. 27), which occupies an area equivalent to that occupied by twelve burghers' dwellings, was built in the days of heavy rubble, and re-modelled when ashlar came into fashion, though the work of reconstruction was never completed. It contains the characteristic magazines found in the other palaces, and the central hall is separated from the corridor by a row of square and round columns in old Cretan style. The palace was built on three rock terraces; on the highest level was simply the ground floor, over the central hall was one storey, and on the west side above the magazines one or two storeys. The influence of Knossian building is very clear in this palace.

In L. M. ii the town fell, and in the period of re-occupation (L. M. iii) the roads were not even paved and only a few scattered buildings remain on the old Acropolis. Among them on the south-west corner of the site Oelmann[2] discovered a house consisting of a room almost square entered through a vestibule which was not quite so deep, with other small rooms separated from the principal room or megaron by a corridor. This arrangement is

[1] Hawes, *op. cit.* p. 22, and cf. plan.
[2] "Ein achaïsches Herrenhaus auf Kreta," *Jahrb. d. arch. Insti.* XXVII. p. 42. Cf. p. 43, fig. 3.

strikingly similar to that at Phylakopi[1] and is another
example of the isolated megaron in Crete in the late
Minoan period.

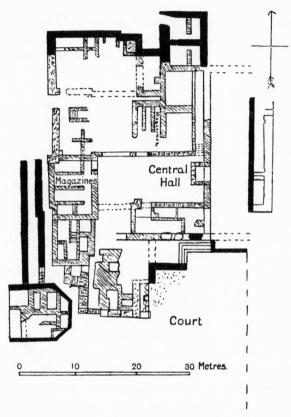

Fig. 27.   "Palace" at Gournia.

Kato Zakro[2].   The site of Kato Zakro, on the east
coast of Crete, was naturally fortified on the north and
east by cliffs, and on the west by the river Zakro but on

[1] *vide* p. 133.   [2] *B.S.A.*, VII. pp. 121 sqq.

the south from which it was easily accessible remains of massive Cyclopean walls have been found, which prove that it was strongly fortified here, where natural protection failed.

The natural pits artificially enlarged, first noticed by Halbherr and Mariani, contained most interesting and abundant finds of pottery, though unfortunately unstratified: the Kamares ware, however, seems to pass without a break into the Mycenean and proves an interesting link in the chain of evidence for the unity of this civilisation.

The exposed position of the district, which is subject to sudden floods, has prevented the survival of many remains of antiquity, but it is clear from the ruins here and also in the northern delta of the Karoúmbes river that the whole region, which was perhaps then more healthy than now, was inhabited.

Its position made it a particularly favourable spot for direct commerce with the North Coast of Africa, and it was probably a trading station established from Knossos, though only one fragment of Egyptian porcelain was forthcoming.

Some most interesting Minoan houses have been discovered on the eastern spur. Fig. 28 (*a*) shows a house with eight rooms and an entrance hall (*A*) containing a pillar, which does not seem to have served any structural purpose, and a curious group of basins possibly intended for devotional uses. Standing in a splendid position on the west face of the hill near the top, it was probably one of a group of buildings occupied by some person of note. The party walls of lightly baked brick on stone foundations are well preserved[1].

Remains of many other houses have been found on this site but in a very denuded condition, so that party

[1] *B.S.A.* VII. p. 130.

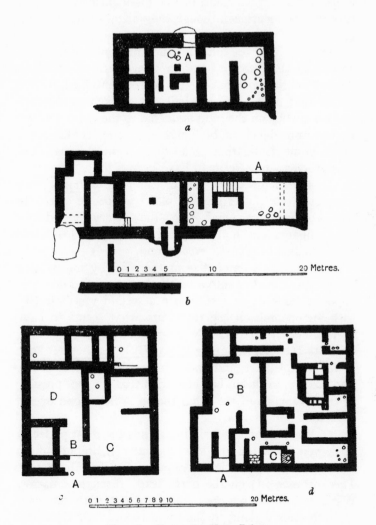

Fig. 28. Houses at Kato Zakro.

walls and doorways could not be distinguished. One or two may be mentioned though they are probably incomplete.

At the foot of the hill was a building entered from the north (*A*) (Fig. 28 (*b*)) containing a group of basins in the hall similar to those in the house mentioned above[1]. On the left of its entrance hall was a room paved with concrete, while on the right stairs led to the upper terrace. In the same block of buildings is a room containing a rough stone foundation of a square central pillar, and other rooms which seem to have been cellars.

Another house to the east of this (Fig. 28 (*c*)) is more complete, though its ground plan cannot be perfectly traced owing to its ruined state: the pottery showed that the occupants were luxurious in their tastes for here alone were remains of painted πίθοι found.

The house[2] is entered from the road by means of a doorway (*A*) leading into a vestibule. A second doorway opposite leads down a step into a second vestibule (*B*), with an opening on the right into what seems to have been a courtyard (*C*). By means of another doorway, opposite the first, a square room (*D*) is reached (17 ft × 17 ft), the largest and most important in the house. The house is in such a bad condition that it is not possible to trace remains of the other rooms, which stood over a basement still *in situ*.

To the east of this building stands the most perfectly preserved house on the site (Fig. 28 (*d*)), important on account of its fine pebble concrete floor and its wall plaster[3]. The entrance (*A*) on the north leads through a narrow vestibule into a large open courtyard (*B*), with doorways at both ends leading to the main rooms. Of these one of the most curious is the plastered room (*C*) with a sunk

---

[1] *B.S.A.* VII. p. 135.   [2] *l.c.* p. 139.   [3] *l.c.* pp. 140–1.

recess in its south-west corner, and two large basins sunk in the west wall, which broadens out as a platform of stones and clay. Whether this room was a bath room or wine press is not clear, but in any case it must be connected with the somewhat similar arrangement in the entrance hall of the house described above. It is interesting to notice several isolated rooms, though common party walls occur in accordance with the usual Cretan plan.

With regard to the chronology, the earliest pottery of the Zakro pit belongs to M. M. ii, but the height of prosperity of the settlement was L. M. i. In the subsequent "Palace" period it fell, together with the other country towns. No pottery was found on the site belonging to any later age.

Houses at Knossos[1]. To the west of the palace site at Knossos, in his search for the early cemeteries, Mr Hogarth came upon the remains of a town, with its houses built on two distinct terraces. Fig. 29 (*a*) shows the ground plan of a large house on the upper terrace. The outer wall, which is built of large well-dressed blocks, is somewhat irregular in shape. The house is divided into numerous rooms by party walls running at right angles to each other, but the arrangement of the rooms is difficult to ascertain with certainty owing to the incomplete state of preservation of the walls. The house was probably entered at (*A*) by means of a passage between it and the next house[2].

A house on the lower terrace (Fig. 29 (*b*)) is especially interesting from the fact that it contains no less than three pillar rooms[3]. Though it is much ruined the remains seem to show that it was even more irregular than the

---

[1] *B.S.A.* vi. pp. 71 sqq. [2] *l.c.* p. 71.
[3] *l.c.* pp. 74, 75.

usual type of this period. The walls run at varying angles and the rooms are of very different shapes. The

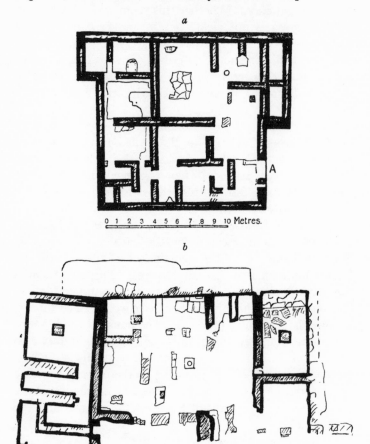

Fig. 29. Houses at Knossos.

south pillar room, though roughly square, nowhere contains a right angle.

Remains of many other houses were found on this site but their ground plans are not clear.

The two houses described above are probably of M. M. period, since Kamares ware was found in both: they were, however, occupied in the L. M. period.

Houses at Goulas[1]. The Cretan city of Goulas affords some good examples of houses of late Minoan period. The city which lies in the neighbourhood of Mt Dicte consists of three distinct parts, viz. the North Acropolis, the South Acropolis and the crater.

It is within the North Acropolis that we find the most important examples of dwelling houses. This hill is faced on the east with a series of terraces, with strong supporting walls of 10 ft or more in length, built of huge rough blocks and filled in with smaller pieces of stone.

The houses built on these narrow ledges are of necessity oblong in plan: the majority of them consist of single chambers, but others have a series of rooms and are more elaborate.

The house shown in Fig. 30 (*a*) contains four chambers of varying size, three of which are regular in form.

Another (Fig. 30 (*b*)) has five rooms and an entrance court reached by steps up the rock[2].

The crater, which lies between the North and South Acropolis, contains some ancient foundations, but no building of importance has been unearthed.

Passing by two square chambered dwellings and a house of the simple prodomos type on the South Acropolis, we come to the most interesting discovery of all (Fig. 30 (*c*)).

A large oblong chamber (*B*), 48 ft in length, is entered by a shallow vestibule (*A*) of the usual type: at its further end it gives access to a similar rectangular chamber (*C*),

---

[1] *B.S.A.* II. p. 169; *J.H.S.* XIV. p. 277.
[2] *l.c.* pp. 182–3.

which is slightly shorter[1].   On both sides of the entrance
to the second chamber are two stone steps, evidently

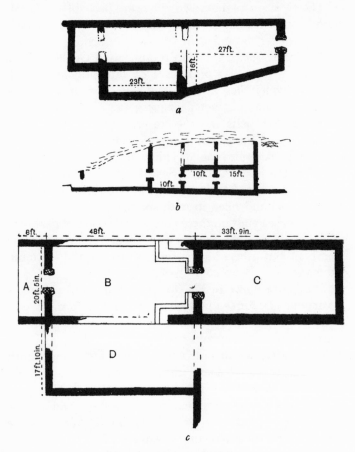

Fig. 30.   Houses at Goulas.

ntended for seats.   Alongside of the first chamber is
another rectangular enclosure (*D*), which must have been

[1] *B.S.A.* ii. pp. 185–7.

entered from it.   The small amount of débris found here
makes it probable that this was not a chamber but a
courtyard.

This dwelling house, with its large megaron approached
through a vestibule, is of the same type as many of the
houses in the second and sixth cities of Hissarlik.

In the shallowness of its forecourt it conforms rather
to the Mycenean type of the sixth city, and may be compared with the megara at Mycenae and Tiryns, though
the hearth is missing.

This building, flanked, as it probably was, by various
chambers and passages, may well have formed the palace
of some chieftain.

Let us now consider a few examples of houses of
Minoan period outside Crete, and in particular the architectural remains at *Phylakopi in Melos*[1], lately brought
to light by the excavations of the British School, which
offer such valuable evidence of the domestic style.

Three distinct periods may be recognised here, though
the methods of construction are not very different.   Of
the first period only a few isolated buildings remain,
scattered over the whole area; the buildings of the later
period show more systematic arrangement, and indeed the
streets of the latest period actually run with the cardinal
points of the compass and are at right angles to each other.

The great town wall, which is supposed to have been
built in the second period of occupation, is constructed
in parallel lines, the intervening spaces being divided
up into chambers by cross walls.   These chambers,
however, do not seem to have been used even in early
times for habitation, but to have been filled up with
small stones to strengthen the fortification.

The remains of houses of Period I, *i.e.* end of the E.M.

[1] *Hellenic Society Supplementary Papers*, No. iv. Phylakopi.

period, are extremely scanty and consist for the most part of irregular walls, which cannot be fitted into any intelligible ground plan. Remains have been found of the walls of one building which seems to have consisted of a single rectangular chamber (Fig. 31 (*a*)). This room however is exceptional: the walls generally run at various angles to each other and the rooms are of very irregular shape. The house shown in Fig. 31 (*b*) is more typical of the style of building of this early period[1].

Of the second (L. M. i) period more evidence is forthcoming, as there are complete plans of ten different houses of this date. The crowded nature of the buildings, and the narrowness of the streets, lead to the inference that not all the spaces enclosed by walls were roofed over, but that the bigger houses at least had open courtyards: it is not however at all possible now to decide which spaces were roofed over and which left open to the air. Though these houses certainly exhibit more design and regularity than those of the earliest period referred to above, there still seems to be an absence of any fixed ground plan and we still notice the walls running at various angles to each other.

One or two may be cited as examples:—

Fig. 31 (*c*) shows a very interesting house[2], resembling as it does in part the Mycenean palace at Phylakopi of the later period. The main apartment (*B*) is entered through a vestibule (*A*), and on the right of this a long corridor (*C*) runs, leading to two rooms at the back, which originally communicated with each other by a doorway at the extreme left of the partition. Fragments of burnt clay bonded with straw found in the principal room seem to be the remains of a hearth floor.

[1] *Hellenic Society Supplementary Papers*, No. IV. Phylakopi, pp. 35–38.
[2] *l.c.* p. 44.

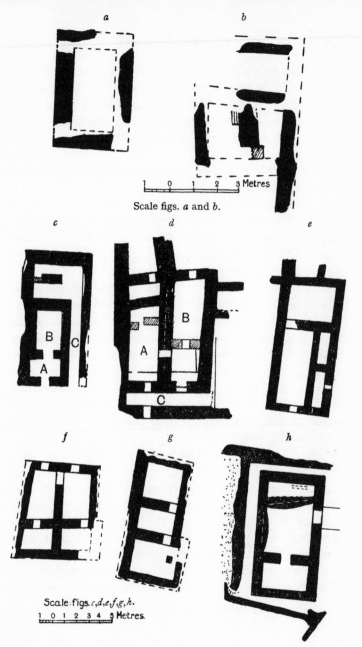

a

b

1 0 1 2 3 Metres

Scale figs. *a* and *b*.

c

d

e

B C

A

B

A

C

f

g

h

Scale: figs. *c*, *d*, *e*, *f*, *g*, *h*.

1 0 1 2 3 4 5 Metres.

Fig. 31. Houses at Phylakopi.

Another house (Fig. 31 (*d*)) has two large rooms (*A* and *B*) side by side with a long corridor (*C*) in front across the breadth of them[1]. There is also a small chamber at the back of one of the rooms. The cross walls are a later addition, when the large rooms were each divided into two parts.

In Fig. 31 (*e, f, g*) will be found other plans showing variety of construction.

The best preserved building of the third city (L. M. ii) is a small house (Fig. 31 (*h*)) consisting of two rooms, the larger of which is entered from the street[2]. For some reason not now clear, a wall was built across the north end of this chamber in later times.

Other houses of interest outside Crete, of somewhat later date than those we have considered, are those at *Mycenae* (Fig. 32). The side of the hill above the grave circle is covered with a labyrinth of houses of rough Mycenean masonry, probably inhabited by retainers of the palace. The walls are for the most part very irregular and the ground plans difficult to ascertain. Many of the houses seem to consist of a single chamber roughly square: sometimes there is a series of rooms as in the plan given.

One house of early date consists of a chamber with square hearth in the middle, and an ante-room to the west looking on to a courtyard. The numerous long narrow passages in the houses are noticeable[3].

Many of these houses on the various sites we have considered exemplify again the wonderful adaptation of plan to environment which we find all through the Minoan period, when endless pains were taken to prepare and utilise a difficult site. The houses at Goulas are built

---

[1] *Hellenic Society Supplementary Papers*, No. iv. Phylakopi, pp. 41, 42.
[2] *l.c.* p. 55.   [3] Cf. Tsountas, Μυκῆναι καὶ Μυκηναῖος Πολιτισμός, p. 44.

on narrow ledges and are accordingly oblong in plan,
while those at Gournia on the edge of the crest have a
system of basement rooms with a back door opening on
to the downward slope, and the entrance to the main floor
on the other side from the street.

The number of rooms varies very considerably, simple
one or two roomed houses often occurring side by side
with elaborate many-roomed dwellings. Many of the
houses have cellars and many two floors.

Though the rectangular plan had evidently been long
established, since we find no remnants at all of curved

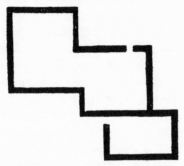

Fig. 32.   House at Mycenae.

walls, yet it had not reached such perfection that all
walls were built at right angles to one another, some
houses being very irregular in this respect.

The style with which we are familiar in the palaces
is generally adhered to in a less perfected form, the
materials are similar, setbacks are noticeable in the walls
from time to time, and even the pillar room and bath
room occur.   A courtyard often forms part of the plan,
and at Palaikastro, as early as the M. M. period, we even
find the mainland arrangement of four columns supporting
a lantern in the centre of the principal room, and pointing

probably to some sporadic connection with the mainland even at this remote date.

The preceding examples are among the most important houses hitherto discovered: it remains to classify them as far as possible, and to point out the chief types. With regard to general characteristics it does not seem possible to draw any sharp distinctions between Cretan and Mycenean houses, for the same traditions seem to have persisted and no unexpected new developments to have occurred.

A wholly scientific classification is not possible since some overlapping is inevitable owing to interacting influences, racial or otherwise, which not only modify types but sometimes produce contamination.

The earliest and most primitive form is the single chamber or simple cell, the house as it were in embryo. In the Neolithic period this may be circular or oval, *e.g.* Orchomenos; in the Minoan age the simplest type, which is found in large numbers in Crete, in the Cyclades and on most of the sites of Mycenean civilisation, is the single chamber approximating to the rectangular and sometimes entirely so. Such a dwelling represents the earliest and most primitive form in rectangular domestic architecture, and persists throughout the Mycenean period in houses of the poorer class. Later we see the same type recurring in some of the early houses of historic times unearthed by Burnouf between the Acropolis and the Pnyx[1].

The elaboration of the single cell type is effected by the addition of cell to cell[2], and results in the house with two connected rooms, the inner entered from the outer. Such a type is enlarged by further addition, as for example in the two houses at Knossos described above[3]. Under

---

[1] *vide* p. 219.
[2] Cf. Meitzen, *op. cit.* III. p. 479, fig. 20, here opposite, not contiguous.
[3] *vide* p. 152.

this type we may also include many of the houses at
Palaikastro, Goulas, Kato Zakro and Phylakopi. A
perfect example of a more elaborate plan developed in
this way, is that of the palace at Arne.

The prodomos type of building consisting of a rectangular chamber entered through a vestibule, so familiar
in the later Greek temple and recently discovered in
Hellenistic houses of the second century at Priene,
should not be regarded as a new type but as part of the
above mentioned elaboration, for the second and more
protected room may now become the more important,
and the first merely be used as an entrance hall. The
Neolithic houses in Syros[1] may be regarded as an
extremely early example, from which the later perfected
type would be developed. They are not quite identical,
by reason of the entrance being at the side of the vestibule,
whereas the normal later type generally has the entrances
on the main axis of the megaron ; the idea is here however
in embryo.

The type is exemplified at Troy, which, though outside
the limits of Greece proper, belonged to the same civilisation. The principal megaron of the palace of the second
city is a good example, as is also the palace of the sixth
city. The principal difference is, as we have seen, in
proportion, the house of the sixth city having its antae
shorter than the earlier building. The very early house
at Phylakopi, and the palaces at Phylakopi and Goulas,
show the same prodomos form, as also the smaller megaron
of the palace at Tiryns.

An apparent elaboration of the simple prodomos type,
which is much less common in existing remains, is that
of an oblong chamber or megaron with two vestibules.
This arrangement is found in the large megaron of the

---

[1] *vide* p. 50.

palace at Tiryns and also at Mycenae. It would appear, however, to be a variation, rather than a ground plan adopted for more important buildings, as we find it in the smaller megaron of the Trojan palace of the second city, side by side with a larger megaron of the simple prodomos type with one vestibule. In the houses it does not occur.

Another interesting feature of the early house is the appearance of λαύραι or passages, the want of which would early make itself felt with a system of communicating rooms or with isolated rooms side by side.

In the great Cretan palaces long corridors leading from one part to another are a noteworthy characteristic. With the isolated room the passage may perhaps be regarded as originating in some such plan as that of the palace of the second city at Troy, where we find three megara parallel to each other with narrow spaces sufficient to form passage-ways between[1].

Sometimes there is a passage on either side of the megaron, as in the palace at Phylakopi, sometimes all round the exterior, as at Tiryns, sometimes at one of the sides or at the end, as in some of the houses at Phylakopi. At Gha two corridors running parallel to each other along the two wings give access to the rooms which lie between them and the bounding wall.

In quite early plans we sometimes find before the room or rooms open spaces, which would be of great practical use to the house owner for his animals, etc., especially where the house was of small dimensions. This court-yard, in its later development, is sometimes entirely sur-rounded by chambers devoted to various uses. Open

---

[1] Prof. Myres considers these spaces too narrow to form passage-ways: according to Dörpfeld's plan (*Troja*, 1893) they are about 1 ft 9 in. wide. Some of the Knossian passages are as narrow.

spaces of the sort are found before several of the houses
at Palaikastro, as also before the five-roomed house at
Goulas, and many of the houses at Phylakopi.

The exact rôle played by the courtyard in Minoan
and Mycenean palace building respectively is another
interesting problem worthy of investigation, but for which
the time is not yet ripe.   The question is naturally bound
up with that of the origin of the Trojan plan.

In the Cretan palaces the large courts have an
importance of their own and the chief rooms do not
necessarily give on to them, whereas on the mainland
the court lies as it were before the house, which is
approached by entering the propylaeum and crossing it:
it therefore assumes a secondary importance here, as
simply leading to the large hall of prodomos type, *e.g.*
Tiryns, Mycenae, etc.

We turn now to the *external appearance of Mycenean
houses*.

A most important piece of evidence on this subject
has been brought to light during the recent excavations
in Crete.   It consists of a series of enamelled plaques[1]
of various sizes, most of them not exceeding 2 in. in height,
in the form of towers and houses.   Though the porcelain
of which they are made resembles Egyptian, Mr Evans
thinks that they are of native Knossian fabric.   These
porcelain tablets evidently formed part of a large mosaic,
of which others were found representing warriors, animals
and trees, and they must have fallen from a room above
as they were in a very broken condition.

It has been found possible, however, to restore about
forty of them with considerable certainty.   The towers
are of strong regularly built masonry with small loop-
holes in the upper part: many have no entrances below

[1] *B.S.A.* VIII. p. 14 and figs. 8 and 9.

and must, like the towers found on Paros[1], have been entered from above by means of ladders.

The two following are typical examples of houses:—

The façade represented in Fig. 33a[2] shows clearly, both by its form and colouring, that if the Mycenean houses were not built of wood and plaster their origin may certainly be traced to wood and plaster construction.

The house has three complete storeys and an attic. On the ground floor are two doors separated by a wide

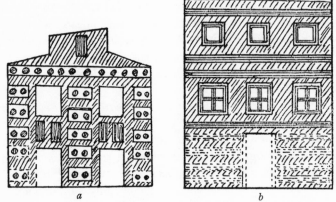

Fig. 33.   Porcelain tablets in form of houses

partition, and immediately above them on the first floor two double windows, filled with red pigment. The red pigment perhaps, as Evans suggests, represents some substitute for glass then in use. Above these again are two large windows, and at the top another small window filled with bright red pigment, which lights what appears to be a small garret.

Fig. 33b[3] shows a façade of a different character:

---

[1] Cf. Ἐφ. Ἀρχ. 1898, p. 175.   [2] *B.S.A.* VIII. p. 17, fig. 9b.
        [3] *l.c.* p. 17, fig. 9a.

the beams are horizontal and probably the rest of the front was rubble and stucco, the favourite materials of Minoan times. On the ground floor, though this part is restored in the plan, there was probably a single door, on the storey above three four-paned windows coloured with red pigment, and on the top floor three openings without any colour.

Most of the other houses show three storeys and many have an attic in addition.

These little models unfortunately do not settle for us the shape of roof employed for Minoan villas. Tsountas supposes that it was pitched[1], and his hypothesis receives some support from the fact that this form was preserved in Hellenic times for the temple, and so would probably be the oldest. At the same time we have no positive evidence on the question.

These houses, which doubtless represent the dwellings of the average Minoan citizen at Knossos itself, are striking in their modernity. As far as appearance goes, with their three floors, their rows of windows and their attic, they find their counterpart in any modern suburb. The façades of course tell us little of inner construction, but in the light of the ample evidence lately forthcoming through excavation this is no longer a difficult problem.

---

[1] On roofs *vide* Tsountas, 'Eφ. 'Aρχ. 1891, pp. 8–10.

CHAPTER XIV

HOMERIC PALACES

THE difficulty of re-constructing the typical Homeric house with any degree of accuracy from the slight indications furnished in the Homeric poems is great, since the poet is dealing with buildings evidently quite familiar to his hearers and is using them merely as part of the background for the events he is narrating.

Accordingly there was no need for elaborate description, and the details given us are not only scanty and few, but are also capable of various interpretations, for the material is handled freely as the background is shown to have been[1]. That the background is in the main historic is now, however, generally admitted[2]. This is a step in the right direction, but we can hardly hope that the time will ever come when scholars will cease to be at variance on the crucial points with regard to the house.

It seems fair to assume in any case that the various palaces alluded to in the Homeric poems conformed roughly to one common type, and belonged to one and the same civilisation, though lack of material in any case prevents a detailed comparison of the palace of Priam of the *Iliad* and those of the earlier books of the

[1] Hercher, *Homerische Aufsätze—Über die Homerische Ebene von Troia*, p. 69.

[2] Cauer, *Grundfragen der Homerkritik*, II. c. I.

Odyssey, on the one hand, with that of Odysseus on the other. Such references as are forthcoming do not seem to point to any contrast.

The contrary opinion is however held by Noack[1], who considers that the hyperoon or upper storey was a very late feature in the Homeric house, even if he does not go so far as Wilamowitz[2], who affirms that it did not make its appearance before the eighth century.

From the apparent simplicity of construction of the Homeric house and from the fact that the αἴθουσα was the regular sleeping place for guests, Noack supposes that the megaron originally served not only as general living room but also as sleeping room to the inhabitants of the house, and that, when the children had their own thalamoi apart, the wedded pair continued to sleep in the megaron[3]. The thalamos of Odysseus, which was clearly outside the megaron, he considers as an exception[4], just as it is an exception to Homeric use for Penelope to sit with her maidens in a separate room above, whereas the normal housewife sits in the megaron, which is common to all. In fact the plan of Odysseus' house is late and many changes are taking place.

The old grammarians do not aid at all, for their criticism is for the most part based on tradition and they hardly distinguish the Homeric age from their own[5].

With the scanty details then furnished by the poems, and with the imaginary house of the fifth century as guide, scholars have constructed the conventional plan of the Homeric palace, which has been adopted by all

[1] *Homerische Paläste*, p. 68.

[2] Wilamowitz-Moellendorf, *Homerische Untersuchungen*, VII. p. 81.

[3] *op. cit.* p. 49.

[4] *ibid.*

[5] Helbig, *Das Homerische Epos aus den Denkmälern erläutert*, p. 2.

the commentators and until quite recent years has not been called into question.

The discoveries, however, of Schliemann and those who have succeeded him, and more recently the finds in Crete, have caused the traditional plan to be re-considered, in view of the supposition that the Homeric palace is of the same type as the Mycenean palaces, a type entirely different from the previously accepted plan.

Both views have been and are still maintained by scholars, though the bulk of opinion inclines more and more to the so-called pre-Hellenic or Mycenean view of the Homeric palace, even though it presents many difficulties.

Reasoning *a priori* we should expect this view to be nearer the truth, since the Achaeans, who were a restless, warlike people, might be expected rather to occupy palaces which they found on the spot, if they were invaders, than in the restlessness of conflict to design and build dwellings of an utterly different type, and if they were indigenous there is no reason for seeking a change. Another view is that of Evans that in Homer we have the material of an earlier Minoan epic taken over into Greek[1].

The question is, whether it is possible for the action of the Homeric poems to take place in a palace of Cretan or mainland type, according to the group with which we identify the Homeric house. If so, we must reject all plans drawn up with reference to a purely imaginary Greek house of the fifth or fourth century, such as has never yet been discovered on any excavated site.

The Ionian remains in Asia Minor unfortunately help us but little, for, except for such monuments as the rock sculptures of Nymphi and Sipylus, practically all the

---

[1] *J.H.S.* 1912, vol. XXXII, "The Minoan and Mycenaean Element in Hellenic life," p. 288.

finds are Hellenistic or Graeco-Roman[1]. It is true that
the Ionian coast towns have not been as yet very
thoroughly explored, but it seems probable that they
had but a faint share in the Aegean culture of the Bronze
Age, and were supposedly under the domination of the
Hatti or some other inland power[2].

The only site in Asia Minor which has yielded rich
Aegean remains is Troy, which had existed for hundreds
of years before the Homeric poems came into being, and
whose civilisation, though in all points analogous to
that of the Aegean, must have developed independently.
In the poems there is also no contrast, the armour and
weapons of the Trojans resembling those of the Achaeans.

Of Asia Minor, with the exception of Troy, we learn
nothing in the poems: and we can only pre-suppose a
sub-Aegean culture there, when the towns were freed from
the inland yoke and the people could rove over the seas
at will, after the withdrawal of Minoan power.

Indeed, if we based our view entirely on internal
evidence, we should rather be tempted to conjecture
that the poems originated in Greece itself, for not only
does the story centre round Agamemnon, lord of Mycenae,
but all the fighting hosts come from Greece on their
hostile expedition and hope thither to return[3].

Moreover they are a race already settled, and leading
a peaceful life in their native land. The Trojan expedition
is an episode which had its origin in special circumstances,
though no doubt the Achaean varied his peaceful pursuits
with a plundering expedition in search of booty from

[1] With the exception of the temple at Branchidae, seventh and
sixth cent. (Newton), and the Artemisium at Ephesus, sixth cent.
(Wood).

[2] Hogarth, *Ionia and the East*, Lecture IV. pp. 65–70, and VI.
pp. 101–2.

[3] Cauer, *op. cit.* II. i. p. 203.   Cf. Lang, *World of Homer*, p. 15.

time to time, even when there was no open war. Cf.
Nestor's frank question to Telemachus (*Od.* III. 71).

> ὦ ξεῖνοι, τίνες ἐστέ; πόθεν πλεῖθ᾽ ὑγρὰ κέλευθα;
> ἦ τι κατὰ πρῆξιν ἢ μαψιδίως ἀλάλησθε,
> οἷά τε ληϊστῆρες, ὑπεὶρ ἅλα;

Strangers, who are ye?   Whence sail ye over the wet ways?
On some trading enterprise or at adventure do ye rove, even as
sea-robbers, over the brine?

The part of the Phoenicians must not be overlooked
though it has been exaggerated in the past, for, though
themselves not originators, they carried cargoes of
beautiful works of art from port to port, and thus
certainly played a great part in the dissemination of
artistic ideas into Homeric society.

It is disappointing that there is no direct light on this
period of transition when the alphabet took final shape
in Ionia, and the classic age was fast approaching.

The poems picture a society of less magnificence and
elegance than that which Cretan discovery prompts us
to imagine, a young, vigorous, natural people with lofty
feelings and ideas, but not that care for outward refinement which we find earlier in Crete.

In contrast to the Cretan palace the Homeric house
was small and often disorderly.   The open hearth stood
in the middle of the megaron, which must therefore often
have been smoky, and on it the food was cooked.

Antinous's words (*Od.* XVIII. 44) show that food was
often left for hours on the hearth to cook.   He says

> γαστέρες αἵδ᾽ αἰγῶν κέατ᾽ ἐν πυρί, τὰς ἐπὶ δόρπῳ
> κατθέμεθα κνίσης τε καὶ αἵματος ἐμπλήσαντες.

These black puddings, a somewhat coarse form of nourish-
ment, were evidently considered a luxury[1].

---

[1] This incident, it is true, takes place in the disorganised household
in Ithaka, but other passages show us that the smell of cooking was
agreeable.   Cf. *Il.* VIII. 549, and *Od.* X. 10, and XII. 369.

At the same time elegance in building was not unknown, *e.g.* the palace of Alcinous, but it aroused wonder.

In this general simplicity of style Noack[1] sees a fatal barrier to any proposed connection of the Homeric house with the Cretan or mainland palaces, which he considers have, with the exception of Arne, far too many rooms to correspond. He is ready to recognise the common features, but the second megaron at Tiryns and the maze of rooms cause him to consider that the mainland type, simple in origin, has been influenced and modified by complicated Cretan forms. Arne, with its simple prodomos rooms giving on to a corridor, approaches more nearly, he considers, to the Homeric type of palace.

Speaking generally, the essential parts would seem to be the same in the Homeric and Mycenean palaces, viz. the courtyard with its propylaeum and the megaron with vestibule abutting on the courtyard. The bath room also occurs in both; and though we may not find any actual palace which we can dub Homeric, yet there is enough in common in the palaces excavated and described, to enable us to recognise a continuity of type from Minoan and Mycenean into Homeric times, and a correspondence in detail of decoration and order.

It is clear that in romantic poems like the *Iliad* and the *Odyssey* we must not look for scientific accuracy with regard to the arrangement of a Homeric palace; indeed, so confusing are some of the details, that it is difficult to reconcile all passages bearing on the subject, whatever be the theory adopted.

The situation is further complicated by the fact that the house of which we know most, viz. the house of Odysseus, is conducted under abnormal conditions, and though this in no wise affects the plan, it does make it

[1] *Hom. Pal.* pp. 69 sqq.

difficult to draw inferences for the position of the women's quarters, etc., in the Homeric house of normal type.

Some points with regard to the general arrangement are quite clear and would fit either plan, others on the other hand are very difficult to explain, if not quite inexplicable, with the conventional plan as guide.

The *conventional view of the Homeric palace* will be given for the sake of completeness, though now practically abandoned. This view, championed though not originated by Professor Jebb in his article in the *Journal of Hellenic Studies*[1] and in his *Introduction to Homer*[2], regards it as a prototype of the ideal Hellenic house of the fifth and fourth centuries, and as having no relation to Mycenean palaces of the Tirynthian type, which are regarded as belonging to an earlier and essentially different stage of civilisation.

The palace is approached by a gate (πρόθυρον) in the wall of the αὐλή or courtyard, in the centre of which is the altar of Zeus Herkeios, the guardian of the home (Fig. 34).

The αὐλή is surrounded by columns, and at its further end is a portico (αἴθουσα), the space occupied by it being called the prodomos. In the centre is a door leading over the ashen threshold (μείλινος οὐδός) into the megaron, with its ἐσχάρα or hearth towards the further end. Here an opening with a stone threshold (λάϊνος οὐδός), on the main axis of the megaron, leads into the women's megaron. Beyond this court are store-houses and chambers.

This view would see in the Homeric megaron the andron of later times, it would regard the aithousa and

[1] VII. pp. 170–80.

[2] *Homer : an introduction to the Iliad and the Odyssey*, Appendix, pp 175 sqq.

the prodomos as identical. The women are assigned a separate megaron immediately behind that of the men and entered through it. The μείλινος οὐδός and the λάϊνος οὐδός are regarded as two separate thresholds, the former at the doorway leading from the αὐλή to the men's megaron, the latter at the doorway from the men's megaron to the women's.

The μυχὸς δόμου, where was the chamber of Odysseus, is put at the far end of the house behind the women's megaron.

Here we have then a long rectangular purely supposititious house with a courtyard and two principal rooms, one behind the other, used for the men and women respectively.

In the *Mycenean view of the Homeric palace*, which is gradually receiving wider adoption, the propylaeum, such as that at Tiryns, leading into the courtyard or αὐλή is regarded as corresponding to the Homeric πρόθυρον. The great hall with its central hearth and four pillars is identified with the Homeric megaron with its ἐσχάρη.

Fig. 34. Homeric House
(conventional plan)

The μείλινος and λάϊνος οὐδός are looked upon as different parts of the same threshold, leading to the principal room. We have the portico (αἴθουσα), while the term πρόδομος is reserved for the second ante-chamber of which we find an example in the large megaron at Tiryns and in that of Mycenae.

The women's apartments are regarded as a set of chambers, quite separate from those of the men, to which they could retire when they wished for privacy, and at Mycenae are identified with a group of chambers abutting on the courtyard to the left of the entrance gate.

The smaller megaron with its fore-courts at Tiryns, which is only accessible from the larger megaron by long and circuitous routes, has, by many advocates of the Mycenean view, been looked upon as the women's quarters of this palace. Another explanation is however possible and will be noted later[1].

Aristotle's account of the socialism prevailing in Crete, where the institution of common tables was as old as the reign of Minos, and even the slaves had the same privileges as their masters, except in the matter of gymnastic exercises and the possession of arms (*Pol.* II. 10), does not preclude the existence of a great central power revered and respected by all; and even if we see in the destruction of the palaces a great socialistic revolution[2], civil war would seem to have been comparatively rare, and the arts and crafts had all the necessary freedom and peace for their perfect development.

On the mainland, it was otherwise. The mighty fortifications alone of Arne, Tiryns and Mycenae, tell their own story the story of a warlike age and of a people ever on the alert, ready to sally forth at a moment's notice, or to defend themselves and their possessions within their own walls. That art suffered in consequence is but a natural result.

---

[1] *vide* p. 203.

[2] Mosso lays great stress on Cretan socialism. Cf. *Palaces of Crete and their builders*, pp. 161 sqq.

In the Homeric poems a similar state of things seems to prevail: each chieftain or king has his stronghold, within which his thegns who dwell around take refuge in times of danger, and if he is called upon to defend his own or another's cause in foreign lands, they follow and support him[1]. A similar polity, though doubtless of a much more primitive order, must be supposed on the evidence of the remains to have existed in Neolithic times at Dimini[2].

The Homeric stronghold was situated on a low hill, of which Troy may safely be taken as an example, whatever be the view adopted of the connection of Tiryns and Mycenae with the poems; it was fortified by a strong outer wall, within which stood the palace and its dependencies with their own ramparts. Although the materials are not mentioned, except in the case of Eumaeus who had built his wall of stones (ῥυτοῖσιν λάεσσι)[3], strengthened with wood, we may conclude, on the analogy of the Homeric city at Troy, that these walls were usually built of large stone blocks, perhaps not always so well finished as those at Troy vi, where the stone was soft and easily worked.

We will glance for a moment at the *Homeric description of Troy*[4].

The Homeric epithet αἰπεινός (lofty) used in many passages of the *Iliad* descriptive of Troy suits well its position on the outlying spur of a chain of hills washed at the foot by the Scamander, whose old bed was much nearer the city than the present.

That it was well-walled (εὐτείχεος) and fortified with fair towers (εὔπυργος) is also clear from the constant

[1] Cf. Isham, *Homeric Palace*, p. 3, and Lang, *Homer and his Age*, c. x. p. 209. [2] *vide* p. 55. [3] *Od.* xiv. 10.
[4] Heinrich, *Troia bei Homer und in der Wirklichkeit*, p. 39.

use of these epithets, as well as from certain scenes
enacted there. Aphrodite, for instance, finds Helen on
the high tower with the Trojan women about her after
the combat of Paris and Menelaus (*Il.* III. 384); again
Hector waiting without the city for Achilles leans his
shield against a projecting tower (*Il.* XXII. 97).

Though the walls of Troy vi have a distinct batter,
it is less pronounced than in the case of prehistoric walls:
a reference to it may be found in the scene between
Hector and Andromache, when she begs her husband
to remain upon the tower and to keep his people beside
the fig tree, "where best the city may be scaled and the
wall is assailable " (*Il.* VI. 434).

The wall is pierced by many gates: "perchance,"
says Zeus to Hera, "wert thou to enter within the gates
and long walls of the stablished citadel of Troy " (εἰ δὲ
σύ γ᾽ εἰσελθοῦσα πύλας καὶ τείχεα μακρὰ, *Il.* IV. 34): two
only however of these gates are mentioned by name, viz.
the Dardanian and the Skaian.

We deduce from *Il.* VI. 392, where Hector was minded
to issue by the Skaian gates upon the plain, that these
gates opened out immediately on to the low lying ground
and were the shortest and most direct way out from the
city.

Hector, being pursued by Achilles round the walls
of Troy, tried in vain to dart under the well-built walls
over against the Dardanian gates (*Il.* XXII. 194), and
through these gates Priam was eager to rush when the
son of Peleus dragged Hector behind his chariot (*Il.* XXII.
413).

Since the Skaian gates apparently led directly on to
the plain, some critics[1] have seen in this latter passage
a reason for identifying the two names. If this be done,

[1] Heinrich, *op. cit.* p. 40.

it is still clear from many other references that the city had several gates.

The Skaian gate was fortified with a tower (*Il.* III. 148), cf. palace at Arne,

> Οὐκαλέγων τε καὶ Ἀντήνωρ, πεπνύμενω ἄμφω,
> ἥατο δημογέροντες ἐπὶ Σκαιῇσι πύλῃσι......
> τοῖοι ἄρα Τρώων ἡγήτορες ἦντ' ἐπὶ πύργῳ.

Oukalegon withal and Antenor, twain sages, being elders of the people sat at the Skaian gates...... Even so sat the elders of the Trojans upon the tower.

Two temples are referred to within the city walls, viz. that of Apollo, where Leto and Artemis healed Aineias (*Il.* v. 445–48), and that of Athene to which Hecabe went to offer the embroidered robe (*Il.* VI. 297), but neither is further described.

The silver bowl from the fourth grave at Mycenae[1] shows a city with massive stone walls surmounted by towers, one above another, such as we may imagine Troy to have been. But here the warriors are exposed to the waist, and are fighting over the walls with bows and arrows, as they must have done at Dimini.

With regard to the palace and dwelling-house more details are forthcoming.

There seems to have been an outer courtyard (ἕρκος), resembling the outer bailey of the medieval castle, to serve as an additional protection: in the house of Eumaeus the inner court or aule is described as great and fair with an open space around it (καλή τε μεγάλη τε, περίδρομος). Here was the dung heap ("till the thralls of Odysseus should carry it away for his wide demesne")[2], on which the faithful Argos lay, and here also the tholos around

---

[1] Ἐφ. Ἀρχ. 1894, pl. 3.
[2] But also in Priam's palace, *Il.* XXIV. 640.

which the rope was flung, on which the unworthy women
were hanged by Odysseus.

Here the swineherd left the three fatted boars to
graze (*Od.* xx. 164), which seems to imply that there was
grass in the ἕρκος, whether through neglect or as a
general custom is not clear.

Here, too, probably the wooers amused themselves
casting weights and spears (ἐν τυκτῷ δαπέδῳ, *Od.* XVII. 169).

The entrance to the inner court or aule was generally
through a propylaeum or covered gateway: through
this Priam drove as he set out on his mission to Achilles
(*Il.* XXIV. 323, ἐκ δ᾿ ἔλασε προθύροιο καὶ αἰθούσης ἐρι-
δούπου), and here Athene stood as she came to visit
Odysseus (ἐπὶ προθύροις Ὀδυσῆος οὐδοῦ ἐπ᾿ αὐλείου, *Od.*
I. 104). This courtyard was probably the place of the
altar at which Priam poured a libation to Zeus (μέσῳ
ἕρκεῖ): we find remains of such altars in the courtyards
both of Cretan and Mycenean palaces, and at Tiryns a
sacrificial pit[1].

Around the aule were porticoes (αἴθουσαι) probably
with wooden columns, and chambers opened on to them.
On the side opposite the prothuron stood the megaron.

The μέγαρον was the chief room of the house and must
have been of no inconsiderable size, since at the house of
Odysseus it accommodated no less than 300 suitors.

The epithet σκιόεις (cf. *Od.* I. 365), constantly applied
to the μέγαρον, may refer to the smoke, or more probably
to the sombre light of the interior as contrasted with
the glare without. A certain amount of light would of
course penetrate into the μέγαρον through the door, and
perhaps even through windows such as we find in the
Cretan palaces: but the principal light probably came
from overhead through a central skylight.

[1] Schliemann, *Tiryns*, p. 339.

In the evening it was lighted by means of λαμπτῆρες or braziers, around which logs were laid and kindled (*Od.* XVIII. 307), and which must have given additional heat as well as light. The lampstand found in the Royal Villa at Knossos[1], and those of the palace at Hagia Triada[2], provide an analogy.

Whether the roof was flat or sloping cannot be inferred from the poems: the roof of Circe's house was certainly flat, for Elpenor slept on it (*Od.* X. 556).

The roof beams are referred to by Telemachus as he goes through the palace with his father and Athene sheds a light before them:—

> ἔμπης μοι τοῖχοι μεγάρων καλαί τε μεσόδμαι
> εἰλάτιναί τε δοκοὶ καὶ κίονες ὑψόσ' ἔχοντες
> φαίνοντ' ὀφθαλμοῖς ὡς εἰ πυρὸς αἰθομένοιο   (*Od.* XIX. 37).

Even the ancients were not agreed as to the distribution of these parts. Schliemann suggests that the δοκοί were the horizontal beams and the μεσόδμαι the long beams[3], most critics affirm the opposite[4]. The μεσόδμαι were taken by Aristarchus to mean the spaces between the columns, and Monro suggests the stone bases on which the columns stood[5], such as were found at Tiryns.

The μέλαθρον seems also to be a beam or rafter: the scholiast connects it etymologically with μέλας, because it became blackened by the smoke from the hearth. Epicaste made fast to this beam the rope with which she hanged herself (*Od.* XI. 278). Athena in the form of a swallow flew up and perched upon it (*Od.* XXII. 239), as did also the eagle in Penelope's dream (*Od.*

---

[1] *B.S.A.* IX. p. 144.
[2] Mosso, *op. cit.* pp. 81, 82 and fig. 36.
[3] *Tiryns*, p. 222.
[4] Buchholz, *Homerische Realien*, II. 2, § 66.
[5] Joseph, *Die Paläste des Homerischen Epos*, pp. 51–53.

XIX. 544). Perhaps it was the main beam, as it is used in a transferred sense of the whole house (*Il.* IX. 204).

The δουροδόκη, in which the spears were placed, seems in the one reference to it in Homer (*Od.* I. 128) to stand here, and has been most satisfactorily explained by Eustathius[1] as a groove in one of the pillars.

Telemachus however leaves his spear leaning against a pillar before he crosses the stone threshold (*Od.* XVII. 29) so that the spear of Athene may also have been left in the prodomos.

The doors (θύραι, θύρετρα, σανίδες) of the megaron were probably. of wood ornamented with metal, and often two-leaved (cf. epithet δικλίς), and on either side stood wooden door posts (σταθμοί) and above the lintel, also of wood (ὑπερθύριον). At Tiryns stone column bases were found, which must have held wooden pillars[2].

There are four Homeric epithets for the threshold (οὐδός) viz. δρύινος, μέλινος, λάϊνος and χάλκεος. There are as yet no remains of metal thresholds, but the charred wood found near the doors, for instance at Tiryns[3], may well be remains of a wooden threshold, and stone thresholds are commonly found[4].

The epithet ξεστός may refer to worked stone as well as to polished wood.

In the simpler houses the floor was probably of beaten earth[5], and in the more luxurious of concrete, as at Tiryns, whereon skins and rugs would be laid. The walls were lined with wooden wainscoting.

---

[1] *Od.* I. 128, "Οτι δουροδόκη ἐστίν· θήκη δοράτων κιονοειδής : ἢ μάλιστα, εἰς κίονα ἐγγεγλυμμένη, ἐν ᾗ πρὸς ὀρθότητα τὰ δόρατα ἵσταντο.

[2] Dörpfeld in Schliemann's *Tiryns*, p. 270.

[3] *ibid.* p. 276.

[4] *ibid.* p. 195.

[5] Helbig, *op. cit.* p. 74.

The general arrangement is then quite clear from the poems, and is borne out by the following Homeric descriptions of the principal palaces.

The Palace of Priam (*Il.* VI. 241).

ἀλλ' ὅτε δὴ Πριάμοιο δόμον περικαλλέ' ἵκανε,
ξεστῇσ' αἰθούσῃσι τετυγμένον, αὐτὰρ ἐν αὐτῷ
πεντήκοντ' ἔνεσαν θάλαμοι ξεστοῖο λίθοιο,
πλησίον ἀλλήλων δεδμημένοι· ἔνθα δὲ παῖδες
κοιμῶντο Πριάμοιο παρὰ μνηστῇσ' ἀλόχοισι·
κουράων δ' ἑτέρωθεν ἐναντίοι ἔνδοθεν αὐλῆς
δώδεκ' ἔσαν τέγεοι θάλαμοι ξεστοῖο λίθοιο,
πλησίον ἀλλήλων δεδμημένοι· ἔνθα δὲ γαμβροὶ
κοιμῶντο Πριάμοιο παρ' αἰδοίῃσ' ἀλόχοισιν.

But when he came to Priam's beautiful palace adorned with polished colonnades—and in it were fifty chambers of polished stone, builded hard by one another, wherein Priam's sons slept beside their wedded wives: and for his daughters over against them on the other side within the courtyard were twelve roofed chambers of polished stone built hard by one another, wherein slept Priam's sons-in-law beside their chaste wives.

This passage describes a great courtyard surrounded with columns under which were various sleeping chambers for the married members of the household. The fact that there were no less than sixty-two chambers opening on to this court, each accommodating a wedded pair, gives some idea of the spaciousness of the palace, if the poet has not exaggerated the number for effect. The maids' sleeping rooms were also probably situated here and even some work rooms, for Odysseus, sleeping in the prodomos, heard a woman grinding at a handmill (ἐξ οἴκοιο...πλησίον).

Palace of Menelaus (*Od.* IV. 20, 37).

τῷ δ' αὖτ' ἐν προθύροισι δόμων αὐτώ τε καὶ ἵππω......
στῆσαν·

Meanwhile those twain made halt at the entry of the gate.

ὣς φάθ'· ὁ δὲ μεγάροιο διέσσυτο, κέκλετο δ' ἄλλους
ὀτηροὺς θεράποντας ἅμα σπέσθαι ἑοῖ αὐτῷ.
οἱ δ' ἵππους μὲν λῦσαν ὑπὸ ζυγοῦ ἱδρώοντας
καὶ τοὺς μὲν κατέδησαν ἐφ' ἱππείῃσι κάπῃσι
πὰρ δ' ἔβαλον ζειὰς ἀνὰ δὲ κρῖ λευκὸν ἔμιξαν,
ἅρματα δ' ἔκλιναν πρὸς ἐνώπια παμφανόωντα
αὐτοὺς δ' εἰσῆγον θεῖον δόμον. οἱ δὲ ἰδόντες
θαύμαζον κατὰ δῶμα διοτρεφέος βασιλῆος
ὥς τε γὰρ ἠελίου αἴγλη πέλεν ἠὲ σελήνης
δῶμα καθ' ὑψερεφὲς Μενελάου κυδαλίμοιο.

So spake he. And he (Eteoneus) hasted from the hall and
called the other ready squires to follow with him.   So they loosed
the sweating horses from beneath the yoke, and fastened them
at the stalls of the horses, and threw beside them spelt and therewith mixed white barley, and tilted the chariot against the shining
faces of the gateway and led the men into the hall divine.   And
they beheld and marvelled as they gazed throughout the palace
of the king, the fosterling of Zeus; for there was a gleam as it were
of sun or moon through the lofty palaces of renowned Menelaus.

This palace though probably not so extensive as the
palace of Priam is evidently on the same plan.   The
gateway is described leading into the courtyard, where
are stalls for the horses, and behind the courtyard is
a hall where guests are entertained and from which
Eteoneus comes forth into the aule to meet them.   The
ornate character of the palace is shown by the impression
produced on Telemachus, who marvelled as he beheld,
for there was a gleam as of sun or moon through the
lofty palace.

αὐτὰρ ἐπεὶ τάρπησαν ὁρώμενοι ὀφθαλμοῖσιν
ἔς ῥ' ἀσαμίνθους βάντες εὐξέστας λούσαντο (*Od.* IV. 47).

But after they had gazed their fill they went to the polished
baths and bathed them.

The ἀσάμινθος seems to have been a bathing tub, perhaps of metal, such as we find in terra-cotta in Crete: whether it stood in a separate bath room or not, is not clear from this passage, but it seems probable that the bath would be taken apart, and the bath rooms of the Cretan and mainland palaces offer an interesting comparison. In the house of Odysseus the bath room must have been on the ground floor, since Penelope ascended to her chamber after bathing (*Od.* IV. 750): footbaths were used in the megaron, for it was here that Eurycleia washed the feet of Odysseus (*Od.* XIX. 386).

The elegance of the architectural decoration in this palace is paralleled by the refinement of the service and appointments, for Menelaus has roamed much and collected many treasures on his travels. The gold and silver vessels recall the wealth of golden cups and bowls found at Mycenae, and show that the poet was familiar with the work even if it could not be reproduced in his own time.

Palace of Paris (*Il.* VI. 313).

Ἕκτωρ δὲ πρὸς δώματ᾽ Ἀλεξάνδροιο βεβήκει
καλά, τά ῥ᾽ αὐτὸς ἔτευξε σὺν ἀνδράσιν, οἳ τότ᾽ ἄριστοι
ἦσαν ἐνὶ Τροίῃ ἐριβώλακι τέκτονες ἄνδρες
οἵ οἱ ἐποίησαν θάλαμον καὶ δῶμα καὶ αὐλὴν
ἐγγύθι τε Πριάμοιο καὶ Ἕκτορος ἐν πόλι᾽ ἄκρῃ.

And Hector was come to Alexandros' fair palace, that himself had builded with them that were most excellent carpenters then in deep-soiled Troy-land; these made him his chamber and hall and courtyard hard by to Priam and Hector in the upper city.

It is interesting to notice by the way that Paris was able and willing to co-operate with the skilled workmen in building his own house, just as Odysseus built his thalamos and fashioned the bed therein, or went into the forest and felled down twenty goodly trees out of which

he made a well constructed raft. May we perhaps look
upon this respect for manual labour as the aftermath
of those healthy socialistic ideas which we found prevailing
at an earlier period in Crete? Professor Gardner is
sceptical, however, about this early Cretan socialism
and does not consider that the remains suggest anything
like a socialistic state. Our chief authority, Aristotle,
idealised, according to Professor Gardner, the Spartan
and Cretan institutions he knew.

The actual house consisted of the three parts, which
we have seen to be essential to the Homeric house, viz.
the courtyard, central chamber and thalamos: other
details are not forthcoming with regard to the plan.

Hector finds Paris however busied with his arms in
the thalamos, and Helen is sitting among her serving
women. As she afterwards summons Hector to enter
and sit upon a bench[1], we may legitimately conclude
that she was sitting at the hearth in the megaron, on to
which the thalamos opened.

Palace of Alcinous (Od. vi. 303; vii. 81).

Nausicaa giving instructions to Odysseus before
leading him back to the city says:—

> ἀλλ' ὁπότ' ἄν σε δόμοι κεκύθωσι καὶ αὐλὴ
> ὦκα μάλα μεγάροιο διελθέμεν, ὄφρ' ἂν ἴκηαι
> μητέρ' ἐμήν· ἡ δ' ἧσται ἐπ' ἐσχάρῃ ἐν πυρὸς αὐγῇ
>
> . . . .
>
> κίονι κεκλιμένη· δμωαὶ δέ οἱ εἵατ' ὄπισθεν
> ἔνθα δὲ πατρὸς ἐμοῖο θρόνος ποτικέκλιται αὐτῇ.

But when thou art within the shadow of the halls and the
court, pass quickly through the great chamber, till thou comest
to my mother, who sits at the hearth in the light of the fire. Her
chair is leaned against a pillar, and her maidens sit behind her.
My father's throne leans close to hers.

[1] *Il.* vi. 354.

αὐτὰρ Ὀδυσσεὺς

Ἀλκινόου πρὸς δώματ' ἴε κλυτά· πολλὰ δέ οἱ κῆρ
ὥρμαιν' ἱσταμένῳ, πρὶν χάλκεον οὐδὸν ἱκέσθαι·
ὥς τε γὰρ ἠελίου αἴγλη πέλεν ἠὲ σελήνης
δῶμα κάθ' ὑψερεφὲς μεγαλήτορος Ἀλκινόου·
χάλκεοι μὲν γὰρ τοῖχοι ἐληλάδατ' ἔνθα καὶ ἔνθα
ἐς μυχὸν ἐξ οὐδοῦ, περὶ δὲ θριγκὸς κυάνοιο,
χρύσειαι δὲ θύραι πυκινὸν δόμον ἐντὸς ἔεργον,
σταθμοὶ δ' ἀργύρεοι ἐν χαλκέῳ ἕστασαν οὐδῷ,
ἀργύρεον δ' ἐφ' ὑπερθύριον χρυσέη δὲ κορώνη.

. . . .

ἐν δὲ θρόνοι περὶ τοῖχον ἐρηρέδατ' ἔνθα καὶ ἔνθα
ἐς μυχὸν ἐξ οὐδοῖο διαμπερές·

. . . .

ἔνθα δὲ Φαιήκων ἡγήτορες ἑδριόωντο
πίνοντες καὶ ἔδοντες.

Meanwhile Odysseus went to the famous palace of Alcinous
and his heart was full of many thoughts as he stood there or ever
he had reached the threshold of bronze.   For there was a gleam as
it were of sun or moon through the high roofed hall of great-
hearted Alcinous.   Brazen were the walls which ran this way
and that from the threshold to the inmost chamber and round
them was a frieze of blue, and golden were the doors that closed
in the good house.   Silver were the door posts that were set on
the brazen threshold and silver the lintel thereupon, and the
hook of the door was of gold.......And within were seats
arranged against the wall this way and that from the threshold
even to the inmost chamber.......There the Phaeacian chieftains
were wont to sit eating and drinking.

The word μυχός, translated by Butcher and Lang
"inmost chamber," will equally well bear the meaning
"inmost part of the hall."   It seems to be used in both
senses.   After the wooers had cast their javelins in vain
and Odysseus began to attack them,

μνηστῆρες δ' ἀνεχώρησαν μεγάροιο μυχόνδε

(*Od.* XXII. 270)

where it clearly means the inmost part of the hall.

On the other hand Eurycleia, relating to Penelope

the arrival of Odysseus and how he took vengeance on
the wooers says:

ἡμεῖς δὲ μυχῷ θαλάμων εὐπήκτων
ἥμεθ' ἀτυζόμεναι, σανίδες δ' ἔχον εὖ ἀραρυῖαι
πρίν γ' ὅτε δή με σὸς υἱὸς ἀπὸ μεγάροιο κάλεσσε
Τηλέμαχος (*Od.* XXIII. 41)

and she went to the megaron and found Odysseus stained
like a lion with blood.   Here the μυχός is clearly a
chamber in the furthest part of the house, quite shut off
from the hall, for the women saw nothing of the slaughter.
It was perhaps in origin a recess in the megaron, later
separated off from it by a partition wall.   In it Münster-
berg[1] would see the origin of the opisthodomos of the
later Greek temple.

This description furnishes us with more details than
the previous ones.   In the principal hall or megaron,
which was entered as before through the aule, was a hearth
with pillars, where the mistress sat with her handmaidens
as well as the master.

Homer does not mention the exact position of the
ἐσχάρα, but the hearth surrounded by four pillars, remains
of which were found in the great hall at Tiryns and at
Mycenae, offers a complete analogy, and the centre of
the room seems its natural position, in any case with a
closed megaron of mainland type.   Such a position would
have been extremely inconvenient in the old conventional
plan, on account of the through draught along the length
of the megaron.

The word ἱστίη (Att. ἑστία) Homer only employs in
oaths, *e.g. Od.* XVII. 155.   Theoclymenus says to Penelope,

ἴστω νῦν Ζεὺς πρῶτα θεῶν ξενίη τε τράπεζα
ἱστίη τ' Ὀδυσῆος ἀμύμονος.

[1] *Jahreshefte des österr. arch. Instit.* III. pp. 137–142.   Prof. Gardner
does not believe it has a definite topographical meaning, certainly not
a consistent one.

The hall was surrounded by seats where the Phaeacian chieftains used to sit, and it was evidently the common hall of the palace free to men and women alike.

So Nestor (*Od.* III. 406) the day after the arrival of Telemachus rose

ἐκ δ' ἐλθὼν κατ' ἄρ' ἕζετ' ἐπὶ ξεστοῖσι λίθοισιν
οἵ οἱ ἔσαν προπάροιθε θυράων ὑψηλάων,

and we have seen frequent examples of such stone benches outside in the Cretan palaces.

The scheme of decoration is particularly interesting in view of the very close parallels afforded in the mainland palaces of Mycenean times. It is generally agreed that the brazen walls and threshold, the silver door posts and lintel, and the golden doors, could not have been solid but were simply overlaid with these metals[1]. Such incrustation was well known in Egypt where the doors were frequently covered with metal, and also in the East, *e.g.* temple of Solomon[2]: "And the whole house he overlaid with gold ...... also the whole altar that was by the oracle he overlaid with gold."

The bronze nails found in the tomb of Agamemnon at Mycenae are supposed to have served to attach such a metal covering[3].

The house of Menelaus must have been decorated in a similar style.

We may perhaps understand in the same sense the descriptions of the houses of Poseidon and Hephaistos, though with the houses of gods the imagination would naturally have freer play. The house of Hephaistos is described as brazen,

Ἡφαίστου δ' ἵκανε δόμον Θέτις ἀργυρόπεζα

. . . .

χάλκεον (*Il.* XVIII. 369)

[1] Helbig, *op. cit.* Excurs. II.   [2] I Kings vi. 22.
[3] Schliemann, *Mycenae*, p. 44.

while the house of Poseidon is golden,

> ἔνθα δέ οἱ κλυτὰ δώματα βένθεσι λίμνης,
> χρύσεα μαρμαίροντα τετεύχαται, ἄφθιτα αἰεί
>
> (*Il.* XIII. 21).

The κύανος frieze has assumed a new interest, since the discoveries at Tiryns[1].

The large frieze found in the vestibule of the men's hall at Tiryns[2] offers a striking analogy to the Homeric description.   It consists of seven alabaster slabs, four narrow and three square, the former overlapping: some have seen in this scheme a proto-Doric series of triglyphs and metopes, though Schliemann thought that the arrangement of the design precluded this.

The narrow slabs are ornamented with sculptured rosettes and the wider with semi-ellipses, both inlaid with blue glass paste, and around the whole design are rows of small rectangular pieces of this same paste.   The pieces

---

[1] The theory, first exploded by Lepsius, that κύανος was blue steel has now been wholly abandoned in face of the true explanation of it, as a blue copper ore or a blue paste made in imitation.   Theophrastus, περὶ λίθων, § 31, says,

> καλεῖται δὲ καὶ κύανος ὁ μὲν ἄρρην ὁ δὲ θῆλυς· μελάντερος δὲ ὁ ἄρρην,

and this darker variety must have been that black κύανος with which was decorated the breastplate of Agamemnon given him by Kinyras of Cyprus.   The true κύανος or lapis lazuli is found in copper mines in the form of crystals but is rare, and in very ancient times in Egypt a substitute for it was found, which was made from copper ore and coloured.   Theophrastus, περὶ λίθων, § 55, tells us that those who wrote about the kings of Egypt recorded the name of the first king who invented artificial κύανος in imitation of the real, and in Egyptian inscriptions the two substances are distinguished.   In Greek, however, the word is used without distinction, but rich and ornate as the palace of Alcinous was we cannot imagine that the frieze of the great hall was of real lapis.   The discovery of the little blue glass cylinders in one of the deep graves at Mycenae (*Mycenae*, pp. 187, 188) shows that the Greeks used this artificial substance even in pre-Homeric times, and in Egypt we find tiles enamelled with it used for walls.

[2] Schliemann, *Tiryns*, pp. 284 sqq.

of glass paste found in the bee-hive tomb at Menidi[1] show the same design.

Such a frieze as this at Tiryns, adorned with smalt, may well have decorated the palace of Alcinous. It is interesting to find the same pattern reproduced on the little temple fresco found in the palace at Knossos[2].

Another passage in *Od.* VI. in connection with this palace sheds additional light on the general disposition.

Nausicaa, sleeping in her chamber in the women's quarters, is visited by Athene, who suggests to her that she should wash her soiled raiment. In the morning she goes to tell her parents

> ἄφαρ δ' ἀπεθαύμασ' ὄνειρον
> βῆ δ' ἴμεναι κατὰ δώμαθ', ἵν' ἀγγείλειε τοκεῦσιν
> πατρὶ φίλῳ καὶ μητρί· κιχήσατο δ' ἔνδον ἐόντας.
> ἡ μὲν ἐπ' ἐσχάρῃ ἧστο σὺν ἀμφιπόλοισι γυναιξίν,
> ἠλάκατα στρωφῶσ' ἁλιπόρφυρα· τῷ δὲ θύραζε
> ἐρχομένῳ σύμβλητο μετὰ κλειτοὺς βασιλῆας
> ἐς βουλήν, ἵνα μιν κάλεον Φαίηκες ἀγανοί[3].

But she marvelled on the dream and went through the halls to tell her parents, her father dear and her mother. And she found them within, her mother sitting by the hearth with the women her handmaids spinning yarn of sea purple stain, but her father she met as he was going forth to the renowned kings in their council, whither the noble Phaeacians called him.

Here again we have the mistress described sitting at the hearth with her handmaidens working near her, so that in this gorgeous palace there seem to have been no special women's quarters, indeed the free equality of women was one of the characteristics of the Homeric age, and it was evidently the usual arrangement that they should work in the megaron. The master is leaving the megaron to go out and Nausicaa, coming from her apart-

---

[1] Lolling, *Das Kuppelgrab bei Menidi*, Tafel III. 24.
[2] *vide* p. 109.   [3] *Od.* VI. 49–55.

ment to the megaron, meets him as he is departing. This passage is proof positive that, in the palace of Alcinous at least, the women's apartments were not situated round a second court at the rear of the first as in the conventional plan, which is shown on the very evidence of the poems themselves, apart from all discovery, to be unnatural.

Several passages in the Homeric poems make it clear that the kingdom of Odysseus consisted of four islands, Ithaka, Same, Dulichion and Zakynthos[1]. Völker[2] had already disputed the identification of Ithaka with the Homeric home of Odysseus, and the controversy has been again raised by Dörpfeld's theory[3] that Leukas or Santa Maura, the island lying to the north of Ithaka, is the home of Odysseus and that in the Doric wandering the inhabitants transferred the name to the island now called Ithaca, a theory which has been vigorously contested by Wilamowitz[4], and which remains in the absence of definite architectural evidence unproved. But whatever be the position of the island, whatever the true meaning of πρὸς ζόφον on which the whole theory seems to turn, the Homeric description of the palace on Ithaca still remains, bearing witness to the general style of the building, though like all the descriptions scanty in architectural detail.

Schliemann[5], in spite of the discouraging results of his excavations on the island, continued to believe in its identity, and considered that the palace must have stood on the level plateau 27 m. × 37 m. at the summit of Mt Aetos, and that the court probably lay between the two enclosure walls, which he discovered at a distance of

[1] *Od.* IX. 21–24, etc.
[2] *Über Homerische Geographie und Weltkunde,* c. 3.
[3] Dörpfeld, *Leukas.*
[4] *Archaeologische Anz.* 1904, pp. 65–75.
[5] *Ithaque, le Peloponnèse, Troie.*

30 m. apart. That the five urns which he himself dug out of a small hole contained the ashes of Odysseus, Penelope and others of the household cannot seriously be believed[1].

Let us turn to the Homeric description. Odysseus in speaking of his house to Eumaeus says (*Od.* XVII. 264):—

> Εὔμαι, ἦ μάλα δὴ τάδε δώματα κάλ' 'Οδυσῆος
> ῥεῖα δ' ἀρίγνωτ' ἐστίν, καὶ ἐν πολλοῖσιν ἰδέσθαι.
> ἐξ ἑτέρων ἕτερ' ἐστίν, ἐπήσκηται δέ οἱ αὐλὴ
> τοίχῳ καὶ θριγκοῖσι, θύραι δ' εὐερκέες εἰσὶ
> δικλίδες   .   .   .   .   .   .
> γιγνώσκω δ' ὅτι πολλοὶ ἐν αὐτῷ δαῖτα τίθενται.

Eumaeus, verily this is the fair house of Odysseus, and right easily might it be known and marked even among many. There is building beyond building, and the court of the house is cunningly wrought with a wall and battlements, and well fenced are the folding doors.......And I see that many men keep revel within.

This account reveals again the same plan of a public hall behind a courtyard, well walled and surrounded with chambers.

As the story of Odysseus's stay in the palace and his gradual revelation of himself unfolds, there are many details given bearing on the arrangement and plan of the palace, some of which are noticed below.

Other important passages bearing on the disposition of the Homeric house.

πρόθυρον. The πρόθυρον or gateway in the wall of the courtyard (ἕρκιον αὐλῆς), already mentioned in the general description, was an essential feature of the Homeric palace, as the frequent mention of it in the

[1] Schliemann, *op. cit.* p. 32.

poems clearly shows. We have seen it referred to in the descriptions of the palaces of Odysseus and Menelaus: again when the princess Nausicaa goes in her mule car to the palace of her father Alcinous, Homer describes her arrival thus:—

> ἡ δ' ὅτε δὴ οὗ πατρὸς ἀγακλυτὰ δώμαθ' ἵκανεν
> στῆσεν ἄρ' ἐν προθύροισι   (*Od.* VII. 3).

And when she had now come to the famous palace of her father she stood in the gateway.

We may then suppose the prothuron to have been always present, and its position before the aule is quite clear from the descriptions[1].

αὐλή. The spacious courtyard with its altar to Zeus Herkeios is also frequently mentioned. Nestor tells how that Peleus was sacrificing to Zeus here, when he and Odysseus approached the palace (*Il.* XI. 772).

> γέρων δ' ἱππηλάτα Πηλεὺς
> πίονα μηρί' ἔκαιε βοὸς Διὶ τερπικεραύνῳ
> αὐλῆς ἐν χόρτῳ· ἔχε δὲ χρύσειον ἄλεισον
> σπένδων αἴθοπα οἶνον, ἐπ' αἰθομένοισ' ἱεροῖσι,
> σφῶι μὲν ἀμφὶ βοὸς ἕπετον κρέα, νῶι δ' ἔπειτα
> στῆμεν ἐν προθύροισι.

And Peleus the old man the lord of horses was burning the fat thighs of kine to Zeus whose joy is in the thunder in the precinct of his court, and held in his hand a chalice of gold pouring forth the bright wine upon the burning offerings, and ye were busy about the flesh of an ox and then stood we in the doorway.

Nestor and Odysseus on arrival stood in the prothuron before the court.

Here, too, Alcinous sacrificed twelve sheep, eight boars and two oxen during the visit of Odysseus (*Od.* VIII. 59).

---

[1] Cf. Joseph, *op. cit.* pp. 11–14.

During the slaying of the suitors Phemius the minstrel, who is trying to devise some way of escape, debates within himself as to the best way of accomplishing it (*Od.* XXII. 333):

δίχα δὲ φρεσὶ μερμήριζεν
ἢ ἐκδὺς μεγάροιο Διὸς μεγάλου ποτὶ βωμὸν
ἑρκείου ἵζοιτο τετυγμένον, ἔνθ' ἄρα πολλὰ
Λαέρτης 'Οδυσεύς τε βοῶν ἐπὶ μηρί' ἔκηαν.

And his heart was divided within him whether he should slip forth from the hall and sit down by the well wrought altar of great Zeus of the household court, whereon Laertes and Odysseus had burnt many pieces of the thighs of oxen.

This passage shows clearly the position of the altar in the aule.

Many passages show that the αὐλή was surrounded by thalamoi or chambers where the married sons slept with their wives, as in the palace of Priam, and also the unmarried sons. In one of these Telemachus slept (*Od.* XIX. 47)

Τηλέμαχος δὲ διὲκ μεγάροιο βεβήκει
κείων ἐς θάλαμον.

And Telemachus passed out through the hall to his chamber to lie down.

Again in *Od.* I. 425, of the chamber of Telemachus,

ὅθι οἱ θάλαμος περικαλλέος αὐλῆς
ὑψηλὸς δέδμητο, περισκέπτῳ ἐνὶ χώρῳ.

Where his chamber was builded high up in the fair court in a place with wide prospect, thither betook him to his bed.

The chamber was therefore probably in the outer wall of the courtyard, commanding a view over the country.

Perhaps the thalamos of Nausicaa was in the same position, for she seems to enter it direct from the court

(*Od.* VII. 7), and she is guarded from disturbance in the exposed position by two handmaidens. In this room a fire was often lighted and even food cooked (*Od.* VII. 13).

The thalamos of the wedded pair has been judged, on account of the almost constant use of the word μυχός hereafter discussed[1], to be in the innermost part of the house. May not that of Odysseus and Penelope however have opened on to the aule, for the olive which Odysseus so cunningly fashioned into a bed was growing ἕρκεος ἐντός (*Od.* XXIII. 190) before Odysseus built the chamber about it?

Phoenix also occupied a room in this position as is clear from his account of his escape (*Il.* IX. 470):—

> εἰνάνυχες δέ μοι ἀμφ' αὐτῷ παρὰ νύκτας ἴαυον·
> οἱ μὲν ἀμειβόμενοι φυλακὰς ἔχον, οὐδέ ποτ' ἔσβη
> πῦρ, ἕτερον μὲν ὑπ' αἰθούσῃ εὐερκέος αὐλῆς,
> ἄλλο δ' ἐνὶ προδόμῳ, πρόσθεν θαλάμοιο θυράων·
> ἀλλ' ὅτε δὴ δεκάτη μοι ἐπήλυθε νὺξ ἐρεβεννή,
> καὶ τότ' ἐγὼ θαλάμοιο θύρας πυκινῶς ἀραρυίας
> ῥήξας ἐξῆλθον, καὶ ὑπέρθορον ἑρκίον αὐλῆς
> ῥεῖα, λαθὼν φύλακάς τ' ἄνδρας δμωάς τε γυναῖκας.

Nine nights long slept they all night around my body; they kept watch in turn, neither were the fires quenched, one beneath the colonnade of the fenced courtyard and another in the porch before the chamber doors. But when the tenth dark night was come upon me, then burst I my cunningly fitted doors and issued forth, and overleapt the courtyard fence lightly, unmarked of watchmen and handmaidens.

This passage shows that slaves male and female also slept in chambers surrounding the courtyard.

At first sight the position of the two fires here, one in the aithousa and one in the prodomos, would seem to support the conventional view rather than the Mycenean. But it seems quite possible to interpret prodomos as the

---

[1] *vide* p. 209. Cf. p. 185.

antechamber of Phoenix's room, which may have been of the type of those at Gha, or the aithousa may be the portico of the aule and the prodomos the vestibule of the megaron. We will proceed to consider the possible interpretations of these two words.

<u>αἴθουσα</u> and πρόδομος[1]. The description of the palace of Priam makes it clear that the courtyard was surrounded by porticoes: we find this arrangement again at the palace of Alcinous (*Od.* VIII. 57)

πλῆντο δ' ἄρ' αἴθουσαί τε καὶ ἔρκεα καὶ δόμοι ἀνδρῶν.

Hither, too, the women carry out the dead after the slaughter in the house of Odysseus (*Od.* XXII. 449)

κὰδ δ' ἄρ' ὑπ' αἰθούσῃ τίθεσαν εὐερκέος αὐλῆς.

Porticoes which correspond have been found on three sides of the courtyard at Tiryns, not a complete peristyle it is true, but there is nothing in the Homeric poems to warrant the assertion that the courtyard was entirely surrounded by porticoes. At Tiryns we find no rooms beneath.

The word αἴθουσα was also evidently used in a more limited sense of the vestibule leading into the hall, and in one passage in Homer is identified with the πρόδομος, which has generally been regarded as the second vestibule where two existed.

When Telemachus and his companion reach the palace of Menelaus they are welcomed, and Helen herself bids her maids prepare beds in the prodomos, the usual place for guests to sleep: at the palaces of Odysseus and Alcinous they also sleep outside

Ἀργείη δ' Ἑλένη δμωῇσι κέλευσεν
Δέμνι' ὑπ' αἰθούσῃ θέμεναι[2].

And Argive Helen bade her handmaids set out bedsteads beneath the gallery.

[1] Joseph, *op. cit.* pp. 25-8.   [2] *Od.* IV. 296-7.

This is the usual Homeric formula for the preparation of a resting place for visitors, and from the fact that Achilles apologises to Priam (*Il.* XXIV. 643) for putting him here, Noack[1] argues that this part is late and was written down at a time when the poet had ceased to understand the old custom, especially as the reason given by Achilles, viz. concealment from the Achaeans, would make some place inside the house seem more fitting. Only in the hut of Eumaeus is a bed prepared for the guest near the fire in the principal room (*Od.* XIV. 518).

According to Helen's instructions the beds are prepared in the aithousa or portico, but the guests are afterwards spoken of as sleeping in the prodomos:

οἱ μὲν ἄρ᾽ ἐν προδόμῳ δόμου αὐτόθι κοιμήσαντο[2].

Possibly prodomos is here used as a more general term which would include the aithousa.

The women's quarters. The moot question of the existence and position of the women's quarters in the Homeric house can never be satisfactorily solved, so long as we look for evidence on one side or the other to the house of Odysseus. The conditions in this house were peculiar in every sense, but more especially so in the question of the women. We know that the free equality of women was an essential feature of Homeric society, that woman was exalted to a noble position, consulted and revered, and apart from the house of Odysseus, where the women could not behave naturally and were obliged through force of circumstances to seclude themselves as much as possible, it seems to me that the assumption of a separate set of apartments, including a women's megaron, to which women were confined, indeed the very idea of exclusion, is altogether foreign to the Homeric poems.

[1] *Hom. Pal.* p. 43.　　　　　　[2] *Od.* IV. 302.

The prevailing state of things seems to have been that the women sat in the megaron or principal apartment at their work, and that the men came in and out freely at will: the women may have had sleeping apartments in a special part of the house.

Iris going to Helen finds her weaving in the megaron (*Il.* III. 125): when Telemachus is in the house of Menelaus she comes down quite naturally into the megaron and begins to weave with her handmaidens (*Od.* IV. 133). When Hector bids his mother go to the temple of Athene, she goes to the megaron and calls her handmaidens (*Il.* VI. 286): when he has sought Andromache in vain he asks the serving women where she went from the megaron (*Il.* VI. 377).

Arete sits with her handmaidens in the megaron (*Od.* VI. 307) and Circe seems also to be there (*Od.* X. 256).

It is true that the chambers of the maiden Astyoche (*Il.* II. 514) and of Polymele (*Il.* XVI. 184) were upstairs, but they were probably single rooms: the women's bedrooms however may quite well have been sometimes upstairs.

The ingrained idea then of separate women's quarters with a megaron where they were isolated seems to be based on insufficient evidence, and to have arisen through the stress laid on the conditions prevailing in the house of Odysseus.

Penelope could no longer sit at her ease in the megaron like Arete or Helen: she had lost her position as mistress of the house and preferred to retire, and her apartments were clearly upstairs, in the ὑπερῷον. Here Penelope slept, for the thalamos on the ground floor had evidently remained uninhabited since the departure of Odysseus, here all the work of the day went on, and even libation was made (*Od.* IV. 761).

The evidence then which may be gleaned on this point from the house of Odysseus is special, and cannot be considered as explaining the normal conditions prevailing in Homeric society. Neither does it lend any support whatever to the conventional view of the Homeric house.

Penelope's visits to the megaron are described in the following terms, which do not make it clear whether she entered the hall from the front or back, and so cannot be used to support the conventional view (*Od.* I. 328):—

> τοῦ δ' ὑπερωιόθεν φρεσὶ σύνθετο θέσπιν ἀοιδὴν
> κούρη Ἰκαρίοιο περίφρων Πηνελόπεια·
> κλίμακα δ' ὑψηλὴν κατεβήσετο οἷο δόμοιο
> οὐκ οἴη· ἅμα τῇ γε καὶ ἀμφίπολοι δύ' ἕποντο.
> ἡ δ' ὅτε δὴ μνηστῆρας ἀφίκετο δῖα γυναικῶν
> στῆ ῥα παρὰ σταθμὸν τέγεος πύκα ποιητοῖο
> .   .   .   .
> ἡ μὲν θαμβήσασα πάλιν οἰκόνδε βεβήκει.

She went down the high stairs from her chamber, not alone, for two of her handmaidens bare her company. Now when the fair lady had come unto the wooers she stood by the doorpost of the well builded roof.......Then in amaze she went back to her chamber.

A passage describing Odysseus's refusal to go to Penelope has been used to support the conventional view. The reason why he is unable to comply is given by Odysseus thus (*Od.* XVII. 564):—

> ἀλλὰ μνηστήρων χαλεπῶν ὑποδείδι' ὅμιλον
> τῶν ὕβρις τε βίη τε σιδήρεον οὐρανὸν ἵκει.
> καὶ γὰρ νῦν, ὅτε μ' οὗτος ἀνὴρ κατὰ δῶμα κιόντα
> οὔ τι κακὸν ῥέξαντα βαλὼν ὀδύνῃσιν ἔδωκεν
> οὔτε τι Τηλέμαχος τό γ' ἐπήρκεσεν οὔτε τις ἄλλος.

But somewhat I fear the throng of the froward wooers whose outrage and violence reach even to the iron heaven. For even now as I was going through the house when this man struck and pained me sore and that for no ill deed, neither Telemachus nor any other kept off the blow.

In reality the passage can be interpreted just as satisfactorily according to the Mycenean view. The reception
accorded to Odysseus by the suitors when he moved about
in the hall was not such as to make him desirous of running
the risk of further provoking their anger by a visit to the
women's quarters. The passage does not in the least
imply that he had to go through the megaron to reach
them.

In *Od.* xx. 387, Penelope's seat is thus described:—

> ἡ δὲ κατ᾽ ἄντηστιν θεμένη περικαλλέα δίφρον
> κούρη Ἰκαρίοιο περίφρων Πηνελόπεια
> ἀνδρῶν ἐν μεγάροισιν ἑκάστου μῦθον ἄκουεν.

Now the daughter of Icarius, wise Penelope, had set her fair
chair over against them and heard the words of each one of the
men in the hall.

κατ᾽ ἄντηστιν, which has been understood to mean
against the wall near the door between the men's court
and the women's, might equally well describe her position
if she sat in the aule facing the door of the megaron.

Immediately before the slaughter of the suitors begins
Eurycleia is bidden to shut the women's quarters.

The swineherd addresses Eurycleia (*Od.* XXI. 381)
thus:—

> Τηλέμαχος κέλεταί σε, περίφρων Εὐρύκλεια,
> κληῖσαι μεγάροιο θύρας πυκινῶς ἀραρυίας
> ἢν δέ τις στοναχῆς γε κτύπου ἔνδον ἀκούσῃ
> ἀνδρῶν ἡμετέροισιν ἐν ἕρκεσι, μή τι θύραζε
> προβλώσκειν, ἀλλ᾽ αὐτοῦ ἀκὴν ἔμεναι παρὰ ἔργῳ.
>
> .   .   .   .
>
> κληῖσεν δὲ θύρας μεγάρων εὖ ναιεταόντων,
> σιγῇ δ᾽ ἐξ οἴκοιο Φιλοίτιος ἆλτο θύραζε
> κληῖσεν δ᾽ ἄρ᾽ ἔπειτα θύρας εὐερκέος αὐλῆς.

Wise Eurycleia, Telemachus bids thee bar the well-fitting
doors of thy chamber, and if any of the women hear the sound
of groaning or the din of men within our walls, let them not go

forth but abide where they are in silence at their work.......
She barred the doors of the fair-lying halls. Then Philoetius
hasted forth silently from the house and barred the outer gates
of the fenced court.

And in *Od.* XXII. 399, after the slaughter :—

ὤϊξεν δὲ θύρας μεγάρων εὖ ναιεταόντων
βῆ δ' ἴμεν· αὐτὰρ Τηλέμαχος πρόσθ' ἡγεμόνευεν.

She opened the doors of the fair-lying halls, and came forth.
Telemachus led the way before her.

It has been supposed that the door referred to here
was at the upper end of the hall, but the passage is quite
as intelligible if we regard the door as being that of the
women's quarters perhaps somewhere in the aule.

Many other passages might be similarly explained. In
short there are no passages which cannot be satisfactorily
interpreted according to the Mycenean view, whereas
there are several which cannot be explained by the old
conventional view.

οὐδός. The account given of the fight between
Odysseus and the beggar Irus gives an adequate idea of
the size and character of the threshold. Irus says εἷκε,
γέρον, προθύρου, "get thee hence old man from the
doorway": to which Odysseus replies, οὐδὸς δ' ἀμφοτέρους
ὅδε χείσεται, "this threshold will hold us both."
Accordingly they fight thereon (*Od.* XVIII. 32)

ὡς οἱ μὲν προπάροιθε θυράων ὑψηλάων
οὐδοῦ ἐπὶ ξεστοῦ πανθυμαδὸν ὀκριόωντο.

Thus did they whet each other's rage right manfully before
the lofty doors upon the polished threshold.

The threshold evidently consisted of a large oblong
polished slab of stone, such as have been found both at
Tiryns and Mycenae.

In conclusion reference must be made to Myres' paper on this subject in the *Journal of Hellenic Studies*[1] where he points out that the four main questions to be answered are whether the apartments of the women were immediately in the rear of the megaron or a distinct group of chambers apart from it, whether the μείλινος, οὐδός and the λάϊνος οὐδός were at opposite ends of the megaron, whether the Homeric megaron had a door at each end, and whether it was entered from the aule by means of a simple portico or through a second ante-chamber.

In connection with the position of the women's quarters, Myres notices that the words used for them are, δόμος, δῶμα, οἶκος, δώματα, θάλαμος, μέγαρα and μέγαρον. The words δόμος, δῶμα, οἶκος, δώματα would not, he considers, be likely to be used of apartments immediately to the rear of the megaron and entered from it, nor the phrases οἴκονδε, εἰς οἶκον, πρὸς δώματα of persons passing from one room to another.

The incidents at the beginning of *Odyssey* xx. referred to by Myres in this connection are conclusive. Penelope after inviting Odysseus to sleep in the house (τῷδ᾽ ἐνὶ οἴκῳ) ascends to her upper chamber (ἀνέβαιν᾽ ὑπερώϊα) and Odysseus lies down to rest in the vestibule (πρόδομος) where he sees the women coming out of the megaron, but whether this is the principal megaron or their own apartments is not clear. Lying here, however, he hears Penelope weeping in her upper chamber, a thing which would seem unlikely if the whole length of the megaron separated him from her chamber. He rises and carries the skins on which he is lying into the megaron and places them on a seat (ἐς μέγαρον κατέθηκεν ἐπὶ θρόνου) and afterwards goes out of doors with an ox-hide (ἐκ δὲ βοείην

[1] xx. pp 128 sqq.

θῆκε θύραζε φέρων) and prays to Zeus, presumably at
the altar of Zeus Herkeios in the aule. From here he
hears the words of good omen of one of the women who
is still grinding corn, and who must therefore have been
at work in one of the buildings in the aule. If the women's
quarters, including Penelope's chamber, were somewhere
in the aule, the narrative here would be quite clear.

Several other passages go against the supposition
that the women's apartments were in the rear of the men's,
as for example when Penelope hears Antinous strike
Odysseus in the megaron, as she is sitting in her thalamos
(*Od.* XVII. 462), or again when she hears Telemachus
sneeze. It would certainly be easier to hear such things
if her chambers were in the courtyard, than if she were
behind the great megaron.

Myres quotes many passages which prove for him that
the singular μέγαρον and also the plural μέγαρα were
sometimes applied to the women's apartments, and from
this he draws the inference that the women's apartments
consisted of a common hall or megaron with a suite of
θάλαμοι annexed. A suitable group of chambers apart
with an upper storey is found in the palace of Mycenae
across the aule exactly opposite to the main megaron,
and Myres thinks that the whole story of the *Odyssey*
as far as it concerns Penelope could have been rehearsed
here.

But what of the palace at Tiryns with its separate
courtyard and megaron on a smaller scale, which have
long been regarded by those who uphold the Mycenean
view of the Homeric house as the women's quarters?
Such a supposition does not seem to rest on any authority.
Not only is it fatal, as Professor Jebb[1] pointed out in his
defence of the conventional plan, to any interpretation

[1] *J.H.S.* VII. p. 187.

of the Homeric house in the light of Mycenean remains, but it is also contrary to all our knowledge of the intercourse of men and women both in the Homeric age and in the Mycenean.

The duplication of the parts of this building, as Professor Ernest Gardner[1] points out (*J.H.S.* XXI. ii.), is strange, unless we are to regard them as two separate buildings (possibly for king and prince) enclosed within the same circuit wall.

Myres regards the second suite of apartments as parallel to the group of chambers at Mycenae and as set apart for the women[2]: if this were the case it would be easy to prove on his own evidence that the palace at Tiryns is not a palace of Homeric type. Even if the word μέγαρον is applied to the women's quarters it need not of necessity imply the existence of a women's court, but may simply refer to the rooms occupied by them.

With regard to the question of the οὐδοί, the mention in the Homeric poems of two thresholds, the stone and the ashen, has lent some support to the Hellenic view of the Homeric house. According to Professor Jebb's plan the μείλινος οὐδός lies between the aule and the megaron, and the λάϊνος οὐδός between the megaron and the gunaikonitis or women's court. But not only does it seem unnatural to have the stone threshold where it would undergo less wear, but there is apparently no passage in Homer to prove this position.

On the other hand, as Myres points out, stone was the usual material employed for the threshold between the aule and the main megaron. Telemachus crosses the stone threshold (*Od.* XVII. 30) when he goes into the hall, and the crossing of the stone threshold would be of importance as the noise would herald the appearance of a new comer.

---

[1] *J.H.S.* XXI. p. 296.   [2] *c.* p. 131.

On the other hand the μείλινος οὐδός is mentioned as the place where Odysseus sat when he entered the house in the guise of a beggar, and was certainly at the lower end of the hall.

Myres' theory that these are but parts of the same threshold removes all difficulties, and moreover is supported by reference to the palaces at Tiryns and Mycenae. Here we find very broad stone thresholds not only between the vestibule and the megaron, but also between the vestibule and the aithousa. Moreover at Tiryns the λάϊνος οὐδός between the prodomos and the megaron has no hinge sockets or signs of wear caused by the opening and closing of doors as the other thresholds have[1], which may be due to the fact that the μείλινος οὐδός rested upon the λάϊνος οὐδός, and that the doors were more in the nature of a French window.

Myres also points out that as the λάϊνος οὐδός must be at the end of the megaron nearest the aule, it is unnecessary to regard Odysseus as being promoted to the further end of the hall when Telemachus gives him a seat παρὰ λάϊνον οὐδόν (*Od.* xx. 258, 899).

It has been assumed, moreover, that the seat of honour was at the further end of the hall, whereas it would seem to be near the fire by the pillars of the roof, where Alcinous and Arete sat and Penelope stood to address the suitors, and later sat to talk with Odysseus. If as seems likely Telemachus sat in this position, it would be comparatively easy for him to join his father at the entrance when the slaughter of the suitors began.

The use of the prepositions κατά and ἀνά Myres considers would be unnatural if there were a door at either end of the megaron; and as to the preposition διέκ, it

---

[1] Schliemann, *Tiryns*, p. 216. Schliemann thinks the doorway was closed by drawing a curtain.

XIV] *Homeric Palaces* 205

means simply "through and out of" and does not in the least prove the existence of a second door. The absence of such a door in the Mycenean isolated megara is therefore no drawback to the interpretation of the Homeric poems in their light.

The fourth question, as to whether the megaron was entered from the aule by means of a simple portico or through a second ante-chamber, is of less significance: there seems, however, to be nothing of importance against the view that the Homeric house had a prodomos between the aithousa and the megaron. The door in the prodomos at Tiryns leading to the bath room[1] would fit in extremely well with the evident proximity of the bath room to the megaron in the Homeric palaces, *e.g.* palace of Alcinous and palace of Menelaus.

Myres' arguments, which have been reviewed at some length on account of their importance, serve to show quite conclusively that there is no insurmountable barrier in the way of regarding the Homeric house as of Mycenean type.

There remain for consideration several terms employed in connection with the Homeric house and omitted hitherto as having less bearing on the plan.

Ὀρσοθύρη[2]. The word occurs only in *Od.* XXII. 126, 132, 332, and would appear from its formation to mean either a raising or trap door, or a door raised above the ground. It is described in Homer thus:—"Now there was in the well-builded wall a certain postern (ὀρσοθύρη) and there by the topmost level of the threshold of the stablished hall was a way into an open passage (ὁδὸς ἐς λαύρην) closed by well fitting folding doors (σανίδες). So Odysseus bade the goodly swineherd stand near thereto, for there was but one approach. Then Agelaus

---

op. cit. p. 215.   [2] Joseph, *op. cit.* pp. 57 sqq.

spoke among them and declared his word to all: 'Friends, will not some man climb up to the postern (ἀν' ὀρσοθύρην ἀναβαίη) and give word to the people?'"

Melanthius answers: "It may in no wise be, for the fair doors toward the court (αὐλῆς θύρετρα) are grievously near to the postern and perilous is the entrance to the passage and one mighty man would keep back an host."

We gather from this passage that the ὀρσοθύρη was a raised door in the wall of the megaron on a level with the top of the threshold, and near the doors between the megaron and courtyard. It led into a λαύρη or corridor, and in the above account the ὀρσοθύρη and the ὁδὸς ἐς λαύρην appear to be two names for the same thing. The door also afforded easy communication with the outside world, as Melanthius is to climb up to it and to tell the people of the terrible plight of the suitors.

Professor Jebb[1] deduces, from the fact that Agelaus proposes to Melanthius that he should go up to the ὀρσοθύρη, when Eumaeus was already guarding it, that the ὀρσοθύρη and the ὁδὸς ἐς λαύρην were two separate doors, and that Eumaeus was really guarding the latter. Both, he says, led into the passage, but the ὀρσοθύρη was at the upper end of the megaron. Melanthius refuses to ascend because the passage is commanded by Eumaeus from the lower door. The reason given by Melanthius for refusing, ἄγχι γὰρ αἰνῶς αὐλῆς καλὰ θύρετρα, which undoubtedly refers to the doors leading to the aule, would seem to be against this view.

The fact that we have only the ground plan of such palaces as those at Tiryns and Mycenae with the walls remaining but a few feet above the ground level, prevents our finding any traces of such a door, but it is noticeable that in the palace of the second city at Troy the founda-

[1] *J.H.S.* VII. p. 181.

tion of the wall is broadened at one spot[1], possibly to
admit of a door of this kind. The small door in the
prodomos at Tiryns leading to the bath room may also
be similar. The λαύρη or side passage is a feature with
which we are very familiar in Mycenean buildings; there
would doubtless be a lower and an upper one in the
Homeric house.

ῥῶγες μεγάροιο[2]. Though Melanthius refuses to give
the alarm by the ὀρσοθύρη, he offers to go and bring
armour from the store chamber (θάλαμος), and to do this
he ascends by the ῥῶγες μεγάροιο (ἀνέβαινε ἐς θαλάμους
ἀνὰ ῥῶγας μεγάροιο). Since this is the only mention
of the ῥῶγες we can but conjecture what they may have
been.

The word has been connected with the root of ῥήγνυμι
and the modern Greek ῥοῦγα meaning a passage. The
old view which regarded it as a clerestory is unsatis-
factory, since Melanthius would certainly have been seen
if he had had to climb up, and also he would have found
it difficult to return this way with a load of armour.

Professor Jebb[3] who supports the former view regards
Melanthius as ascending to the ὀρσοθύρα and then turning
to the inner part of the house and going by narrow passages
(ῥῶγες) to the store chamber. The second time that he
makes the attempt he is seen and followed. The ῥῶγες
have been also variously explained as beams, ladders,
holes in the back wall of the megaron, etc. The solution
can only be conjectural.

The θάλαμος ὅπλων, which was accessible because
Telemachus had in forgetfulness left the door open, must
have been in the inner part of the house and of a fair
size, since Melanthius on his first visit brought twelve

[1] Schliemann, *Troja*, p. 79, plan 25u.
[2] Joseph, *op. cit.* pp. 62–4.   [3] *J.H.S.* VII. p. 182.

shields, twelve helmets and twelve spears, and could presumably have brought many more had he not been intercepted and killed.

The θησαυρός or treasure chamber is also in the inner part of the house as we learn from *Od.* XXI. 9, for though the word θάλαμος is used, it is evidently a store chamber that is indicated. In several other references the verb used is καταβαίνω, as though the chamber were partially if not wholly underground (*Od.* XV. 99, etc.).

Concerning the much discussed θόλος[1] mentioned in *Od.* XXII it is difficult to come to any satisfactory conclusion. It was certainly a circular building and stood somewhere in the aule (*Od.* XXII. 442, 466). This is all that can be known of it for certain. It has been regarded severally as a kitchen[2], which is unlikely as food was certainly cooked in the megaron (*Od.* XX. 280); as a treasury[3] for articles of household use, but the thalamoi where arms, etc., were stored seem to have been within the house (*Od.* XXII. 138); as a burial place[4] on the analogy of the circular tombs found at Mycenae, or as a chapel where the household gods were stored. The words of Odysseus "God forbid that I should take these women's lives by a clean death, these that have poured dishonour on my head and on my mother," before he fastened the rope with which he would hang them around the pillar of the θόλος, have caused Joseph to make the likely suggestion that it was the privy.

With our present knowledge it is impossible to verify any of these conjectures, and no buildings of the kind have been unearthed in the courtyards of Mycenean palaces hitherto discovered.

[1] Joseph, *op. cit.* pp. 21–24.
[2] Lange, *Haus und Halle*, p. 36.
[3] Buchholz, *op. cit.* II. ii. p. 103.
[4] Gardner, *J. H. S.* III. p. 267.

μυχός. This word is used commonly of the inmost part[1] and does not necessarily imply a separate chamber, though indeed employed with this meaning, as of the bed-chamber of Alcinous and his wife (*Od.* VII. 346). Therefore in such a passage as that in which the palace of Alcinous is thus described (*Od.* VII. 86, 87),

> χάλκεοι μὲν γὰρ τοῖχοι ἐληλάδατ᾽ ἔνθα καὶ ἔνθα
> ἐς μυχὸν ἐξ οὐδοῦ

"brazen were the walls which ran this way and that from the threshold to the μυχός," the word translated by Butcher and Lang "inmost chamber" may merely mean "inmost part of the hall," and there is no need to postulate a chamber at the back in the same building axis with the megaron, as Professor Jebb does in his plan.

Speaking generally the weight of evidence on the question of the Homeric house seems to lie in favour of an interpretation on the lines of recently excavated Mycenean palaces. This does not mean that every detail of the Homeric palaces can be satisfactorily explained with reference say to the palace at Tiryns—which indeed would leave little room for local variation—but that in the absence of any satisfactory remains in Ithaka, or Leucas if the action of the *Odyssey* took place there, we may interpret the palace of Odysseus and the other Homeric palaces in the light afforded by the plan of such a palace as that at Tiryns, and may regard the latter as belonging essentially to the same epoch and stage of civilisation, though not identical in every particular.

[1] Cf. Winckler, *Die Wohnhäuser der Hellenen*, p. 35.

CHAPTER XV

GREEK HOUSE OF THE FIFTH AND FOURTH CENTURIES

THE remains of houses of the classical period in Greece are unfortunately too scanty to enable us to construct a ground plan of the normal type. In Athens for instance, in spite of the luxuriousness of public buildings, the streets seem to have been for the most part narrow and tortuous and the houses poor. Of the many hundreds of houses discovered by Burnouf[1], the majority consisted of a single cell, or sometimes two or three built round a courtyard, cf. Ps. Dicaearch. I. i:—

αἱ μὲν πολλαὶ τῶν οἰκιῶν εὐτελεῖς, ὀλίγαι δὲ χρήσιμαι. ἀπιστηθείη δ᾽ ἂν ἐξαίφνης ὑπὸ τῶν ξένων θεωρουμένη, εἰ αὕτη ἐστὶν ἡ προσαγορευομένη τῶν Ἀθηναίων πόλις.

The majority of the houses are mean but a few are commodious. If strangers were to come upon it suddenly, they would scarcely believe that this is the talked-of city of the Athenians.

Nevertheless efforts were made to improve the arrangement of the streets, as for example by Hippodamus of Miletus[2], the champion of parallel streets and rectangular intersections, who lived in the latter half of the fifth century and left his mark at Peiraeus, Thuria and Rhodes.

No remains of houses of the prodomos type belonging

[1] Burnouf, *Archives des missions scientifiques*, v. pp. 71 sqq.
[2] Arist. *Pol.* II. v. I.

to this period have come to light, but in view of recent discoveries at Priene[1], it is no longer safe to say that the type was entirely abandoned, in so far as the ordinary dwelling-house was concerned, and was only retained for the temples of the gods.

The conservatism ever promoted by religion will easily account for the persistence of the type for sacred buildings, whereas the poverty of individuals in an age of war and the gradual abandonment of private dwellings of the luxurious type of the Homeric palace, due to altered political and social conditions, would naturally lead the way to a simpler form of dwelling, though the more elaborate prodomos type may quite well have continued to exist side by side with it.

It is indeed a far cry from the ornate and spacious Homeric palace to the small simple dwelling of the fifth century, but this complete change in domestic architecture is concomitant with the vast changes in social and political conditions.

The great Homeric chief with his thegns is no more, and the expeditions and adventures of the great heroic age have been replaced by all the bustle and competition of the narrow life of towns. The very necessity for the accommodation of thousands within a tiny space made the roomy Homeric palace an utter impossibility, common party walls had to be built to economise space and the megaron appears to have vanished entirely from domestic architecture.

Want of evidence makes it impossible to say whether it survived in the country, where the houses were in any case more beautiful and spacious (cf. Is. *Areop.* 52):

ὥστε καλλίους εἶναι καὶ πολυτελεστέρας τὰς οἰκήσεις καὶ τὰς κατασκευὰς τὰς ἐπὶ τῶν ἀγρῶν ἢ τὰς ἐντὸς τείχους.

[1] *vide* p. 241.

In the city of Athens, which may be taken as typical, the private houses were mostly of only one storey, but there must have been many blocks of dwellings of three or four storeys (συνοικίαι) to accommodate the poorer classes, slaves, etc.[1]: these were sublet by the ναύκληρος. The agora in the inner Kerameikos had become the centre of civic life[2], consequently the house had lost in importance, and the glad feasts and re-unions which were the keynote of the Homeric age had altogether vanished[3].

The woman still sat at home with her maidens weaving and spinning, but the man spent most of his time abroad and only returned home to eat and sleep.

The streets and public buildings were in charge of a magistrate known as an ἀστυνόμος; five of these were appointed for the city and five for the Peiraeus[4].

In Athens the oldest settlements were upon the Pnyx hill[5] on small and large terraces along two defiles, hence the scholiast derives the name from πυκνόω. These buildings were of the simplest character with clay floor, clay walls and flat clay roof, and according to Vitruvius[6] were shown in later times as a curiosity. Some of them had been deserted and had fallen into decay even in classic times.

The great Panathenaic way was so narrow that only five could walk abreast in it, and the chariots must have been forced to go single file[7].

There were certain spaces which, through chance or superstition, had been rejected in spite of the crying need for room[8]. Thucydides (II. 17) tells us how the

[1] Walther Lange, *Das antike griechisch-römische Wohnhaus*, p. 9.
[2] Curtius, *Stadtgeschichte von Athen*, p. 169.
[3] Winckler, *op. cit.* pp. 61–63.   [4] Liddell and Scott, ἀστυνόμος.
[5] Curtius, *op. cit.* p. 25.   [6] XXXV. 12.
[7] Harrison, *Primitive Athens*, p. 131.
[8] Thuc. II. 17, τὸ Πελαργικὸν καλούμενον.

Athenians who had always loved a country life were with difficulty persuaded by Pericles to come to the city at the time of the first Peloponnesian invasion, and how few of them had houses or could settle with friends. Some brought with them the woodwork of their country houses, οἱ δὲ πολλοὶ τά τε ἐρῆμα τῆς πόλεως ᾤκησαν καὶ τὰ ἱερὰ καὶ τὰ ἡρῷα πάντα. Even the so-called "Pelasgian" ground at the foot of the citadel which was under a curse was occupied at this time. The space between the Long Walls was also built over in parts, as is evidenced by a passage in Justinian, stating that when the thirty tyrants suspected all the Athenians of treason they drove them all out and ordered them to live there (Just. v. 9, 12).

The love of space and open air caused those of the richer citizens who found it possible to make for themselves gardens. We learn for instance from Isaeus, περὶ τοῦ Δικαιογένους κλήρου, that Dicaeogenes, after purchasing the house of Theopompus, pulled it down, dug up the garden on which it stood and made a garden for his own house in the city. The existence of such gardens attached to the houses of the rich disproves Pliny's statement (*Nat. Hist.* xix.) that Epicurus, *otii magister*, was the first to institute such gardens at Athens.

With regard to the materials used for building houses, Xenophon's oft-quoted military metaphor mentions the chief (*Mem.* III. I. 7):—

πολὺ γὰρ διαφέρει στράτευμα τεταγμένον ἀτάκτου, ὥσπερ λίθοι τε καὶ πλίνθοι καὶ ξύλα καὶ κέραμος ἀτάκτως μὲν ἐρριμμένα οὐδὲν χρήσιμά ἐστιν, ἐπειδὰν δὲ ταχθῇ κάτω μὲν καὶ ἐπιπολῆς τὰ μήτε σηπόμενα μήτε τηκόμενα, οἵ τε λίθοι καὶ ὁ κέραμος ἐν μέσῳ δὲ αἵ τε πλίνθοι καὶ τὰ ξύλα, ὥσπερ ἐν οἰκοδομίᾳ, συντίθεται, τότε γίγνεται πολλοῦ ἄξιον κτῆμα, οἰκία.

For a well arranged army is very different from a disorderly one; as stones and bricks, wood and tiles if thrown together in confusion are of no use whatever; but when the stones and tiles, materials not likely to rot or decay, are placed at the bottom and the top and the bricks and wood are arranged in the middle, a house which is a valuable piece of property is formed.

In *Cyrop.* VI. 3. 25, he speaks of the necessity of strong foundations, as well as of a roof:—

ὥσπερ γὰρ οἰκίας οὔτε ἄνευ λιθολογήματος ὀχυροῦ οὔτε ἄνευ τῶν στέγειν ποιούντων οὐδὲν ὄφελος.

The general mode of construction then, as we find also in early times, was a strong foundation of stone with brick or woodwork above, surmounted by the roof composed of tiles.

The prices of houses varied according to their position and size. In Is. XI περὶ τοῦ ʼΑγνίου κήπου, we read of a house at Melite sold for half a talent or 30 minae (*circ.* £120) whereas one at Eleusis is worth only 5 minae (*circ.* £20). Again Dicaeogenes (Is. V) sells a house in the city to Philonicus for 50 minae. It is also clear from the first mentioned speech that houses could be rented for as little as 3 minae per annum.

On his travels Pausanias saw many celebrated houses, such as the house of Adrastus[1] at Argos, the ruins of the house of Amphitryo[2] at Thebes, the house of Menelaus[3] at Sparta, Pindar's[4] house over the Dirce near Thebes, etc., but he is content with simply mentioning them, and gives us no description at all of their plan and arrangement.

The façade was probably never imposing, for the house was approached by a narrow passage and all its beauty was within. The furniture[5] was of a very simple character and consisted of couches, chairs and folding stools and tables, with various rugs and cushions: the

[1] Frazer, *Paus.* II. 23. 2.   [2] *ibid.* IX. 11. 1.
[3] *ibid.* III. 14. 6.   [4] *ibid.* IX. 25. 3.
[5] Lange, *op. cit.* p. 41.

standard of comfort could not have been very high judged
from a modern standpoint but was no doubt adequate
to the needs of the times.

The beauty of the house lay in its simple open arrangement, and something of its brightness and charm may
be imagined to-day in such a town as Seville, where the
houses are mostly built on the courtyard plan and where
the gay little court with its waving palms may be seen
through the open grating of the doorway. The Athenian
houses, on the contrary, as seen from the street presented
a dead wall with a heavy solid door in the middle. The
charm was added to by the beauty of the perspective in
such of the larger houses as possessed a garden or added
a second court.

The host of vases and vessels of all kinds which remain
to us from this period give us a very adequate idea, by
the beauty and simplicity of their forms, of the taste and
artistic sense which displayed itself even in the routine
of ordinary existence.

Such heating as was required was obtained by means
of braziers of charcoal, and the open courtyard lighted
all the surrounding rooms[1]. That this light was perfectly
adequate is clear to-day from such a building as the
Alhambra, whose large rooms opening off the courtyards
are lighted in exactly the same manner, and lighted so
well by the strong southern light that all the myriad
colours of the decoration of tiles and walls may be perfectly
distinguished.

Many of the important towns of this period were
founded in an age when piracy was rife, and accordingly
we often find them a few miles away from the sea with
a high rock as citadel. In historic times this fortress
was often dismantled, as at Athens, and used for sacred

[1] Lange, *op. cit.* p. 51.

purposes, and the agora or market place, which was a prominent feature of every Greek town of importance, became the civic centre. The various sacred precincts provided open spaces throughout the city, and varied the monotony of the long rows of mean houses.

Before reviewing the monumental and literary evidence for the actual plan of the classic Greek house, we will take a glance at the accepted view of the normal type, such as we find in Becker's *Charicles*[1] (Fig. 35), a view supported by no extant remains and in utter conflict with the clear and concise account given by Vitruvius and noted below.

Becker considers that, whereas in Homeric times the women's apartments were usually situated in an upper storey, the normal position in classical times was on the ground floor. They consisted of a court (*B*) surrounded by rooms behind the first court, which he calls the andronitis (*A*), and entered through it. He accepts the Vitruvian account involving two courts, except in regard to their relative position. The gunaikonitis he thinks may have been mentioned first by Vitruvius because it was regarded as being of more importance, since it contained the household stores and the treasure chambers.

The view that the Greek classic house had two courts, the andronitis for the exclusive use of the men, and the gunaikonitis behind it and entered through it, for the exclusive use of the women, is also adopted by Bau-meister[2], Gardner and Jevons[3], and Smith, *Dictionary of Antiquities*[4], and is commonly received.

[1] Vol. II. p. 105, *Excurs zur dritten Scene. Das griechische Haus.*
[2] *Denkmäler des klassischen Altertums*, Haus, p. 627.
[3] *Manual of Greek Antiquities*, pp. 36–39.
[4] *Dict. of Antiq.*, Domus, pp. 424–6.

Such an account of the Hellenic house as is given in Daremberg and Saglio[1] is somewhat more modified.

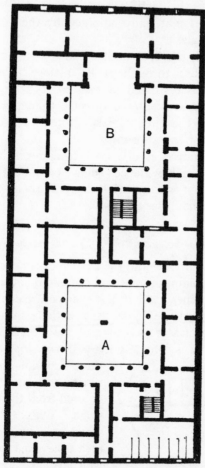

Fig. 35. Conventional fifth century house

There are two types recognised here, viz. (*a*) the peasant's hut, such as that described by Galen, with its courtyard

[1] *Dict. of Antiq.*, Domus, pp. 337 sqq.

and hearth; in the towns the dwellings of the poor were similar and consisted of a house with one court: (*b*) the dwellings of the rich, where the primitive house is developed and materially enlarged by the addition of a second peristyle.

In short, it has been understood that the normal type of Greek house throughout its history from Homeric times upwards consisted of two courts, the first called the andronitis and entered directly from the street, the second called the gunaikonitis entered by a door at the further end of the andronitis.

This account does not seem to agree in its principal features with such evidence as has been obtained through excavation, nor with many literary allusions which have reference to the house of this period.

Remains of houses of the fifth and fourth centuries.

In 1875 Burnouf[1] and the French excavators in Athens unearthed remains of some eight hundred houses belonging to historic times, which however, on account of their fragmentary nature, give very little assistance in the construction of a ground plan of the normal type.

A flat area is generally made in the slope of the rock,

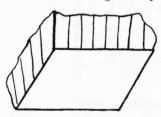 three side walls are continued up the rock and the house is entered from the front of the slope. Where two houses stand side by side a larger area is levelled, and a party wall is built between, either on the level or on a foundation of rock which has been left for the purpose in levelling.

[1] Burnouf, *Archives des missions scientifiques*, v. pp. 71 sqq.

There are remains of one or two doors and the stair-cases leading to them, but the walls have almost entirely disappeared. They nearly all appear to have been at right angles, even in the smallest dwellings (Fig. 36).

The remains show that some Athenian houses consisted of a single cell, others of two or three grouped together

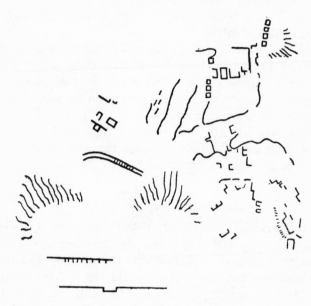

Fig. 36.   Houses near the Pnyx

in lines, or so that they seem to communicate with each other and form a whole.   Some of the houses with their many rooms, spaces for courts, cisterns and burial places, seem to have belonged to the rich.   Speaking generally we find the smallest and most irregular houses near the Acropolis, whilst the largest, which are of no considerable size, are in the plain.

One house on the Pnyx[1] is interesting from the fact that it contains four tombs, showing the survival of the ancient custom of burial within the house. The entrance is at the southern angle; several steps lead to a door which opens on to the first enclosure, on the left of which are two rooms containing tombs; on the right is a second enclosure used for the same purpose.

On the North Pnyx we also find a little room with a tomb in the middle[2].

On the Museum hill to the north-east are remains of another interesting house[3]: it has three doors with chambers corresponding. The north door gives on to a square room with a round doorway in its west corner leading into a circular room.

The remains are interesting but of little practical value in bringing before our eyes the average dwelling house of a Greek citizen of the fifth century.

Houses in Melite (Fig. 37).

The ancient suburb of Melite[4] lying in a valley surrounded by the Acropolis, the Areopagus and the Pnyx, has been very thoroughly excavated by Dörpfeld in his search for Enneacrunus. He has opened up the ancient road which runs north and south between the Acropolis and the Pnyx, and has laid bare remains which by their architecture and inscriptions are shown to belong to the sixth and fifth centuries B.C.

These include shrines and sacred precincts of gods or heroes, walls, boundary stones, cisterns, a lesche and remains of houses of the period.

---

[1] Burnouf, *op. cit.* p. 76.   [2] *ibid.*
[3] p. 77 and figs. 3 and 4, "prison of Socrates."
[4] *Antike Denkmäler*, II. T. 37 and 38. *Ath. Mitt.* XVII. 1892, pp. 439 sqq.

A house near the lesche[1] shown by its two inscriptions to have belonged to the fourth century B.C. and to have been heavily mortgaged, is of polygonal masonry, but too little remains to enable us to reconstruct its ground plan. Unfortunately this is also the case with most of the remains: there are fragments of walls of squared or polygonal masonry, and open paved spaces, but any attempt to glean from them the nature, plan and construction of the average fifth century house is practically futile.

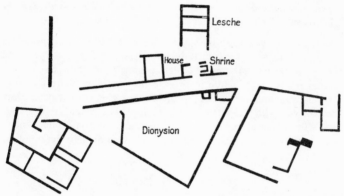

Fig. 37.   Houses in Melite

It was in Melite that Phocion lived in a house more ornate than the others, if Plutarch is to be trusted: the temperance and simplicity of his character are certainly against this (Plut. *Phoc.* 18):

ἡ δὲ οἰκία τοῦ Φωκίωνος ἔτι νῦν ἐν Μελίτῃ δείκνυται χαλκαῖς λεπίσι κεκοσμημένη, τὰ δὲ ἄλλα λιτὴ καὶ ἀφελής.

And the house of Phocion is shown yet at this day in Melite adorned with brass plates, but in other respects plain and simple.

Themistocles also had a house here (Plut. *Them.* 22), and the ruined house of Epicurus, which he left by will

---

[1] *Ath. Mitt.* XIX, p. 503.

to his followers (Diog. Laert. x. 10), was to be seen here in Cicero's days (*Ep. ad fam.* XIII. 13).

The houses in general, like Burnouf's houses, would seem to show that the dwellings of Athenians of historic times were very modest, and to add confirmation to the words of Demosthenes (*Ol.* III. 25):—

δημοσίᾳ μὲν τοίνυν οἰκοδομήματα καὶ κάλλη τοιαῦτα καὶ τοσαῦτα κατε-
σκεύασαν ἡμῖν ἱερῶν καὶ τῶν ἐν τούτοις ἀναθημάτων ὥστε μηδενὶ τῶν
ἐπιγιγνομένων ὑπερβολὴν λελεῖφθαι. ἰδίᾳ δ᾽ οὕτω σώφρονες ἦσαν καὶ σφόδρα
ἐν τῷ τῆς πολιτείας ἤθει μένοντες ὥστε τὴν Ἀριστείδου καὶ τὴν Μιλτιάδου
καὶ τῶν τότε λαμπρῶν οἰκίαν εἴ τις ἄρα οἶδεν ὑμῶν ὁποία ποτ᾽ ἐστὶν, ὁρᾷ τῆς
τοῦ γείτονος οὐδὲν σεμνοτέραν οὖσαν.

In public then they completed for us edifices and ornaments of such beauty and magnitude in temples and the dedications set up in them, that none of their posterity has now the means of surpassing them, while in private they were so modest and so thoroughly constant to the principles of the constitution that those of you who know the kind of house that Aristeides inhabited and Miltiades and the other illustrious men of that time, realise that it was no more elaborate than the houses of their neighbours.

Houses in the Peiraeus.

In digging the foundations for a new theatre in Peiraeus[1] in 1883-4 many ancient walls were found, which were thought from inscriptions to be a temple of Dionysus, but which proved to be the remains of a dwelling house of some kind (Fig. 38).

The remains consist of two parts, a large rectangle 40 m. × 23 m. with many rooms, and a court (*A*) surrounded by halls with columns.

The court is at a considerably lower level than the rectangle with rooms, which are all on one level, and the two parts are connected by a staircase. The building

[1] *Ath. Mitt.* IX, pp. 279 sqq.

was entered from the south-east through a vestibule (*B*) containing a rectangular altar; before this vestibule stood two columns between antae; and a doorway, the position of which is not quite determined, led from it into the south hall (*C*). On the west and north of the small court (*D*) were two other halls (*E* and *F*), and the roof was probably carried by columns which surrounded the court.

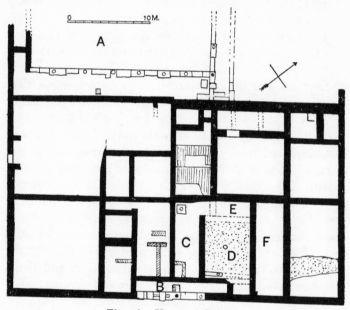

Fig. 38. House at Peiraeus

At the west end remains of columns seem to show that there was another peristyle (*A*) here of great size: the breadth was 21·15 m. without the surrounding halls, the length unknown.

The inscriptions show that in the neighbourhood of the building stood a temple of Dionysus, Dörpfeld[1]

[1] *Ath. Mitt.* IX, p. 286.

thinks probably in the middle of the great court. The
surrounding rooms and open court may have been the
priests' dwelling.

Palace at Palatitza.

The Macedonian building at Palatitza[1], described in
Daremberg and Saglio as a Hellenic palace of the fifth
century, must be noticed before we pass on to the literary
evidence for the Greek house of classic period.

On a raised plateau between the villages of Palatitza
and Krontlaes is a deserted Byzantine chapel: within its
walls and on the soil surrounding it M. Heuzey discovered[2]
in 1855 remains of Greek architecture, which prove that
there was a large building here (Fig. 39), rectangular
in form (78 m. wide by 110 m. long), divided into two
parts by a passage (*A*) 10 m. wide running right through
the courtyard from east to west, and cutting the palace
in two. Rooms of different sizes were on the north and
south. The passage was divided into three vestibules
(*B, C, D*) at its entrance, the first and second being each
7 m. long: the third and largest is entered by three
doors formed by two piers with Ionic engaged columns
and mouldings. The lines of division of the passage are
continued to divide the rooms on either side, and there
seems to have been a covered portico round the courtyard.

Fragments of the architecture had been used as
materials for building the Byzantine chapel and were
found on the soil or in the neighbouring village. The
remains though scanty showed that the following orders
were employed in the original building:—Doric order
with columns, little Ionic order with columns, large

[1] Daremberg and Saglio, *Dict. of Antiq.*, Domus, p. 346. *Mission de Macédoine*, 1875, Heuzey et Daumet.

[2] Heuzey et Daumet, *Mission Archéologique de Macédoine*, p. 184 ff. pl. 7–14.

Ionic order with columns, large order of piers with engaged
Ionic columns and little order of piers with engaged
Ionic columns.   One fragment of a Corinthian capital
was also found.

In the absence of epigraphical and historical evidence,

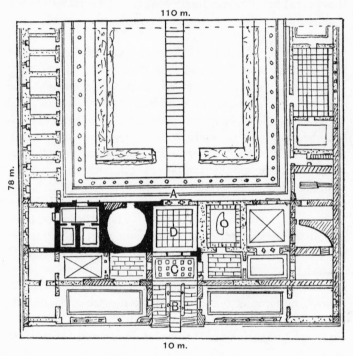

Fig. 39.   Palace at Palatitza

the date of this building must be determined with reference
to its plan and architectural details.

Heuzey discusses the various hypotheses, that it was
a propylaeum to a sacred precinct, or a palace devoted
to public use or inhabited by a monarch, like the palace
at Pella mentioned by Livy, and finally concludes that

it was what he designates a royal prytaneum, *i.e.* a prytaneum made use of by a king.   He regards it as dating
from the second half of the fifth century[1].

If this view were correct the building would be not
only interesting but quite unique, since the remains of
this period are so exceedingly scanty.   Unfortunately the
architectural evidence seems to indicate a much later
date.

The Doric column is slenderer than is usual in the
fifth century and the profile of the capital, if one may
judge from the drawings given, is almost a straight line
and lacks the graceful curve of fifth century work.

The large Ionic order has piers with Ionic half columns
attached on two opposite sides : these are apparently
not found in fifth century buildings.   Engaged columns
occur as early as the temple at Phigalea and we are
familiar with them in the Erechtheum, though it is not
certain whether they formed part of the original design
or were a later Roman addition.   These however have
a wall as background.   We find somewhat of a parallel
in the theatre, where the supports for the proscenium
take the form of square or oblong pillars with an engaged
column on one face.   This form is found at Epidaurus[2],
Assos[3] and Oropus[4] : and even if the theatre at Epidaurus
does not belong to the second century it is certainly not
earlier than the fourth[5] : those at Delos and Oropus are
later.

With regard to the details of the Ionic capital, the lines
running across from volute to volute are quite straight
at the top and bottom and the volutes have no cushion ;
the side and front are the same, just as at Bassae.

---

[1] Heuzey et Daumet, *op. cit.* p. 225.

[2] Dörpfeld und Reisch, *Das griechische Theater*, T. vi.

[3] *ibid.* p. 149.   [4] *ibid.* T. vi.   [5] *ibid.* pp. 129–31.

It therefore seems probable that this palace, like the palace at Nippur[1], is not fifth century work at all, but belongs to the succeeding Hellenistic period.

Literary evidence for Greek house of fifth century.

The contemporary evidence therefore for the Greek house of the fifth and fourth centuries is almost entirely literary, and seems for the most part to have reference to the houses of the middle or upper class.

The house is approached by a gateway (πρόθυρον): here the guests stand and have a discussion at the house of Hippias, before knocking at the door and being admitted by the porter (Plato, *Protag.* 314 c sqq.):

ἐπειδὴ δὲ ἐν τῷ προθύρῳ ἐγενόμεθα, ἐπιστάντες περί τινος λόγου διελεγόμεθα...δοκεῖ οὖν μοι ὁ θυρωρός, εὐνοῦχός τις, κατήκουεν ἡμῶν...... ἐπειδὴ......ἐκρούσαμεν τὴν θύραν, ἀνοίξας......ἔφη.

And when we were in the porch, we stood there and discussed a certain question.......Now the doorkeeper, a certain eunuch, heard us I think......when we had knocked at the door......he opened it and said——.

The door was called αὐλεία θύρα, as many passages bear witness, of which one or two may be quoted:

Plat. *Symp.* 212 c

ἐξαίφνης τὴν αὔλιον θύραν κρουμένην πολὺν ψόγον παρασχεῖν ὡς κω-μαστῶν.

Suddenly there was a knocking at the door leading into the court which caused a great din as though of revellers.

Pind. *Nem.* I. 19:

ἔσταν δ' ἐπ' αὐλείαις θύραις
ἀνδρὸς φιλοξείνου.

And they stood at the doors leading into the court of a hospitable man.

[1] *vide* p. 239.

Menand. fragm.

> τοὺς τῆς γαμετῆς ὅρους ὑπερβαίνεις, γύναι,
> τὴν αὐλίαν· πέρας γὰρ αὔλιος θύρα
> ἐλευθέρᾳ γυναικὶ νενόμιστ᾽ οἰκίας.

Thou art going beyond the bounds assigned to a married woman, lady: for the door of the house that leads into the court is the customary limit beyond which a free woman may not go.

This door opened into the αὐλή or courtyard as in the house of Socrates (Plato, *Protag.* 311 A):

> δεῦρο ἐξαναστῶμεν (*i.e.* from the sleeping-chamber) εἰς τὴν αὐλὴν καὶ περιιόντες αὐτοῦ διατρίψωμεν.

Let us arise and go into the courtyard and spend our time there in walking round.

The courtyard was apparently surrounded or flanked by a colonnade and by sleeping chambers and other rooms of various kinds. The guests at the house of Hippias found Protagoras walking round the portico and Hippias sitting there (Plato, *Protag.* 314):

> ἐπειδὴ δὲ εἰσήλθομεν, κατελάβομεν Πρωταγόραν ἐν τῷ προστῴῳ περι-
> πατοῦντα......τὸν δὲ μετ᾽ εἰσενόησα......Ἱππίαν καθήμενον ἐν τῷ κατ᾽ ἀντικρὺ
> προστῴῳ......καὶ μὲν δὴ καὶ Τάνταλόν γε εἰσεῖδον.

And when we had gone in we found Protagoras walking about in the portico.......And afterwards I noticed Hippias sitting in the portico opposite......and also I saw Tantalus.

The term περίστυλον or peristyle, as applied to this colonnade, is not a contemporary one but is first found in Diodorus (*flor.* B.C. 8).

In the courtyard there stood an altar as we gather from Plat. *Rep.* 328 C, τεθυκὼς ἐτύγχανεν ἐν τῇ αὐλῇ, 'he happened to have performed the sacrifice in the courtyard.'

Among the various chambers surrounding the courtyard must be especially noticed the ἀνδρῶν and παστάς.

The ἀνδρῶν was clearly in its origin a room for the entertainment of male guests, cf. Aesch. *Cho.* 712 ἄγ᾽ αὐτὸν εἰς ἀνδρῶνας εὐξένους δόμων, where Clytemnestra commands a slave to lead in Orestes.

It was frequently employed as a dining room, cf. Ar. *Eccl.* 676:

B. τὸ δὲ δεῖπνον ποῦ παραθήσεις;

Π. τὰ δικαστήρια καὶ τὰς στοὰς ἀνδρῶνας πάντα ποιήσω·

"And where will you serve dinner?"
"I shall make the law courts and the arcades all dining rooms."

Again at the arrival of Philippos Xen. *Sympos.* I. 13 ὁ δὲ στὰς ἐπὶ τῷ ἀνδρῶνι, ἔνθα τὸ δεῖπνον ἦν, 'and he stood in the andron where the meal was spread.'

παστάς. The exact nature of this part of the house is exceedingly difficult to ascertain, since the word occurs in but few passages and without any clear explanation. The word is used by Herodotus (II. 169) in his description of the tomb of Amasis. It was further, he says, from the μέγαρον than the other tombs, but was in the courtyard (αὐλή) of the temple and consisted of a great stone pastas fitted with columns in imitation of palm trees and with other ornamentation: and within the pastas were doors (θυρώματα) and within the doors the tomb.

This description seems to indicate a separate building in the temenos, consisting of a chamber with doors and a portico (παστάς), corresponding to the Homeric αἴθουσα.

In another passage (II. 148) describing the labyrinth near Lake Moeris, with its twelve courtyards all with colonnades, and its three thousand chambers, he speaks of the wonderful impression produced by the various winding passages, as one passes from the courtyard into the houses, and from the houses into the παστάδες, to other houses from the παστάδες and to other courtyards

from the houses.   The παστάδες here seem to be colonnades or passages with pillars connecting different sets
of rooms.   The word also occurs in an inscription of the
fourth century B.C. (*C. I.* 1688, 22) recording a decree of
the Amphictyones concerning Delphic administration.
The words are τὰς δὲ παστάδας κοινὰς εἶμεν πάντεσσι,
but there is nothing in the context to aid in the solution
of the meaning.   Possibly it was used here of colonnades,
as in the passage of Herodotus referred to above.

In the following passage from Xenophon the word
παστάς is generally interpreted, according to the use of
Vitruvius, as the recess opposite the front door, an
interpretation which is somewhat at variance with its
apparent meaning in other contemporary passages.   It
seems possible that here also it may bear the meaning
it bears in Herodotus, viz. the portico in front of the
house equivalent to the Homeric aithousa.

The passage is as follows (Xen. *Mem.* III. 8):—

ἐν ταῖς πρὸς μεσημβρίαν βλεπούσαις οἰκίαις τοῦ μὲν χειμῶνος ὁ ἥλιος εἰς
τὰς παστάδας ὑπολάμπει, τοῦ δὲ θέρους ὑπὲρ ἡμῶν αὐτῶν καὶ τῶν στεγῶν
πορευόμενος σκιὰν παρέχει.

In houses with a southern aspect in winter the sun shines
into the παστάς, but in summer, going over our heads and the
roof it causes a shadow.

In another passage (Eur. *Or.* 1371) it seems to bear the
meaning of porch.   A Trojan slave comes from the house
and describes the murder of Helen.   He speaks thus:—

πέφευγα
κεδρωτὰ παστάδων ὑπὲρ τέρεμνα
Δωρικάς τε τριγλύφους.

I escaped over the chambers of the porch inlaid with cedar
wood and over the Doric triglyphs.

Later writers use παστάς as equivalent to θάλαμος
the bridal chamber.   It is thus used of the bed-chamber

of Amphitryon and Alcmena in Theoc. XXIV. 46—
ἀμφιλαφὴς δ᾽ ἄρα παστὰς ἐνεπλήσθη πάλιν ὄρφνας, 'and
the large chamber was filled with darkness.'

This is the probable use, according to Jebb in the
Antigone[1], where the rocky chamber in which Antigone
was confined is spoken of as ἀκτέριστος παστάς, the
bridal chamber without funeral rites (*Antig.* 1207). It
seems clear, from the earlier passages quoted, that the
word παστάς had some connection with columns or
pillars, and it is possible that the later use of the word
of the marriage chamber may be derived from the earlier
with reference to some arrangement of pillars, perhaps
round the bed in the thalamos[2].

Vitruvius (VI. 10) in describing the Greek house refers
to a recess with antae, which was common on the north
side facing the front door and which was called προστάς
or παστάς (v.l. παραστάς).

In ea parte, quae spectat ad meridiem, duas antas inter se
spatio amplo distantes, in quibus trabes invehuntur, et quantum
inter antas distat, ex eo tertia dempta spatium datur introrsus.
Hic locus apud nonnullos προστάς, apud alios παστάς nominatur.

On that side which faces the south are two projecting walls
with an ample space between them, on which beams are placed,
and the depth of the recess is two-thirds of the space between
the two projecting walls. Some call this space προστάς, and
others παραστάς or παστάς.

The Greek houses of the second century B.C. unearthed
in Delos[3] possess such a recess, but that the recess existed
and was called παστάς in classical times there is no
adequate evidence to prove. Vitruvius is the first writer
to explain it thus.

Pollux (*flor.* A.D. 186) explains:—παστάδας δὲ ὁ Ξενο-
φῶν ἃς οἱ νῦν ἐξέδρας, 'what we now call the exedra

---

[1] Jebb, *Antigone*, p. 264, note on l. 1207.
[2] So Jebb, *op. cit* p. 265.   [3] *vide* p. 248.

Xenophon called the παστάς.' The term exedra had lost in Roman times its earlier meaning of arcade and indicated a sitting room or saloon. Suidas (*flor.* 1100 A.D.) is apparently nearer the original use: πρόδομος· ἡ τοῦ οἴκου παστάς.

Aristotle's account of the various things to be considered in building a house is interesting, if it does not furnish us with many details. In his *Economics* (I. 6, 7) he says·—

οἰκίαν δὲ πρός τε τὰ κτήματα ἀποβλέποντα κατασκευαστέον καὶ πρὸς ὑγίειαν καὶ πρὸς εὐημερίαν αὐτῶν. λέγω δὲ κτήματα μὲν, οἷον καρποῖς καὶ ἐσθῆτι ποῖα συμφέρει καὶ τῶν καρπῶν ποῖα ξηροῖς καὶ ποῖα ὑγροῖς καὶ τῶν ἄλλων κτημάτων ποῖα ἐμψύχοις καὶ ἀψύχοις καὶ δούλοις καὶ ἐλευθέροις καὶ γυναιξὶ καὶ ἀνδράσι καὶ ξένοις καὶ ἀστοῖς. καὶ πρὸς εὐημερίαν δὲ καὶ πρὸς ὑγίειαν δεῖ εἶναι εὔπνουν μὲν τοῦ θέρους εὐήλιον δὲ τοῦ χειμῶνος. εἴη δ' ἂν ἡ τοιαύτη κατάβορρος οὖσα καὶ μὴ ἰσοπλατής.

In building a house consideration must be had for possessions, health and happiness. For possessions that there is fitting store room for fruits dry and moist and clothes, and proper accommodation for other possessions animate and inanimate, for slaves and free men and women and men and guests and citizens. And with regard to health and happiness, the house should be airy in summer and sunny in winter. Such a house would have a south aspect and not be equal in breadth.

The south aspect was always adopted if possible, with a view to obtaining the maximum of sun in winter and shade in summer. Examples are numerous in the Hellenistic houses in Delos and at Priene.

The expression μὴ ἰσοπλατής may be used of a house which is wider at one end than at the other, as for example the house near the sacred lake in Delos (*infra*), though it is not clear how such a plan would promote health and well being. Perhaps it may be referred to such plans as we frequently find in Hellenistic houses, where the court is not situated in the middle but rather to the south of the house, with the result that the surrounding rooms are not all of the same breadth.

ἀνδρωνῖτις and γυναικωνῖτις. Let us now consider the question of the men's and women's quarters and the use of the terms ἀνδρωνῖτις and γυναικωνῖτις, which Professor Ernest Gardner (*J.H.S.* xxi. ii)[1] regards as being mainly responsible for the invention of the two-court theory of the Greek house.

Ischomachus, in conversation with Socrates (Xen. *Oec.* ix. 4) describes how he showed his wife the plan and construction of their house:

καὶ διαιτητήρια δὲ τοῖς ἄνθρωποις ἐπεδείκνυον αὐτῇ κεκαλλωπισμένα τοῦ μὲν θέρους ψυχεινὰ, τοῦ δὲ χειμῶνος ἀλεεινά· καὶ σύμπασαν τὴν οἰκίαν ἐπέδειξα αὐτῇ ὅτι πρὸς μεσημβρίαν ἀναπέπταται......ἔδειξα δὲ καὶ τὴν γυναικω-νῖτιν αὐτῇ, θύρᾳ βαλανωτῇ ὡρισμένην ἀπὸ τῆς ἀνδρωνίτιδος, ἵνα μήτε ἐκφέρηται ἔνδοθεν ὅτι μὴ δεῖ.

And I began to show her the dwelling rooms of the men which were beautifully decorated, warm ones for winter and cool for summer. And I pointed out to her that the whole house looked south.......And I showed her the women's apartments cut off by a door with a bolt from the men's apartments, so that nothing could be carried out which ought not to be.

Two different and distinct sets of apartments are mentioned here, but there is nothing to point to the existence of two courts. A strong door completely shut off the part of the house set apart for the women from that set apart for the men.

The house that was plundered by Energus and Mnesibulus is clearly described thus (Dem. *Energ.* 53):—

καταβαλόντες τὴν θύραν τὴν εἰς τὸν κῆπον φέρουσαν......εἰσελθόντες ἐπὶ τὴν γυναῖκα μου καὶ τὰ παιδία ἐξεφορήσαντο ὅσα ἔτι ὑπόλοιπά μοι ἦν σκεύη ἐν τῇ οἰκίᾳ......πρὸς δὲ τούτοις......ἔτυχεν ἡ γυνή μου μετὰ τῶν παιδίων ἀριστῶσα ἐν τῇ αὐλῇ......ἀριστώντων δὲ ἐν τῇ αὐλῇ, ὡς ἐπεισπηδῶσιν

[1] pp. 299–300.

οὗτοι......αἱ μὲν ἄλλαι θεράπαιναι (ἐν τῷ πύργῳ γὰρ ἦσαν, οὗπερ διαιτῶνται) ὡς ἤκουσαν κραυγῆς, κλείουσι τὸν πύργον, καὶ ἐνταῦθα μὲν οὐκ εἰσῆλθον.

They broke down the door leading into the garden......they came upon my wife and children and carried out all the furniture that I still had left in the house......moreover my wife happened to be having breakfast with the children in the court.......And as they were breakfasting in the court when these men came in......the maids, who happened to be in the tower where they live, when they heard the noise shut the tower, and they did not enter there.

This passage shows very clearly that in this house there was one court with two doors, one leading into the street and the other into the garden. The women used this court freely, but they also had apartments exclusively for their own use (πύργος), which could be shut off entirely from the main court.

The fact of the free use made by the women of the main court is also borne out by the passage of Plutarch in which he states that it is not considered correct to enter another man's house without knocking at the door; 'in our time,' he says, 'there are porters but in olden days knockers were used so that a stranger might not come upon the mistress of the house or the daughter or a slave being chastised or maid servants screaming' (Plut. *de curios.* 516).

From this passage it is also clear that the front door opened directly on to the courtyard, where the women were often to be found.

The women's quarters were often situated in an upper storey, as we learn from such a passage as the following (Eur. *Phoen.* 89). The paidagogos enters, after Jocasta's prologue, and addresses Antigone thus:—

> ἐπεί σε μήτηρ παρθενῶνας ἐκλιπεῖν
> μεθῆκε μελάθρων ἐς διῆρες ἔσχατον
>
> .   .   .   .
>
> κέδρου παλαιὰν κλίμακ᾽ ἐκπέρα ποδί.

When thy mother has given thee leave to quit the maidens'
apartments and go to the uppermost part of the house, do thou
climb up the ancient staircase of cedar wood.

Several other passages might be cited, *e.g.* Ar. *Eccl.*
693, ἑτέρα φήσει τις ἄνωθ᾽ ἐξ ὑπερῴου, 'another will call to
you from above from the upper storey,' and again Ar.
Eccl. 961, καὶ σύ μοι καταδραμοῦσα τὴν θύραν ἄνοιξον 'and
you please run down and open the door.'

A similar situation for the gunaikonitis is found in
the house described in Lys. *de caede Erastos* (1. 9). The
speaker says:—

οἰκίδιον ἐστί μοι διπλοῦν, ἴσα ἔχον τὰ ἄνω τοῖς κάτω, κατὰ τὴν γυναικω-
νῖτιν καὶ κατὰ τὴν ἀνδρωνῖτιν· ἐπειδὴ δὲ τὸ παιδίον ἐγένετο ἡμῖν, ἡ μήτηρ
αὐτὸ ἐθήλαζεν· ἵνα δὲ μή, ὁπότε λοῦσθαι δέοι, κινδυνεύῃ κατὰ τῆς κλίμακος
καταβαίνουσα, ἐγὼ μὲν ἄνω διῃτώμην, αἱ δὲ γυναῖκες κάτω· καὶ οὕτως ἤδη
συνειθισμένον ἦν ὥστε πολλάκις ἡ γυνὴ ἀπῄει κάτω καθευδήσουσα ὡς τὸ
παιδίον.

I have a little house of two storeys the upper and lower of
equal size, with the women's apartments upstairs and the men's
downstairs.   And when our child was born his mother nursed
it, and in order that she might not run the risk of falling downstairs every time she went to wash, I lived upstairs and the
women downstairs.   And this had come to be our custom that
my wife often went downstairs to sleep with the child.

In this house there was evidently no second court, but
the women used the main court and retired to their own
apartments when they wished.

The speaker goes on to tell of the events of one particular evening:—

ἀναστᾶσα καὶ ἀπιοῦσα προστίθησι τὴν θύραν, προσποιουμένη παίζειν, καὶ
τὴν κλεῖν ἐφέλκεται……ἐπειδὴ δὲ ἦν πρὸς ἡμέραν ἧκεν ἐκείνη καὶ τὴν θύραν
ἀνέῳξεν.   ἐρομένου δ᾽ ἐμοῦ τὶ αἱ θύραι νύκτωρ ψοφοῖεν, ἔφασκε τὸν λύχνον
ἀποσβεσθῆναι τὸν παρὰ τῷ παιδίῳ, εἶτα ἐκ τῶν γειτόνων ἐνάψασθαι……καὶ
μεστὸς ἦν ὑποψίας ἐνθυμούμενος μὲν ὡς ἀπεκλείσθην ἐν τῷ δωματίῳ, ἀνα-
μιμνησκόμενος δὲ ὅτι ἐν ἐκείνῃ τῇ νυκτὶ ἐψόφει ἡ μέταυλος θύρα καὶ ἡ αὐλεῖος.

And when she had got up and gone away she put to the door pretending that she was in joke and drew the bolt.......And when it was nearly daybreak she came back and opened the door. And when I asked her why the doors had creaked in the night she said that the light near the baby had gone out and that she had re-lighted it from a neighbour's.......And I was full of suspicion because I had been shut in that night and because on that night I remembered that the θύρα μέταυλος and the θύρα αὐλεῖος had creaked.

The θύρα αὐλεῖος as we have seen is the door between the courtyard and the street: there remains the question of the θύρα μέταυλος, which some scholiasts and late grammarians, misled by false etymology, have regarded as the door between the two courtyards (μεσ—αυλος), and which has therefore lent support to the two-court theory.

The passage quoted above, which is the sole contemporary evidence we possess on this point, except a passage in Eur. *Alc.* 549[1] which does not help, would seem to contradict this view of the μέταυλος θύρα, since the wife, who was occupying the andronitis, says that she went to a neighbour's for a light. Consequently it was as she passed from the andronitis to the street that the two doors creaked. The θύρα μέταυλος then must have been situated between some part of the andronitis and the θύρα αὐλεῖος. Professor Ernest Gardner, in the article referred to above, suggests that the meaning of μέταυλος is 'behind the aule'[2] on the analogy of many other compounds with μετά, and that the door was situated at the back of the courtyard between the apartments occupied by the wife and the court.

If this is the case, it would seem better not to identify the θύρα μέταυλος with the θύρα βαλανωτή which, on the

[1]   ἐν δὲ κλείσατε
                        θύρας μεσαύλους.
[2] *J.H.S.* XXI. ii. p. 300.

evidence of other passages, cut off the gunaikonitis from
the apartments of the men.

To sum up, from these and other passages we deduce
that certain rooms were set apart for the exclusive use of
the women and female slaves, and that these were denoted
by the name γυναικωνῖτις as distinguished from the

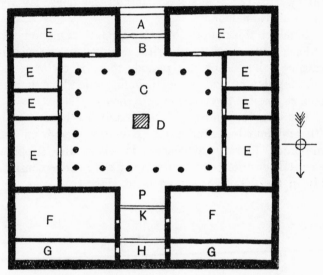

Fig. 40.   Imaginary house of the fifth century B.C.

A   πρόθυρον.   F   Andronitis.
B   ἡ αὐλεῖος θύρα.   G   Gunaikonitis.
C   αὐλή.   H   ἡ βαλανωτὴ θύρα.
D   Altar.   K   ἡ μέταυλος θύρα.
E   Sleeping rooms, store rooms, etc.   P   ? Pastas.

apartments of the men called ἀνδρωνῖτις. The γυναικωνῖτις was entirely cut off from the ἀνδρωνῖτις by a
strong door (θύρα βαλανωτή). Other evidence further
shows that the γυναικωνῖτις was frequently situated in
an upper storey called πύργος, ὑπερῷον, διήρες, and was
approached by a steep staircase.

At the same time it must be recognised that there are a few passages where the usage does not seem to be quite consistent, as for example Lys. III. 7, ἐκκόψας τὰς θύρας εἰσῆλθεν εἰς τὴν γυναικωνῖτιν, 'he knocked at the door and entered the gunaikonitis,' where the term seems to be applied to the court, as it is later by Vitruvius[1]. But perhaps the women's quarters in this house lay very near the front door.

Finally if it is not possible, through lack of monumental evidence, to re-construct with exactitude the normal scheme of houses of this period, there is certainly not sufficient literary evidence forthcoming to lend the slightest support possible to the two-court theory.

The plan appended of the imaginary house of the fifth and fourth centuries B.C. is constructed from contemporary literary evidence. It gives the supposed general disposition; the houses must have varied considerably in the details of arrangement (Fig. 40).

[1] *vide* p. 263.

CHAPTER XVI

GREEK HOUSE OF THIRD AND SECOND CENTURIES, POMPEIAN HOUSES, VITRUVIAN ACCOUNT, SUMMARY

THOUGH there is no literary evidence to aid us in the reconstruction of the Greek house of the third and second centuries, the excavations at Delos and Priene[1] give a very adequate knowledge of the type of building which prevailed.

The only palace of the period as yet unearthed on Greek soil is that at Palatitza described above[2]. Like the houses of the period it has the long vestibule and the courtyard surrounded with columns; in common with earlier Minoan palaces it has the large courtyard with a number of rooms around but in detail the resemblance is not very close.

It is otherwise with the palace at Nippur discovered in 1889 and published by Dr Peters[3] (Fig. 41). Though probably belonging to this same epoch it does show certain definite resemblances to Mycenean forms. These caused Mr Clarence Fisher, writing in the *American Journal of Archaeology*, 1904[4], to describe the building as Mycenean, and to compare it in detail with the palace at Tiryns. His theory has, however, been conclusively

---

[1] *vide* pp. 248 and 241.   [2] *vide* p. 224.
[3] *A.J.A.* x. 1895, pp. 439 sqq.   [4] pp. 403 sqq.

disproved by Dr Marquand (*A.J.A.* 1905)[1].   We certainly
have in this palace the megaron (*A*) and prodomos (*B*)
set behind a courtyard (*C*) surrounded with columns,
but this was an arrangement, as we now know from the
Priene excavations, which persisted right through the

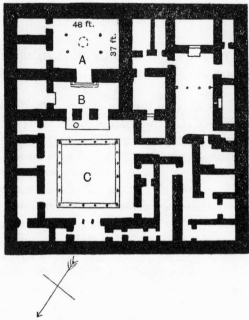

Fig. 41.   Palace at Nippur

history of Greek domestic architecture and was common
in Hellenistic times.

The compound piers at the angles of the peristyle
and the elliptical columns of the πρόθυρον betray the
late origin of the palace, and may be compared with

---

[1] pp. 7 sqq.   Hilprecht, *Explorations in Bible Lands*, 1903, p. 337,
dates it *circ.* 250 B.C.

the similar piers of the Hellenistic agora at Priene[1]. The columns again are cylindrical and tapering towards the top, whilst the Mycenean shaft tapered from the top downwards uniformly. The resemblances of plan, however, serve to show that certain traditions persisted, and that Hellenistic work was a direct descendant of that of prehistoric times. This continuity is still clearer in the case of the houses.

Houses at Priene[2].

Many groups of houses of peculiar interest have been brought to light during the recent excavations at Priene, which have laid bare the entire western part of the town. The town appears to have grown up soon after the dedication of the temple to Athena by Alexander, and thus dates from the third century B.C. The houses certainly belong to the same epoch, since no layers have been found beneath them, and by the character of their walls, their decoration, etc., they are thought to date from about the second century B.C., *i.e.* they are roughly contemporary with the Hellenistic houses of Delos.

The town must have presented a similar appearance to Pompeii, the streets being long and straight and the houses without windows, lighted entirely from within, with a very unobtrusive entrance very often opening on a side street.

The normal plan which occurs in almost all the Priene houses, even in those of the poorer class, is as follows. The house is approached by a long narrow passage, presumably covered, with the door set back a little from the street, so as to leave a vestibule or πρόθυρον. This passage gives access to a square or rectangular courtyard,

---

[1] Wiegand und Schrader, *Priene*, Blatt II.
[2] Wiegand und Schrader, *op. cit.* pass.

open to the air. On the north side of the court is the largest and most important room of the house, approached through a vestibule with two columns standing between antae. On the other sides of the courtyard are store rooms and sleeping chambers, and sometimes a recess on the south side.

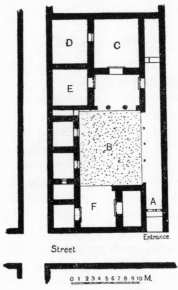

Fig. 42. House at Priene.

Some of the principal houses may be noted in detail. The house in the Theatre street (Fig. 42)[1], near the temple of Athena, is quite typical. A narrow passage (*A*) with a vestibule and front door leads to the open court (*B*), which is surrounded on three sides by rooms, while on the fourth the entrance corridor is continued and three columns alongside of the court support a

—————
[1] Wiegand und Schrader, *op. cit.* p. 285.

lean-to roof. On the north side of the court is a large
room (*C*), 7·1 m. long by 7 m. wide, entered by a
vestibule 5·3 m. deep with two columns standing between
antae. Between this room and the side street are two
large rooms (*D* and *E*), and five smaller ones along
the west side. On the south side of the court is a deep
recess (*F*) with a sitting room opening out on its east

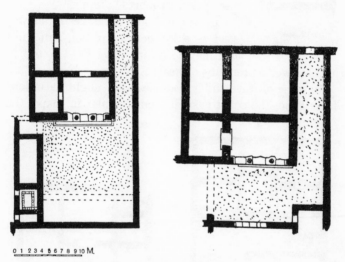

0 1 2 3 4 5 6 7 8 9 10 M.

Fig. 43. Houses at Priene.

side. The plans of two other important houses are also
given (Fig. 43). They exhibit the same characteristics,
viz. the vestibule with columns leading into the principal
room behind a square courtyard[1].

The smaller houses show the same essential features,
the long passage, the court, and the room with vestibule
and columns.

[1] Wiegand und Schrader, *op. cit.* pp. 287–8.

16—2

One quite small house (Fig. 44)[1] is of exceptional interest since it not only exhibits the features enumerated,

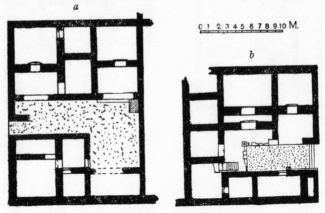

but remains of a hearth have been found in the room behind the vestibule. Hearths have also been found in this position in two other houses on the site.

Several altars have been found near the entrances of houses, one bearing an inscription to Zeus Olympios.

In some houses the vestibule was used as a kitchen, as pithoi, handmills and marble basins have been found in them, as well as remains of hearths.

Fig. 44.
House at Priene.

In some of the smaller houses we find slight variations of the type, the court is small and irregular in shape, the

Fig. 45. Houses at Priene.

vestibule is frequently narrower than the room behind it, and the rooms surrounding the courtyard are fewer and smaller, but the essential features remain.

Two houses (Fig. 45)[2] are peculiar in plan in that

---

[1] Wiegand und Schrader, *op. cit.* p. 288.　　[2] *ibid.* p. 295.

they contain respectively two rooms with vestibules, in
one case separated by other rooms (Fig. 45 *a*), in the other
side by side (Fig. 45 *b*).   In neither case do they communicate with each other, but both open on to the
courtyard, so that it has been thought that they were set
apart for men and women respectively, and represented
the andronitis and gunaikonitis[1].

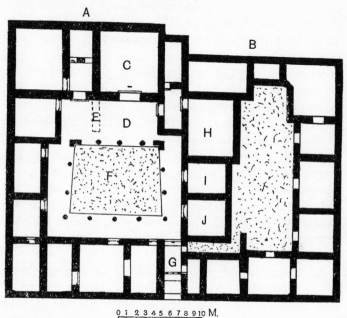

Fig. 46.   House at Priene.

Another large house (Fig. 46)[2] shows further variation and throws great light on the description of the
Greek house given us by Vitruvius and noticed below.
The house (*A*) has clearly been altered and enlarged,
and the neighbouring house (*B*) has been put into

[1] But see p. 233.   [2] Wiegand und Schrader, *op. cit.* p. 295.

communication with it and used as an annex. The large room (C) has been left untouched, but the vestibule leading to it (D) has now three columns of which the most westerly by its diminished diameter is seen to be an addition. The west wall (E), moreover, of the vestibule has been pulled down, and the court (F) has been changed into a peristyle by the addition of columns. The rooms on the west side of the house have also been enlarged. The next house (B), which was included in the scheme of enlargement, is entered from the same passage-way as the first (G), and three of its rooms (H, I, J) could be entered after the alteration by doorways from the courtyard of the first house. The remains show that this annex was very elaborately decorated, and it seems probable that it formed the andron, *i.e.* chambers specially set apart for the entertainment of male guests.

The discovery of these Hellenistic houses of the second century B.C., with a common plan of such great interest, must alter the general conception of the history and development of the house. Here we have monumental evidence of the persistence of a type of building previously regarded as long extinct in domestic architecture.

In the mainland palaces of the Mycenean epoch we have seen that a very usual plan included a courtyard with colonnades, having a hall on its north side entered through a vestibule with columns between antae, the so-called prodomos type of building. At Priene the same essential features re-appear as over two thousand years before at Troy, and that, not only in one or two houses, but in nearly all on the site, showing that the type was a normal and common one. We can no longer assert, then, that the prodomos type of building persisted only in ecclesiastical architecture, but there is every probability that its history is continuous from prehistoric times, through the Homeric and classical period up to the Hellenistic age.

A curious piece of evidence in this connection has come to hand from Sicily. An interesting house shown by the perfection of its architectural details and other indications to belong to the Hellenistic period, though it

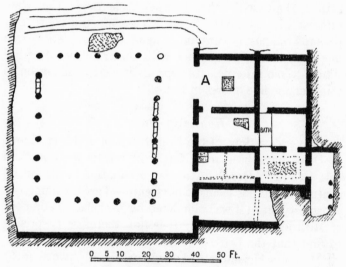

Fig. 47. House at Girgenti.

is possible that it may be yet earlier in date, has been partially excavated at the expense of the owner at *Girgenti*[1], a little to the north of the Temple of Concord (Fig. 47). The unfinished state of the excavations makes it impossible to draw any deductions with regard to the complete building: it has a courtyard 70 ft square with rooms abutting on the north side, and beyond them

[1] *Journal of Hellenic Studies*, 1906, p. 210.

indications of a similar peristyle. There are no passages, the rooms being entered from each other or from the peristyle, and, though parts were clearly built in Roman times, the general plan does not seem to have been modified in any way.

Professor Ernest Gardner[1] points out that the Doric capitals would be fourth century in Greece, and that the house must be compared with those at Priene and Delos, rather than with the Pompeian houses. The chief interest of this house is the recess off the court (*A*), perhaps the pastas, containing remains of a square hearth in the middle in accordance with the tradition of earlier times. This intermediate type, as it were, leads us on to consider the fine houses in Delos.

Houses in Delos[2].

The excavations of the French school under M. Couve in Delos have been most fertile in results for houses of this period. After the Athenian occupation in the second century B.C. Delos seems to have enjoyed great commercial prosperity, until it was plundered by Archelaos, lieutenant of Mithridates, in B.C. 86; it is not therefore surprising to find that the houses are rich and luxurious.

M. Couve has unearthed five houses in all; two near the sacred lake, one at the top of the hill to the west of the lake, one in the street leading to the theatre, and one near the Inopus. All these houses, which were probably the abodes of rich merchants, are thought on account of the similarity of their ground plans, their decoration and their method of construction, to belong to the same epoch. They all alike exhibit a central court surrounded by Doric, or as in one case Ionic columns, with various

---

[1] *J.H.S.* 1906, note by Gardner, p. 211.

[2] *B.C.H.* XIX. pp. 460 sqq.

rooms grouped around: the court is entered through a narrow passage with a door opening on the street. The bedrooms and kitchen, which open directly on to the aule, are small but there is always one magnificent room with mosaic floor and elaborate decoration, opening on to the peristyle by three large doors, or by one door between two large windows; this room was doubtless used for habitation in winter when the winds made it too cold to live in the open air of the courtyard, and also for the reception and entertainment of guests. It has therefore been identified as the andron.

The court, which seldom lies in the middle of the house, has a large recess usually opposite the entrance, which has been called the pastas, as answering to the definition given by Vitruvius of that term[1].

Some of the houses show signs of an upper storey, though the staircases, which were doubtless of wood, have for the most part disappeared.

It is not possible to draw from these houses any certain inference with regard to the Greek house of the fifth century B.C., although it seems probable that the earlier type would be imitated. If this were so, we should expect it to be elaborated rather than simplified, especially in luxurious houses of this kind, so that the absence of any traces of a second court would lend some support to the view adopted of the classical house.

Though the connection with the Homeric plan is not here so clear as at Priene, yet the large recess on the north side of the court, though it has no ante-chamber, is analogous to the megaron of the Priene houses. There is no hearth here; the houses were luxurious and had separate kitchens, and heat must have been supplied when necessary by a portable brazier.

[1] *vide* p. 260.

Let us now glance at the plan of these houses a little more in detail.

The house near the sacred lake is characteristic[1] (Fig. 48 *a*). It is irregular in plan, the courtyard not being square and none of the rooms rectangular. The

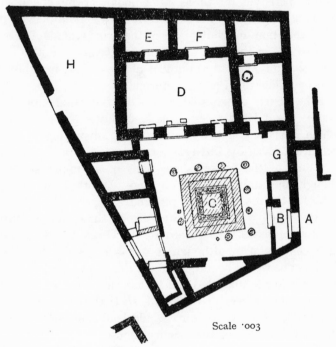

Scale ·003

Fig. 48 *a*. House at Delos near the sacred lake.

house is entered by a door (*A*) on the south-east leading into a vestibule (*B*) on the right of which is a roughly paved room, which was possibly the porter's lodge; on the left is a bench where visitors could sit while waiting. A door leads from the vestibule to the court-

[1] *B.C.H* XIX., *op. cit.* p. 485.

yard (C), which is surrounded by twelve columns: in the centre, as in Roman houses, is the impluvium, a square space covered with mosaic for the reception of rain water which now collects there to the detriment of the wonderfully preserved mosaics, but was formerly carried away into a cistern.

The large room (D) which opens on to the court by three doors was doubtless the andron and the principal

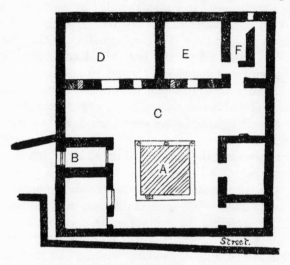

Scale ·003
Fig. 48 *b*. House at Delos at the summit of the hill.

living room in winter: behind it are two small rooms (E and F) probably used as sleeping chambers. The kitchen was the room to the left of the entrance according to M. Couve, for though no hearth was discovered there were traces of smoke on the walls. On the east side of the court is the recess (G) or pastas as it has been called, which is common to all these houses, and was probably used as a sitting room. Though it contains no central hearth, it is doubtless the survival of the megaron of Homeric times. The large room (*H*) on the west side really formed part of the original house, but now has a separate entrance on the street.

The house at the summit of the hill[1] is much more regular in plan than the preceding (Fig. 48*b*). The court (*A*) which lies, as usually in these houses, towards the south of the building, is entered on its west side (*B*) through a vestibule. It was surrounded by eight columns and had an impluvium in the centre. To the north of the court a large gallery (*C*), corresponding to the customary recess, runs across the breadth of the house, and on to it open two large rooms (*D* and *E*) and one smaller (*F*). There are three other rooms around the court and there was probably another storey: the rooms in this house were all lighted by means of windows looking on the street.

The house near the theatre[2] (Fig. 49*a*), which is the best preserved of all, has two entrances, the principal (*A*) on the street leading to the theatre and another (*B*) on the side street. The general disposition is similar to that of the preceding houses. The long vestibule leads by two steps into the courtyard (*C*): opposite it on the other side of the aule is the large andron (*D*) (8·6 m. × 5·6 m.) very richly decorated, and on the north side the familiar recess (*E*). Various other rooms are grouped around.

The same general plan is adhered to in the house near the Inopus (Fig. 49 *b*), but it is entered by two doors (*A* and *B*) which open directly on the court without any vestibule. The remains also seem to show that the colonnade extended along two sides only of the court.

[1] *B C.H.* XIX., *op. cit.* p. 492.　　　[2] *l.c.* p. 497.

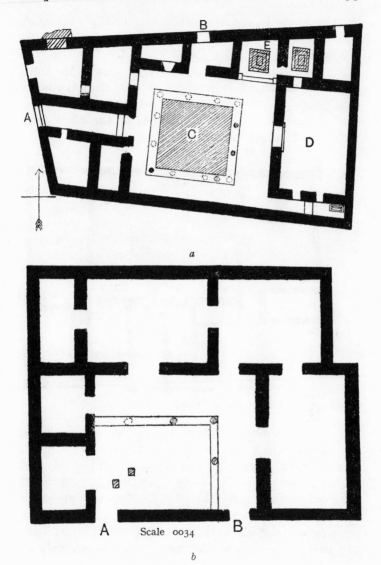

Fig. 49. Houses at Delos. (*a*) near the theatre; (*b*) near the Inopus.

The house to the west of the sacred lake[1] (Fig. 50*a*), which contained many works of art, is somewhat different from the other four. From the fact that two of its rooms communicate directly, both with the court and with the street, it has been thought that the house was public or semi-public. The entrance on the east side is through a long vestibule (*A*) of the usual type, while on the south side are two doors (*B* and *C*) leading

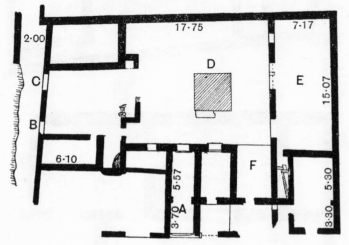

Fig. 50 *a*.   House at Delos.

into a vestibule with entrances into the courtyard (*D*). The court, which was neither square nor rectangular, was probably a peristyle, and the usual andron (*E*) and pastas (*F*) are present. The two cisterns in the courtyard have led some to think that this building was an annex of a gymnasium, while M. Couve suggests that it was possibly a sculptor's workshop. It is much larger than any of the others, and the many remains, not only of

[1] *B.C.H.* XIX. *op. cit.* p. 509.

sculptures but also of capitals, drums of columns and other architectural fragments, lend support to the theory.

Another house, later cleared, probably belonged to a community of merchants (Fig. 50 b). The vestibule leads into a courtyard without columns, paved with black and white mosaic with some colour. Facing the front door is the usual recess, and the large andron is entered by a door at the side of the court: beyond it are other rooms.

So much for the Hellenistic plans which have opened up a world of possibilities in the field of Greek domestic

Fig. 50 b.   House at Delos.

architecture, pointing to a widespread union and persistence of recognised Mycenean-Hellenic types before only dreamt of. We may hope that excavation will open up other settlements bearing out the same facts, but meanwhile the chain of evidence in the three above mentioned is singularly complete. At Priene we have the actual Mycenean type of a megaron with prodomos opening on to a courtyard, and even the hearth is not lacking in several cases to make the analogy complete: in Delos we have only the survival of this in the recess or pastas without a hearth on the north side of the courtyard, while at Girgenti we see the intermediate stage of a recess without prodomos opening off the courtyard, with a hearth in the middle.

Before quitting this period brief mention must be made of a Hellenistic house found at *Praesos*[1], though whatever be its nature it does not appear to be a private dwelling house (Fig. 51). The massive character of its masonry, the width of its doorways and other indica-

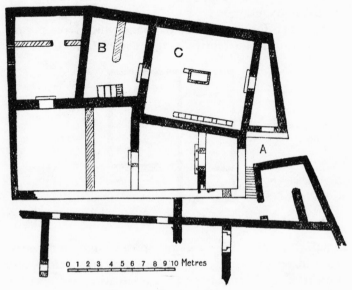

Fig. 51.   House at Praesos.

tions, have caused Mr Bosanquet to suggest that it may have been a κοιμητήριον or house of public entertainment[2]. On the evidence of the pottery it has been dated as belonging to the third century B.C.

The house, which is very irregular in plan, probably because the space available was limited by streets, has

---

[1] *B S.A.* VIII. p. 259.   [2] *l.c.* p. 260.

a fore-court (*A*) with two entrances. To the left of the approach steps descend to a basement, and in one of the rooms (*B*) are remains of a wooden staircase leading to an upper storey. In another room (*C*) are remains of an oblong tank which, although it resembles an impluvium, was probably a store tank for oil, since the house was used as an oil factory before it was abandoned. The peristyle is absent and the plan generally does not conform to any normal type of dwelling house.

Pompeian houses[1].

In conclusion a brief reference must be made to the arrangement of the Pompeian houses, which seem at first sight to be analogous in plan to the conventional Greek house, though the resemblance is only superficial.

Here we commonly have two courts, one behind the other; there is, however, no differentiation in use in the manner of the supposed andronitis and gunaikonitis, for the second court is a luxurious annex of the first.

In reality the house shows the union of the Greek and Italic plan, which was accomplished in the second century B.C., and which it is natural to find in a city such as Pompeii, which was subject at the same time to Greek and Roman influence. The front part of the house consists of the atrium with alae, tablinum and fauces, and rooms arranged according to the usual Roman plan, whilst in the rear is the Greek peristyle with its subsidiary rooms.

The earlier houses, which are roughly contemporary with the Greek houses found in Delos, and sometimes bear an apparent likeness in plan, prove on closer examination to belong to an essentially different type. The house

[1] Mau's *Pompeii*, trans. by Kelsey, II. pp. 245 sqq. Overbeck's *Pompeii*, II. c. iv. pp. 230 sqq.

of the surgeon[1], for example, which was built before
200 B.C. and retains its original plan, is wholly Italic
(Fig. 52 *a*). It consists of the usual roofed court (atrium)
surrounded by smaller rooms with a garden in the rear.
The presence of alae, tablinum and fauces, as well as
the roofed courtyard without columns, shows this house
at once to be of Roman type.

The house of Sallust[2] also built in the second century
B.C. resembled in original plan the house of the surgeon.

The house of Pansa[3] (Fig. 52 *b*) shows very clearly
the union of the two plans. The atrium of the usual
type, with alae and tablinum, is entered through a
vestibule: at the further end access is given to the
peristyle and rooms surrounding it.

The house of the faun, which is the largest and most
elaborate, has an atrium and two peristyles.

In the house of Meleager[4] (Fig. 53) we find the atrium
and peristyle side by side with most of the rooms grouped
behind.

Some of the earlier houses have no peristyle, while a
few are built without an atrium, but the normal plan
at Pompeii includes both atrium and peristyle, and shows
the complete union of Greek and Italic types.

The account of Vitruvius.

There remains for consideration the account given of
the Greek house by Vitruvius, a celebrated architect of
the age of Augustus and the only ancient writer on
architecture. His description has been the cause of much
dispute, and many have been the attempts to emend the
passage, but in the light of recent excavations it now
seems clearer.

[1] Mau, *op. cit.* p. 280.   [2] *ibid.* p. 284.
[3] *ibid.* p. 350.   [4] Overbeck, I. 282.

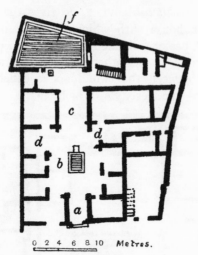

0 2 4 6 8 10 Metres.

a = fauces; *b* = atrium; *c* = tablinum; *d* = alae; *f* = garden.

a

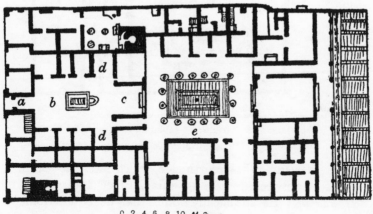

0 2 4 6 8 10 Metres.

a = fauces; *b* = atrium; *c* = tablinum; *d* = alae; *e* = peristyle.

b

Fig. 52. Houses at Pompeii. (*a*) House of the surgeon; (*b*) House of Pansa.

In his *de architectura*, VI. 7, he gives the simple plan of the Greek house with which we are familiar. It is entered by a passage, flanked by stables on one side and a porter's lodge on the other, with a door at each end. The space between the two doors is called θυρωρεῖον. This leads to the peristyle, which has a colonnade on

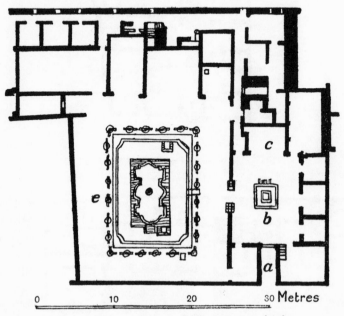

0   10   20   30 Metres

a=fauces; *b*=atrium; *c*=tablinum; *e*=peristyle.

Fig. 53. House of Meleager at Pompeii.

three sides and on the fourth side, which faces the south, a recess between projecting antae, called the προστάς or παστάς. He specifically states that he is describing the Greek house: the following are his words:—

Atriis Graeci quia non utuntur, neque aedificant, sed ab janua introeuntibus itinera faciunt, latitudinibus non spatiosis, et ex una parte equilia, ex altera ostiariis cellas; statimque januae interiores finiuntur. Hic autem locus inter duas ianuas graece θυρωρεῖον appellatur. Deinde est introitus in peristylion: id peristylion in tribus partibus habet porticus; in ea parte quae spectat ad meridiem, duas antas inter se spatio amplo distantes, in quibus trabes invehuntur, et quantum inter antas distat, ex eo tertia dempta spatium datur introrsus. Hic locus apud nonnullos προστάς, apud alios παστάς nominatur.

The Greeks do not build atria because they do not use them, but they make passages from the entrance door of no great breadth, and on one side stables and on the other the porters' rooms: and immediately after the inner doors are placed. But this place between the two doors is called in Greek the θυρωρεῖον. From there is the entrance into the peristyle: this peristyle has colonnades on three sides; and on that side which looks south two antae at a considerable distance apart on which beams rest, and the space within is one-third less than the distance between them. This place is called by some the προστάς, by others the παστάς.

This description is hitherto quite clear and tallies in all its features with the remains of houses found in Delos, belonging to the second century[1]. He continues,

In his locis introrsus constituuntur oeci magni, in quibus matres familiarum cum lanificis habent sessionem. In prostadii autem dextra ac sinistra cubicula sunt collocata, quorum unum thalamus, alterum amphithalamus dicitur—circum autem in porticibus triclinia quotidiana, cubicula etiam et cellae familiaricae constituuntur. Haec pars aedificii gynaeconitis appellatur.

Within are built large reception rooms where the mistresses sit with the wool-spinners. On the right and left of the προστάς are situated the bedrooms, one of which is called the thalamus, and the other the amphithalamus. Moreover around in the colonnades are built dining rooms for daily use, also bedrooms and rooms for the slaves. This part of the building is called the gynaeconitis.

Rooms for the use of the women and slaves were thus apparently behind the pastas ('in his locis introrsus'),

[1] *vide* p. 248.

sleeping chambers on either side of it, and dining rooms, bedrooms, and store rooms around the court. This part of the building, *i.e.* the court and the rooms surrounding it, is described as the gynaeconitis, a use of the term which indeed occurs once in Lysias (*supra*), but will not fit the conventional view of the Greek house, nor the view adopted.

The rest of the description appears at first to militate against the view we have taken of the classical house, in that it distinctly postulates a second court.

Coniunguntur autem his domus ampliores habentes lautiora peristylia, in quibus pares sunt quattuor porticus altitudinibus, aut una, quae ad meridiem spectat, excelsioribus columnis constituitur. Id autem peristylium, quod unam altiorem habet porticum, Rhodiacum appellatur. Habent autem eae domus vestibula egregia et ianuas proprias cum dignitate porticusque peristyliorum albariis et tectoriis et ex intestino opere lacunariis ornatas, et in porticibus quae ad septentrionem spectant, triclinia Cyzicena et pinacothecas; ad orientem autem bibliothecas; exedras ad occidentem; ad meridiem vero spectantes oecos quadratos tam ampla magnitudine, uti faciliter in eis tricliniis quattuor stratis ministrationum ludorumque operis locus possit esse spatiosus. In his oecis fiunt virilia convivia; non enim fuerat institutum matres familiarum eorum moribus accumbere. Haec autem peristylia domus andronitides dicuntur, quod in his viri sine interpellationibus mulierum versantur. Praeterea dextra et sinistra domunculae constituuntur habentes proprias ianuas, triclinia et cubicula commoda, uti hospites advenientes non in peristylia sed in ea hospitalia recipiantur.

Adjoining this are larger buildings with more spacious courts in which the four colonnades are equal in height, or one, which looks south, is built with higher columns. That court which has one colonnade higher is called Rhodian. Moreover those buildings have splendid vestibules and special doors of imposing aspect and the colonnades of the courts ornamented with white stucco and plastering and inlaid ceilings, and in the colonnades which look north Cyzicene dining rooms and picture galleries,

in those looking east libraries; in those looking west sitting
rooms; in those looking south square reception rooms sufficiently
large to allow easily of there being room in them for the service
with four tables spread, and the games. In these rooms are
held the men's banquets, for it was not formerly the custom,
according to the manners of the Greeks, for women to be present.
Moreover these courts are called andronitides because in them
the men spend their time without interruption from the women.
Furthermore on the right and left are built little buildings with
their own doors, dining rooms and convenient bedrooms, so that
guests on their arrival may be received not in the court but in
those guest rooms.

From this passage we gather that larger buildings
are built on to the part of the house first described, with
more luxurious peristyles, which are highly decorated
with stucco and panels of inlaid work, and abutting on
them are dining rooms, libraries, picture galleries, sitting
rooms, etc. These peristyles are called andronitides,
because in them the men spend their time without interruption from the women. On the right and left are
annexes with their own doors, dining rooms and comfort-
able bedrooms, so that guests might be received not into
the peristyle but into these guest chambers.

It is quite clear that Vitruvius is here describing
Greek houses of a luxurious type with two courts or
peristyles, libraries, picture galleries, etc. The first court
and the chambers around are designated the gunaikonitis,
a use of the term which is very rare in classical times but
does occur. The second court and chambers surrounding
it he designates the andronitis because it was set aside
for the men.

With regard to the relative position of the two courts
he does not commit himself; he merely says 'coniunguntur
his,' and it seems likely, as Lange[1] suggests, that the

[1] *Haus und Halle*, p. 138.

position of the andronitis and gunaikonitis would be influenced by exigencies of space as a rich man enlarged his house.

Professor Ernest Gardner's suggestion (*J.H.S.* XXI.)[1] that the second peristyle and surrounding chambers should be regarded as an expanded andron, receives singular confirmation from one of the later houses discovered at Priene (fig. 7)[2]. Here we see the transition from the one court to the two court house. The owner in his scheme of enlargement has included the house next to his, which he has decorated elaborately evidently with a view to using it for entertainments.

The type of house with two courts, which seems to have been adopted by the Greeks and the Romans about the same time, viz. second century B.C., would be familiar to Vitruvius and is evidently the type he is describing. His description, therefore, lends no support whatever to the two court theory of the classical Greek house, with the court for the women behind that of the men.

Vitruvius concludes his account by a reference to certain passages which he calls mesauloe, the position of which is not very clear. These are his words:—

Inter duo autem peristylia et hospitalia itinera sunt, quae mesauloe dicuntur, quod inter duas aulas media sunt interposita; nostri autem eas andronas appellant.

Moreover between the two peristyles and the guest rooms are passages which are called mesaulae because they are placed in the middle between the two aulae: but we call them androneos.

Thus the passages are situated between the two peristyles and the guest chambers, and are called by the Romans androneos. 'Sed hoc valde mirandum est,' as he justly remarks, for it does not suit the use of the word in Greek or Latin.

[1] p. 302.   [2] *vide* p. 245.

This passage is obscure and it does not seem possible to derive any satisfactory conclusion from it with regard to the mesauloe.

The account, however, in so far as it bears on the general disposition of the Greek house, is quite clear in the light of recent evidence, since the discovery of the Hellenistic development of the Greek fifth century house has now removed all difficulties of interpretation.

SUMMARY.

Finally, a brief summary may be given of our study of the Greek house throughout its history, as it appears in the light of recent discoveries.

Our main object has been to show a certain uniformity and continuity of type from the earliest Neolithic period up to the Hellenistic age, a type based broadly speaking on the courtyard with principal room.

In the Neolithic period we have shown the general resemblance of architectural forms in the West Mediterranean basin, and how the earliest architecture of Greece was intimately connected therewith; and in the Eastern Mediterranean, in Asia Minor, we have seen in the beehive tombs the aftermath of this influence.

With regard to lacustrine dwellings in Greece, evidence is as yet too scanty to make any conclusion possible as to their importance or the part they played in Greek architectural history.

In the consideration of the three early styles of building, viz. round, elliptical and rectangular, we have not reached any absolute conclusion with regard to priority: on the site of Orchomenos we have seen them in succession, and have regarded this as being, in general, the probable order of development with some exceptions on scattered sites.

Crete, where our study of regular architecture must begin, gives us buildings of surpassing magnificence and bewildering complication with certain Semitic and Eastern analogies, but at the same time very character-istic and original in structure. These show the early Aegean system of communicating rooms, as do also most of the houses of this period.

Passing to the mainland we come to the plan which we have considered essentially Greek, viz. the principal room or megaron quite isolated, standing on the north side of the courtyard. The actual origin of this plan, found as early as Troy II, we have been unable to trace, but we have pointed out the resemblances which exist with Cretan building, proving a certain connection with the south, and also possible affinities with the Nordic house, where the central hearth in the isolated room was indispensable from the earliest times.

The Homeric palace has been shown to be almost certainly of the same type as that of the mainland palaces, in general construction and arrangement.

Then follows a gap of several centuries, and when we reach classic Greece of the fifth century evidence is utterly lacking of houses of the Homeric type, though they may have persisted in the country: some were still built on the courtyard system, *e.g.* house of Kallias, though far less luxurious than their Mycenean predecessors.

The houses of the average citizen were small and crowded, frequently having common party walls; through these the Plataeans dug so that they might not be seen in the streets at Plataea (Thuc. II. 3).

That the Mycenean-Homeric type, however, was a national one, and no short-lived fashion, is proved up to the hilt by the discovery of the houses of the second century at Priene, which preserve the identical form, and make the chain of evidence complete. At Delos the type has undergone some modification, but the recess off the court is analogous to the old megaron and is a survival of the earlier type.

About this time (second cent. B.C.), arose the type with two courtyards described by Vitruvius, doubtless built by rich Greeks as an elaboration of the simple type: the enlarged house at Priene is a prototype of the two court plan.

The final development is in Italy. The Roman house, after having passed from the simple peasant hut to the atrium type, finally in the second century B.C. under Greek influence, added a second court to its plan. At Pompeii we have many examples of the combination of the two distinct types, viz. the Roman atrium with the Greek peristyle added.

Though the theory that there was no break in the historical development of the Greek house may be contested—as what theory may not?—yet the foregoing study may perhaps have its use in that it is for the most part a statement of actual facts, from which each may draw for himself his own conclusions.

Our sole object has been to throw some new light on the nature of the abodes of the Greek race throughout its history, and to make a complete review of architectural development possible, by collecting and colligating scattered information and facts.

INDEX